Keats and Romantic Celticism

Other Publications by this Author

TABOOED JUNG: Marginality as Power, 1996

SHELLEY'S AMBIVALENCE, 1989

COLERIDGE'S THEORY OF IMAGINATION TODAY (*editor*), 1989

BLAKE AND THE ASSIMILATION OF CHAOS, 1978

Keats and Romantic Celticism

Christine Gallant

First published 2005 by
PALGRAVE MACMILLAN
Houndmills, Basingstoke, Hampshire RG21 6XS and
175 Fifth Avenue, New York, N.Y. 10010
Companies and representatives throughout the world

PALGRAVE MACMILLAN is the global academic imprint of the Palgrave Macmillan division of St. Martin's Press, LLC and of Palgrave Macmillan Ltd. Macmillan® is a registered trademark in the United States, United Kingdom and other countries. Palgrave is a registered trademark in the European Union and other countries.

ISBN-13: 978–1–4039–4851–9
ISBN-10: 1–4039–4851–8

This book is printed on paper suitable for recycling and made from fully managed and sustained forest sources.

A catalogue record for this book is available from the British Library.

Library of Congress Cataloging-in-Publication Data
Gallant, Christine, 1940–
Keats and romantic celticism / Christine Gallant.
p. cm.
Includes bibliographical references (p.) and index.
ISBN 1–4039–4851–8 (cloth)
1. Keats, John, 1795–1821—Knowledge—Mythology. 2. Keats, John, 1795–1821—Knowledge—Folklore. 3. Keats, John, 1795–1821—Knowledge—Celts. 4. English poetry—Celtic influences. 5. Mythology, Celtic, in literature. 6. Supernatural in literature. 7. Romanticism—England. 8. Fairies in literature. 9. Celts in literature. I. Title.

PR4838.M83G35 2005
821′.7—dc22

2004065754

10 9 8 7 6 5 4 3 2 1
14 13 12 11 10 09 08 07 06 05

Contents

Acknowledgements

I am glad to express here my appreciation to my colleague John Burrison, Regents Professor of English and Director of Folklore Curriculum at Georgia State University, who shared his expertise with me and provided many useful insights on contributions that folklore might make to the analysis of literature. I should add of course that any errors I have made are all my own. I also gratefully acknowledge the support I have received from Georgia State University with a research leave in 2000, and also the fellowship from the National Endowment for the Humanities in 2003 that enabled me to write this book.

The quotations from Sir Walter Scott's ballads in *Minstrelsy of the Scottish Border* are taken from the four-volume edition edited by T.F. Henderson, which was published by William Blackwood and Sons (Edinburgh and London) and Charles Scribner's Sons (New York) in 1902, and reissued by Singing Tree Press in 1968. The verses from Scott's *Lay of the Last Minstrel* are taken from the 1913 edition of *The Works of Sir Walter Scott* by Houghton Mifflin and Company (New York).

Copyright acknowledgements

1
The Evidence for Celticism in Keats

Keats was born on Hallowe'en. This was Samhain of the old Celtic calendar, the time when the veil between the mortal world and the world of faerie grew porous and thin, a dangerous time. And indeed Romantic Celticism, its culture and politics, was central to his major works. Woven in and out of his poetry are faeries, demons, and spirits. These are "the Good People," "the wee folk," and "the Little People" long known in the folklore of the British Isles, so named to propitiate any that might be lurking nearby unseen.[1] Terming them thus also quieted one's own fears of the capricious, amoral powers of these beings that half belonged to the world of the dead and half to the world of the mortal.[2] The presence of the faerie in Keats's writings is accompanied by the centuries-old feeling of dread at their menace mixed with fascination by their timeless allure, rather than the more modern notion of them as small, tricksy aliens. Keats was not emulating Spenser, Shakespeare, and Milton with their literary rendering of contemporary faerylore; nor was he revealing some supposedly pervasive anxiety to fit into their aristocratic literary culture by using faerylore as they did.[3] He drew on an earlier and more primitive lore of the faerie.

Throughout the text of this book, I use the word *faery* to mean an individual spirit; and *faerie*, the general realm of the Otherworld, or an adjective pertaining to this realm, or its magic. I am purposely using the older, more archaic spelling that derives from the French word *fey* and dates back at least to the Renaissance, in order to suggest the great antiquity of these beings that go back to pre-Christian days. As the *Oxford English Dictionary* observes of the word *faerie* or *faery*: "In present usage, it is practically a distinct word, adopted . . . to exclude various unpoetic or undignified associations connected with the current form *fairy*."[4] Keats himself uses "faery" and "fairy" interchangeably, for the slippage between the words was already common by then.

Traditional faerylore is an integral part of his major poems, early to late: "Calidore: A Fragment," *Endymion: A Poetic Romance*, "The Eve of St. Agnes," "La Belle Dame sans Merci: A Ballad," "Ode to a Nightingale," *Lamia*, and *The Fall of Hyperion: A Dream*. The first poem he wrote, "Imitation of Spenser," has as its setting the land of faerie and so does the very last, "The Cap and Bells; Or, The Jealousies. A Faery Tale, by Lucy Vaughan Lloyd." Many epistolary poems that span his poetic career employ some theme relating to the faerie. Some present a faery's persona relating the poem, such as "Had I a man's fair form," "Ah! woe is me! poor Silver-wing," "Song of Four Fairies: Fire, Air, Earth, and Water," and "Shed no tear." "Old Meg she was a gipsey" most likely is about a Highland faery.

The realm of the faerie in folklore is always a timeless place.[5] One of the most common tales is that of the mortal who is lured away to faeryland and stays for a short time, to find on leaving that centuries have passed back in the human world while the mortal has remained caught out of time.[6] "Calidore" from his 1817 *Poems* alludes to this and so do many of his epistolary poems: "Unheard, unfelt, unseen," "Dear Reynolds, as last night I lay in bed," and "There is a joy in footing slow across a silent plain." Obviously, this is true of the more well-known poems, "La Belle Dame sans Merci" and *Lamia*. But *Endymion* also relates this experience again and again with the stories of Adonis, Glaucus, Alpheus, and especially Endymion. It's the outcome just beyond the conclusion of "The Eve of St. Agnes." The narrator of *The Fall of Hyperion* enters the faerie realm of Moneta due to the faery feast he recklessly consumes in the opening lines, and there's a good chance that he'll remain as a captive there forever.

Keats drew extensively upon folklore motifs concerning the faerie. He could have known them from Sir Walter Scott's works, particularly the ballads and accompanying essays on folk-beliefs in the multi-volume *Minstrelsy of the Scottish Border* that was so commercially successful, as well as Robert Burns's poems and transcribed songs from the folk, and the many antiquarian collections of folk materials that were popular in the early nineteenth century. The modern study of folklore began during the early nineteenth century, and derived from the absorbing interest of eighteenth-century antiquarians in relics of the British past. What had been the random but enthusiastic collecting of anything associated with the ancient Britons became, during the Romantic period, the more systematic recording of the British past through the orally transmitted ballads and beliefs of the native folk. Celticists in particular were concerned with the preservation of the old Gaelic literature, beliefs, and traditions that seemed in danger of dying out because of the English pressure to assimilate to their dominant culture and language.

We know from Keats's letters that he greatly admired Scott's ballads, and from Charles Brown's posthumous cataloguing that his small library included Burns's *Poems*. Both Scott and Burns were passionately partisan in their desire to record the old native beliefs through their poetry; and Scott also accompanied his transcribed and "reconstructed" ballads with long, detailed essays on the faerie beliefs that were the ballads' background. Keats's poems contain at least 250 folk-motifs relating to faeries or faeryland (also known as the Otherworld in Stith Thompson's definitive *Motif-Index of Folk-Literature*). They appear in his epistolary minor verses as well as those considered his major works. It's noteworthy that according to the *Motif-Index* these motifs used by Keats usually are of Celtic origin, most often Irish myth.

Some motifs flicker through his works once or twice, creating the atmosphere or reinforcing the narrative; but variants of a few main motifs appear again and again. Surely their recurrence is significant. Further, some motifs that appear in his early poems become predominant in the late works while others fade and hardly reappear at all. Motifs relating to the habits and appearance of faeries are fairly common. Those relating to the taboo against looking at faeries (Motif C311.1.2) appear from his earliest poems to the very late *Lamia*; most often variants on the motif of the faeries' revenge on the person who spies on them (Motif F361.3). Motifs relating to the nature of faeryland also appear in most of his faerie poems, and so do motifs relating to captives in faeryland (Motif F375). However, the motif that appears most often, from his first poem to his last (excluding the final unfinished *Cap and Bells*) is the one that associates faeryland with the world of the dead (Motif F160.0.2).

Keats's reliance on regional folklore about the faerie has been generally neglected by the literary critics. The prominent British folklorist Katharine Briggs states that "Keats wrote in the folk-fairy tradition," as opposed to the literary-faery tradition that began in the Elizabethan and Jacobean periods with Spenser and Shakespeare.[7] There is also a long chapter on Keats in *The Erotic World of Faery* by Maureen Duffy, beginning forthrightly: "If ever a personality may be said to be bewitched it was his.... His vocabulary is elf-shot."[8] However, her book is heavily Freudian, with faerylore reductively seen as the projection of all that has been censored and suppressed into the unconscious. Otherwise, there are only a few articles. The medieval scholar J. Burke Severs noted that "Keats's interest in fairies extended through his poetic life" but by that he meant Keats's scattered references to Oberon and Titania; and he primarily discusses these in the early works from the 1817 *Poems*. He concludes that these references show the strong influence of Shakespeare's *Midsummer Night's Dream*.[9] Other articles and essays consider Keats's use of folk-legends in "La Belle Dame," "Eve of St. Agnes," and *Lamia*, or note fleeting references to faerylore in the poetry.[10] These critics have picked up the presence of the faerie here and there, but only as elusive traces that vanish like magic fern-seed.

Faerylore serves as more than a rich source of allusions for his literature, however. Many of his poems take well known, popular literary works about the faerie as their basis for Keats's own version that in some way revises or amplifies the original, with details from the original inserted into Keats's own work as clues pointing to his source. Thus the early "Calidore" extends an incident in Book VI of Spenser's *The Faerie Queene*; *Endymion*, "The Eve of St. Agnes," and "La Belle Dame sans Merci" amplify supernatural ballads from Sir Walter Scott's *Minstrelsy of the Scottish Border*; the epistolary poem "When they were come unto the Faery's court" continues a ballad about the faerie in Scott's *Lay of the Last Minstrel*; and "Ode to a Nightingale" is Keats's own abbreviated version of Shakespeare's *A Midsummer Night's Dream*.

It was for ideological as well as artistic reasons that he drew systematically and extensively upon the folk-beliefs about the faerie held in England and its periphery Celtic countries of Ireland, Scotland, and Wales.[11] The modern study of folklore began during the Romantic period; and to antiquarians of the time and their enthusiasts the oral lore of the "folk" contained surviving remnants of past history. To them, the faerylore still kept its Celtic origins that predated the coming of Christianity to the British Isles and went back before the Roman conquest. Transcribing the orally transmitted folktales was a way of preserving the traditions and past that were fast disappearing. Sir Walter Scott was especially important in this regard. We know that Keats read him and admired the poems he had "reconstructed" from their original form as Gaelic folk-ballads. He must also have been familiar with the enormously popular *Minstrelsy of the Scottish Border* in which they appeared. Scott's introductory essays that supplied those ballads' underlying folk-beliefs would have been an excellent source of faerylore for Keats.

And to a much larger extent than has been acknowledged, this entire Celtic, pre-Roman period of British history held a fascination for Keats from the time of his early reading at Enfield School. Over and over in his poetry he evoked that period of ancient Britain, as well as the regional folklore believed to derive from its Celtic past. In many of his works, the pre-Roman period of Britain is conflated with the ostensibly classical setting. Sometimes the native mythology underlies and supplements the more familiar classical mythology. A poem that is first set in ancient Latmos or Corinth or in a sanctuary of the defeated Titans shifts to another Celtic realm closer to home. Endymion himself is a figure as much based upon Thomas the Rhymer of Scottish legend as upon the Carian youth from Greek myth. The account of Endymion's quest for Cynthia is unexpectedly interrupted by the poet's invocation of the "Muse of my native land!" This Muse is prior to the classical Greek Nine, being "first-born on the mountains ... before the first of Druids was a child" (*End.* IV.1–7) — a Celtic Muse, in other words. It should be kept in mind that there are many old folk connections between the faeries and the Druids with many believing that the Druids controlled the faeries, or that faeries *are* Druids.[12]

Behind both *Hyperion* and *The Fall of Hyperion* is the old tradition, drawn on by Milton in *Paradise Lost*, that identifies the mythic Titans with the historic Celts. Ossianic melancholy pervades Keats's rendering of the Titans in the two *Hyperion* fragments. In *Hyperion* they are explicitly compared to Druids (*Hyp.* I.137 and II.34–5); and the "High Prophetess" Moneta (*Fall.* I.145) in *The Fall of Hyperion* becomes the last of the Druids. The rather conventional Romantic account of the Titans' defeat by the Olympians becomes the vastly more original attempt to re-create the end of the Celtic Empire of antiquity with the defeat of the Celtic Britons by the Romans. *Lamia* too, when we deduce its time frame from clues within the poem and its concluding note provided by Keats, proves to be set during the period of the British Celtic revolts against the Roman invaders. Celticism is as intimately a part of Keats's poetry as the classicism that may seem to fill his poems at every turn.

In many ways, Keats's readers up to the present time have read his poetry to be as unchanging as though it too was caught in faeryland, with the poems like elegies that are haunted by his early death. This emotional freight that Keats and his poetry continue to carry for his readers is the focus of Jeffrey Robinson's recent perceptive study of the reception of Keats by the readers who have loved Keats and by the nineteenth- and twentieth-century poets.[13] He argues that these all helped to create the "closed" canonized Keats, and the great problem for his readers of "over-familiarity: we swallow his poems, life and career as if we have always known what they meant."[14] The entire enterprise of Keats criticism for the last few decades has been to break down this sense of his "over-familiarity." The story of the dramatic shift in his critics' perspective of him to a historically oriented Keats is familiar by now, and his early association with the radical culture of the Hunt circle is at the foreground of present critical attention.[15] However, as Robinson points out, the discussions seem to center on cultural, political, and thematic issues rather than the poetics, and "the poem itself remains secure."[16] An unexamined aspect of Keats's poetry that may make it less familiar and more uncanny is his Celticism.

Viewing Keats as a Celticist is not a familiar perspective. It has long been settled, supposedly, that his sources, myths, and inspiration were solely to be found in ancient Greece and Rome. This is the primary reason that he has long been considered apolitical and uninterested in contemporary history. He did indeed seem to have an unending appetite for classical Greek and Roman mythology, as well as Roman history. The books in his small personal library that Charles Brown catalogued posthumously included several on Roman history and antiquities, and the popular mythology handbooks such as Lemprière's *Classical Dictionary* and Tooke's *Pantheon.*[17] He probably first encountered Lemprière and Tooke at Enfield School, for its headmaster Charles Cowden Clarke said he seemed to know them by heart. All of this may take a different twist if we look at it in a different way. The Romantic Celticist did.

Very early indeed, Keats had begun reading writers who would have been good sources for a knowledge of the history and culture of the Gauls (as the Celts were called in the classical world), and the Celts of the British Isles. The books we can be sure he read were those in the library for the students at Enfield School, in the personal library of Clarke, and in his small personal library. The books at Enfield School were not scholarly or esoteric, but solidly informative. They would have given him a general knowledge of the customs of the pre-Roman Celts in England, as well as the later history between England and its stubborn Gaelic neighbor Scotland. Many of the books in Keats's own library that relate to the Celts of the British Isles are not well known today but were in his time, with some running to many printings.[18]

Latin authors were a mainstay of his reading at Enfield, along with classical mythology.[19] The reviewer John Lockhart may have ridiculed Keats for his inability to read the Greek classics in their original language; but he knew the other classical language. Charles Cowden Clarke later recalled that at Enfield School Keats had translated all 12 books of Virgil's *Aeneid*, and "the quantity he wrote of translation during the last 18 months or two years of his stay at Enfield was surprising."[20] Several of the books in his private library had Roman history or antiquities as their subject, including Livy's *Roman History*; and a few were written in

Latin. Necessarily, the accounts of Roman history included the Romans' encounters with the Gauls. It seems clear that his reading of the Roman historians would not have been restricted to those found on his shelf. If he knew Latin well enough to translate Virgil, then quite probably he read that equally famous writer on Roman history, Julius Caesar.

Caesar's commentaries on his Roman conquest of Gaul are the only primary source on the Gauls and their society; and he included first-hand accounts of the British Celts in the first century BC. It is particularly likely that Keats read his *Gallic War*, given his other interests in reading about the British Celts. And if so, he would have learned a great deal of what the classical world knew about the Druids from direct contact with their society of the Gauls. Caesar in particular described their habits in great detail.

Livy and Lemprière both contained detailed information about this chief enemy of ancient Greece and Rome. Livy contained a detailed, dramatic narrative of the successful Gallic invasion and sacking of Rome in the fourth century BC. Lemprière's *Classical Dictionary*, a compact but thorough little book, opens with a long history of significant dates in European history beginning with the Trojan War. These include Rome's Gallic Wars, the invasion of Gaul and Britain by Rome, and then the occupation of Britain by Roman forces. The dates are followed by the dictionary proper that defines the usual characters, places, events, and terms from the classical cultures. Many of the extended definitions refer to the ancient Gauls and the Iron Age Celts of Britain: "Bardi," "Celtae," "Druidae," "Galli," "Gallia" (or ancient Gaul, called Galatia by the Greeks).

Allusions to Druids appear in *Endymion* and the two *Hyperion* poems. In addition, of course, "bard" is a fairly common term in Keats's poetry. It could refer to that class of the ancient Celtic society that was closely allied with the Druids as well as to the Greek Homeric bard — in fact, for Keats the word probably always carried this underlying Celtic meaning. Lemprière's definition for "Bardi" only states that it was "a sacerdotal order among the ancient Gauls," with no mention of the classical Greeks (or Homer).[21] Keats certainly had access to a basic knowledge of the Celts in Lemprière's book that Clarke said "he appeared to *learn*." Tooke also included material about "the Druidae, Priests of the Gauls."[22]

Spence's *Polymetis*, another one of Keats's favorites in the Enfield library, is an iconographical study of Greek and Roman mythology.[23] Like the *Classical Dictionary* and *The Pantheon*, and most of the other mythological handbooks of the period, it was designed for readers who could not take a Grand Tour to see the ancient art for themselves. Clarke, as have most later critics, considers Lemprière, Tooke, and Spence to be significant as "the store whence [Keats] acquired his intimacy with the Greek mythology" and confidently asserts that "his amount of classical attainment extended no farther than the 'Aeneid.'"[24] Yet here, as in those other two, there is also an account of history closer to home.

Polymetis is an eighteenth-century gentleman entertaining friends at his country villa that has the usual outdoor bric-a-brac of classical antiquity. His guided tour provides the book's 21 "dialogues." However, Dialogue the Seventeenth is not a learned discourse on the artistic representations of Roman poetry, but rather a "long digression" concerning "our forefathers," the native Celts who were subjugated by those Romans and who are characterized as "a rough, barbarous, *valiant*, and restless people.... always ready to rebel; and endeavoring, on every opportunity, to recover what they had lost" [italics mine].[25] Spence argues that the present-day British reverence for Latin could be traced to the survival tactics of the Celts who had been conquered by the Romans and needed to learn their language. For him, Latin was the language of the colonizer and studying the Roman classics in English is equivalent to throwing off the yoke of the invader.[26]

For several folio pages, Spence justifies exactly the kind of education that Keats was getting for himself by acquiring his knowledge of classical culture through translations and handbooks. By implication, Spence refutes the aristocratic idea that classical mythology is a preserve of the upper classes. More, there were class implications to this privileging of the native tongue, since classical learning was considered the province of the upper classes and the aristocracy throughout the eighteenth and early nineteenth centuries. The ignorance of Latin usually seen as a mark of inferior class background instead reveals a closeness in spirit to the original "valiant" and resisting Britons.

The link in all of Keats's early reading was the native culture of the British Isles, its language, and its history. His interest in this continued into his adult life, as we can tell from the books found in his library. One was Burns's *Poems*. Several others are by Celtic writers or on Celtic subjects. The presence of "Hist. of K. Arthur" may not seem surprising given Keats's general interest in medieval literature. However, this historical figure turned by Malory into fictionalized myth in reality had been the leader of the Celts in the south and west of England near the end of the fifth century, uniting them against the invading Saxons. A persisting folk-legend holds that upon his death he was borne off by faeries, and still dwells in faeryland until he can return to free the Celts once more.[27]

A major Celtic presence in Keats's library was Edward Davies's *Celtic Researches*, to be discussed at greater length in Chapter 2.[28] Davies was a well-known figure among antiquarians and historians of his time, with his hermeneutics well within the mainstream. In *Celtic Researches* he read *The Book of Genesis* literally to propose an ingenious theory of ancient history, also held by a great many antiquarians during this period just prior to the development of modern archaeology with its scientific instruments of excavation and dating. Davies held that after the Flood, Noah and his three sons, Shem, Ham, and Japheth, began populating all of the world. Japheth and his offspring settled in Europe. Britain was "probably colonized by those who were born within a century of the deluge";[29] and thus Japheth was the direct ancestor of the Gauls, or Celts.[30] The Celts were the original Europeans. Thus far, Davies's theories were generally familiar ones believed by many contemporary antiquarians.

Davies went on to discuss Druidism, which he thought was exclusively native to the British Isles. As the learned class of the Celts, these British Druids had preserved the religion and sciences of Noah and his sons.[31] They were the mythical priests of classical legend who lived in "the land of the extreme north," and taught the Greeks religion and philosophy — *they* were the Hyperboreans, and the British Isles their mysterious country of antiquity.[32] In other words, the British Celts were the true source of classical Greek and Roman mythology. *Celtic Researches* was not some eccentric treatise by a country curate in Wales (which Davies in fact was), but quite in line with the spirit of the larger movement of Romantic Celticism. One can see how this book would refocus Keats's understanding of classical mythology — for evidently it was the original native Celts who were the learned ones, and the Greeks and Romans who were the barbarians.

Only a few critics have recognized the significance of Davies's circuitous, digressive work as a source for Keats's poetry. Bernard Blackstone considers it to be a major one.[33] However, he only demonstrates this in several footnotes where he cites parallels between Davies's book and phrases or general ideas in *Endymion*. He does not pursue any possible similarities between the Titans of Davies and of Keats, except to note that a few of the fallen Titans in *Hyperion* have the Celtic names given by Davies.[34] (The names for these Titans are also given by Milton and Lemprière, however.) This neglect of Davies's influence on Keats was redressed thirty years later by Fiona Stafford in her essay on Romantic Titanism. Primarily concerned with the place of Macpherson's Ossian in the political movement of eighteenth-century Celticism, she also considers Keats's *Hyperion* to be a significant part of that movement in its Ossianic echoes of hopeless nostalgia for a lost past. She attributes Keats's underlying association of the Titans and the Celts to his knowledge of Davies's book.[35]

There were potent reasons for Keats's early absorption in Celticism. Celticism had strong contemporary political implications, for it was pre-Roman as well as pre-Christian in its origins. Since the eighteenth century there had been an increasing nationalistic emphasis upon the native peoples of the Isles, the Britons that included the early Celts and went back through them to the ancient Gauls who were a major enemy of classical Greece and Rome. As Chapter 2 will show, this growing enthusiasm for all things Celtic during the eighteenth and early nineteenth century has been designated a "Celtic Revival" that foreshadows the more well-known one a century later in Ireland.[36] Celtic scholars of this earlier period held that the British Celtic culture predated the classical one of ancient Greece and Rome; and they fervently believed that the Celtic culture was superior to it too.[37] This interest in the pre-colonized Celtic past implied a sympathy for the present debased and impoverished Celtic "colonies" of England; and it pointed to an anti-monarchism.[38] Keats was as much a Celticist as a classicist, though not so overtly.

This Celticism went back very far and was evident throughout his life, to be seen in the books he read, the letters he wrote to friends and relatives, and the limited number of journeys outside London that he could afford to take. It was also evident among his circle of friends.

In a general way, Leigh Hunt and his circle influenced Keats's Celticism with their liberal counterculturalism and advocacy for groups colonized by the English. Most famously, Hunt's prison term for libel in 1813 was occasioned by his *Examiner* article that not only attacked the Prince Regent but was strongly partial to the Irish; and he continued to campaign for Irish rights into the Victorian era. One of Keats's earliest poems was the sympathizing sonnet "Written on the Day That Mr. Leigh Hunt Left Prison." This was composed in 1815, a year before he met Hunt and joined Hunt's circle, so his motivation in writing it must have been ideological rather than personal. We know that he was familiar with *The Examiner* from his days at Enfield School, and the likelihood is strong that he read the offending essay.[39] Here Hunt described a St. Patrick's Day banquet held in 1812 among the Irish nobility, where he defended the justice of their "hisses" and "clamors" when a toast was proposed to the Prince Regent. ("It might have been proper in the meeting, had it been possible, to distinguish between the Prince of Wales as a subscriber to the Irish charity, and the Prince of Wales as a clincher of Irish chains . . .")[40]

Hunt and his friends were not only concerned with the political rights of the native-born in the periphery countries, but were also interested in the folk-traditions of those countries.[41] Such traditions harkened back to the pre-Christian days, as did those of the more patrician classical mythology, and thus they were doubly congenial to the Hunt circle. As Jeffrey Cox has commented, the circle's general use of Greco-Roman myth was "ideologically charged" and used for political as well as literary ends.[42] They had "a larger ideological project," which was the general questioning of Christianity and exploration of alternative myths.[43]

Hunt himself had an interest in Celtic nationalism and its connected bardic culture that went back to his schooldays. Thomas Gray was one of his favorite poets in his early years at Christ's Hospital.[44] The Gray he admired was not the composer of the familiar "Elegy Written in a Country Churchyard," but the later Gray who admired Ossian and wrote poetry inspired by the ancient bards of Wales. Hunt must have read Ossian in these days also, for *Juvenilia*, his collection of poems written between the ages of 12 and 16, contained several with heavy obligations to both.[45] Hunt later dismissively noted in his *Autobiography* that these early works were "for the most part . . . mere trash. . . . I wrote 'odes' because Collins and Gray had written them."[46] But *Juvenilia* proved successful enough that when he visited school friends at Oxford he was introduced to the literati, which included the Welsh bards Richard Llwyd and William Owen, both involved with Welsh nationalism. The latter had a Welsh harp along, which he played for Hunt.[47]

Later, Hunt wrote that his earliest memories of Keats were the times when they talked and read together soon after their first meeting in 1816: "No imaginative pleasure was left unnoticed or unenjoyed; from the recollection of bards and patriots of old, to the luxury of a summer rain at the window or the clicking of the coal in winter-time."[48] These bards clearly were Celtic and not Greek, as their association with the "patriots of old" shows. When the Celtic bards recounted the tales of ancient heroes and battles, the histories of their countries assured that they were doing so to incite their listeners to oppose some present tyranny. An event evoked again and again in the literature of later Celticists — most famously by Thomas Gray in "The Bard" — was the order by Edward I, when conquering Wales, to massacre the bards to prevent them from composing patriotic poems of resistance. *Juvenilia* was one of the books in Keats's small library.[49]

Keats's earliest poems, included in his 1817 volume *Poems*, easily draw upon faerylore as part of a context in which such allusions would be caught and understood. These poems were written at the time when Keats had first joined the Hunt circle and to a large extent should be read within this framework. Those that refer specifically to faeries were based on literary works all had read, or they were included in letters to friends.[50] In a way, *Poems* was a celebration of his newfound friendship with the group and his place within it.[51] Familiarity with folklore was common to this circle, as can be seen from the running references to it in Keats's letters to friends and relatives.[52] In early 1818 when Keats was visiting Devon, a region bordering the ancient Celtic area of Cornwall and rich in traditional faerylore, he sent John Reynolds the first of many poems about the faerie that he enclosed in letters to friends and relatives over the next few years.[53] Others were sent to his sister Fanny and brother Tom during his 1818 walking tour through Scotland, and to his brother George after he settled across the ocean with his newly married Georgiana in 1819. This lore evidently was part of the general knowledge of Keats's family as well as friends.

Keats's strong republican political bent was established quite early. Nicholas Roe has amply demonstrated the grounding in English radicalism that Keats would have received at Enfield School from 1803 through 1811, his only formal schooling aside from Guy's Hospital.[54] Clarke's school followed the tradition of republicanism and political dissent of the 1790s. It would have provided the intellectual climate for a sympathy and then advocacy for Celtic nationalistic aims by Keats. Clarke has told us which books in the Enfield School library particularly absorbed Keats, who during his last 18 months there read constantly.[55]

> Voyages and travels of any note . . . Robertson's histories of Scotland, America, and Charles the Fifth. . . . His constantly recurrent sources of attraction were Tooke's "Pantheon," Lemprière's "Classical Dictionary," which he appeared to *learn*, and Spence's "Polymetis." . . . He asked me to lend him some of my own books; and, in my "mind's eye," I now see him at supper (we had our meals in the schoolroom), sitting back on the form, from the table, holding the folio volume of Burnet's "History of his Own Time" between himself and the table, eating his meal from beyond it. This work, and Leigh Hunt's *Examiner* . . . no doubt laid the foundation of his love of civil and religious liberty.[56]

Consider these histories that were such favorites of Keats.

Robertson and Gilbert were both Scottish, and their partisan histories are written from the viewpoint of the eighteenth-century Scot under the yoke of England. Both portray Scotland as fiercely independent, always battling England's monarchism. Robertson begins *The History of Scotland* with the mythic period of Dalriada that was followed by the successful repulsion of the Roman invaders by the Gaelic Scots.[57] Most of his two-volume work centers around the complicated machinations of power surrounding Mary Queen of Scots, and it is easy to see why the young Keats read it with such enjoyment. Our sympathies lie with Mary and her country, not England and its scheming kings. There is a running criticism of the English bias against the Gaelic language; and Robertson concluded that the Scots' present seeming "ignorance and obscurity... must be imputed to the unhappiness of their political situation, not to any defect of genius."[58]

Bishop Burnet's zeal even more clearly points toward Gaelic nationalism.[59] His anecdotal, sometimes gossipy, autobiography is a first-hand account of the English monarchies of the period. The first volume records the political maneuvering by Mary Queen of Scots, as well as the later reign of James II, much despised by Burnet as "a king who ran counter to the sentiment of the Scottish people... contrary to the bent and genius of the nation."[60] Decidedly anti-monarchist, Burnet details the profligacy of James II and Charles I, as well as James II's general suppression of Scottish rights. He relates the seamy and tyrannical acts of the English monarchy against the background of the continuing resistance of the Highland clans and the Scots in general.

These books fired Keats's imagination before he left Enfield School at age 14. Six years later when he left London for a country sojourn to begin composing *Endymion*, he headed south for the Isle of Wight. It was his first such expedition entirely alone, and he brought company in the form of three inspiring pictures to hang wherever he went: one of Milton and his daughters, one a sketch by his friend Benjamin Haydon, and one of Mary Queen of Scots.[61]

Beyond Keats's own reading of Scottish history and the influence of the Hunt circle, however, the broader social context supported Keats's strong interest in Celticism, most notably through the linked cultural phenomena of Ossian, Sir Walter Scott, and, to a lesser degree, Robert Burns. All of these Scottish figures were wildly popular among wider European and even American audiences, for they seemed connected in various ways to the ancient Gaelic traditions that were in danger of being forgotten and extinguished.[62]

Today, most literary scholars consider Ossian's *Fragments of Ancient Poetry* and *The Works of Ossian: "Fingal" and "Temora"* as cultural curiosities. Ossian himself, the ancient Gaelic bard, was the subject of genuine legend. However, his mysteriously intact epics were supposedly found in the Western Highlands of Scotland and "translated" into English 1400 years later by James Macpherson, in what soon became apparent was a forgery. But many cultural historians are coming to read the situation quite differently, and see the resulting controversy over the epics' authenticity as an important index of rising Gaelic nationalism. Fiona Stafford holds that at a deep level the epics supposedly by Ossian were authentic because Macpherson (himself a clansman as a youth) was drawing here on the Celticist's authentic grief at the passing of the Highland clans and their way of life extending back a thousand years.[63]

It is very likely that in 1817 or early 1818 Keats read Macpherson's popular first volume of supposed translations from the Gaelic, the *Fragments of Ancient Poetry* (1760) that actually was his translation of old Gaelic ballads and lays that he had collected in the Highlands, and then the epics of Macpherson's "discovered" Ossian, probably *Fingal* which was the best known. It was later in 1818 that Keats began writing *Hyperion*; and Ossianism, with its doomed nostalgia for a vanished noble past, clearly shows throughout this epic fragment.[64]

Ossian may only be a literary and cultural footnote now, but in the late eighteenth century, as Jerome McGann has remarked, "Ossian's influence… eclipsed all others."[65] This alone would have insured Keats's familiarity with him. In addition, Chatterton whom he greatly admired — one of Keats's earliest sonnets was "Oh Chatterton! How very sad thy fate" and *Endymion* was dedicated to him — "translated" some very Ossianic and supposedly ancient Saxon poems. Hazlitt too was highly enthusiastic about Ossian. He gave a series of public lectures in 1817, published in 1818 as "Lectures on the English Poets," and Keats eagerly attended them. In his introductory lecture "On Poetry in General," Hazlitt remarks on "four of the principal works of poetry in the world, at different periods of history — Homer, the Bible, Dante, and let me add, Ossian."[66] As would the Celticist, he praises "Ossian" for his melancholy witnessing of an ancient Gaelic nobility that has long since passed away: "He is a feeling and a name that can never be destroyed in the minds of his readers…. The feeling of cheerless desolation, of the loss of the pith and sap of existence… is here perfect."[67]

At some point during these years, Keats read Scott. The old Gaelic worlds created by both Macpherson and Scott had much in common with the world of English medieval romance that so attracted him. The supposed Gaelic past celebrated by "Ossian" was an idealized version in which warriors, maidens, kings, and foes all operated according to a strict code of chivalry and honor. If Stafford is right, it is a romanticized and partisan picture of the clan society that was essentially medieval in its outlook. Scott too reconstructed the medieval romance in his Border ballads, and clan life in many of his novels. We know that Keats admired both Scott's poetry and his novels, for he wrote to his brother

George in 1818 alluding to both: "We have seen three literary kings in our Time — Scott — Byron — and then the scotch nove[ls.]"[68] It is significant that Keats termed him a "literary king" for his poetry as well as his historical novels, for he could only have meant the widely read *Minstrelsy of the Scottish Border* (1803) and the even more popular *Lay of the Last Minstrel* (1805), originally intended as one of the romantic Border ballads to be included in *Minstrelsy.*

Keats's reading at Enfield on Scottish history would have been well-supplemented by these contemporary best-sellers; and given their widespread fame he surely was familiar with them.[69] Scott would have given him a more literary rendering of early Scottish history with *Minstrelsy*, and a keener focus on the bard who had sung this "minstrelsy" with *Lay of the Last Minstrel.* Both works would have met with strong enthusiasm from this young lower middle-class reader who aspired to be a poet now, *pace* Scott's minstrel who is "last," for as Scott stated in *Minstrelsy*: "... though these aboriginal poets [the Gaelic bards] showed themselves at festivals and other places of public resort, it does not appear that, as in Homer's time, they were honoured with high places at the board, and savory morsels of the chine; but they seem rather to have been accounted fit company for the feigned fools and sturdy beggars, with which they were ranked by a Scottish statute."[70]

Minstrelsy would have given Keats more than an understanding of early Scottish history. He would have received an excellent grounding in English as well as Scottish folk-beliefs about the faerie world, through Scott's long introductory essays accompanying the old folk-ballads collected and "reconstructed" here. Scott dwelt in several of these essays upon one ballad in particular as "antique" and "long current ... in Scotland," the "ballad of Thomas of Ercildoune, and his intrigues with the Queen of Faery Land" that was titled "Thomas the Rhymer."[71] This old Celtic ballad proved a later inspiration for Keats in "La Belle Dame" as well as *Endymion*, a re-imagined version of "Thomas the Rhymer."[72] Quite possibly "The Daemon-Lover" that Scott included in Volume III was the basis for Keats's poem "The Eve of St. Agnes."

Scott was in line with those eighteenth-century antiquarians who collected and studied all the forms of the past that they could locate, although Scott's interests were focused enough on one area of the past — that relating to the Scottish Border country — to make him a very early folklorist as well. One modern folklorist has termed him "in the front ranks of all British antiquarians."[73] Another states that "even if Scott had never published anything else ... his name would have been spoken with admiration by students of sung folk-narrative all over the world. . . . Much of that respect would probably be in acknowledgement of the painstaking and thoughtful editorial commentaries which introduce and surround the individual texts [in *Minstrelsy*]."[74]

Scott's antiquarian interest went back to his childhood spent in his grandparents' farm in the Border country, when he collected artifacts and the oral traditions of the area. Scott felt, like many contemporary Celticists, that the traditional Gaelic way of life was disappearing; and he traveled through the Borders area of Scotland in the 1770s to collect Gaelic ballad literature from individuals and from local manuscript collections. For *Minstrelsy*, his first and best antiquarian work, Scott presented his versions of the old Gaelic ballads that he had in some cases rewritten into "improved," more literary versions in the Scots dialect. Since he considered them to be literary records of Scottish history, he included long introductory essays relating the surrounding events and the supporting folk-beliefs. His long introductory essays on "Popular Poetry" (Scottish folk-ballads) and "The Minstrelsy of the Scottish Border" would have seemed as partisan a version of Scottish history as the accounts by Robertson, Gilbert, and Burnet, and possibly more convincing in its appeal to a contemporary reader. His "Introduction to the Tale of Tamlane, on the Fairies of Popular Superstition,"[75] would have supplied Keats with all that he needed to know about traditional British folk-beliefs surrounding the faerie and its world.

An additional source of knowledge, if one were needed, would have been Robert Burns, whose *Poems* Keats owned. If Keats admired Scott, there would have been a much closer fellow-feeling between him and Burns. Nearer to Keats in class, Burns was closer too in his quick satiric republicanism. A high point of Keats's walking tour was visiting Burns's tomb at Dumfries, with Keats describing "the Bardie's country" in a letter to Reynolds in terms of Burns's folk-ballads and "Tam O'Shanter" and noting that, "One of the pleasantest means of annulling self is approaching such a shrine as the Cottage of Burns."[76] Many of Burns's poems, including "Tam O'Shanter," used the same Scottish folk-beliefs that Scott later collected; and he relied strongly upon folklore for the content, language, and sometimes structure of his poems.[77]

Born about a decade before Scott, Burns too had the antiquarian's interest in the past Gaelic times that were fast vanishing, to be seen for him in the folksongs. Today we may not think of him as an early folklorist, but he has a significant place in the history of folksong study.[78] When his *Poems, Chiefly in the Scottish Dialect* was published in 1786 and he was able to move beyond the scope of tenant-farming, Burns attracted his Edinburgh patrons because his poems seemed part of the larger nationalistic movement of Celticism that they ardently supported. For that reason the next year they sponsored his tours through the Borders and Highlands to collect traditional folk-ballads before they were forgotten; and also encouraged him to collect, edit, and annotate folksongs for *The Scots Musical Museum*. On these tours he most likely picked up the folklore of the areas as well, if he had not already known it; and after this Edinburgh experience he collected the old practices and customs as well as the folksongs. Burns's antiquarianism can be seen in his many renderings of the old folksongs, "reconstructed" by him much as Scott did somewhat later, and also in his longer poems with their reliance on the traditional folk-beliefs in magic such as "Tam O'Shanter," "Address to the Deil," and "Hallowe'en." If Scott gave Keats the intellectual knowledge of "the Fairies of Popular Superstition," Burns supplied the bite of the experience.

All of this formed the background for Keats's 1818 walking tour with Brown through northern England and Scotland, with a brief excursion into Ireland. He began reading *Celtic Researches* sometime after he met Brown in 1817, for his copy apparently was borrowed from Brown.[79] Brown himself was of Scottish descent, for his grandfather came from the Hebrides. He evidently knew some Gaelic, enough to converse with natives when he and Keats reached Scotland.[80] This long trek gave Keats an immediate experience of the lands and the people that he had only known through books. His close association with Brown from 1817 through 1819 would have reinforced his Celticism.

Most of Keats's country journeys in England were to areas rich in Celtic or Cornish history. A few months before the 1818 walking tour when Keats was visiting Devonshire, he wrote to Reynolds of his intent to visit "Kent's Cave at Babbicun."[81] The weather prevented him then, but he evidently visited it at some point, for in September 1819 he wrote again of "Babbicomb" to Reynolds who was then journeying through Devonshire: "If you can get a peep at Babbicomb before you leave the country, do. — I think it the finest place I have seen, or — is to be seen in the South."[82] Kent's Cavern in Torquay, a city on Babbacombe Bay, is the archaeological site of a Paleolithic cave-dwelling that was first investigated in the early nineteenth century. Keats's continuing interest in viewing it suggests his wish to find out what he could about the supposed Celtic period before the Romans came.

Keats and Brown decided upon this tour in the spring of 1818. By that May, Keats had received his apothecary's license, published *Endymion*, and made the momentous decision to abandon the practical profession of medicine for the uncertain vocation of poetry. As he wrote to Haydon that April, the tour was "to make a sort of Prologue to the Life I intend to pursue — that is to write, to study and see all Europe at the lowest expence [*sic*]....I will get such an accumulation of stupendous recollolections [*sic*] that as I walk through the suburbs of London I may not see them."[83] In other words, he would get the images, observations, and experiences that would serve as materials for his future poetry. The "Europe" he would see was briefly northern England but primarily Scotland, whose history he knew so well. Something pulled him to this Celtic country all of his life. Even in May 1820, a month before his deteriorated health forced him to move in with Hunt and his family, he was considering another visit to Scotland.[84]

Tours in the Celtic periphery countries in the early nineteenth century had replaced the aristocratic Grand Tour of the early eighteenth century for many middle-class Englishmen with an antiquarian interest.[85] The trip was not a healthy one for Keats. They walked almost 700 miles in six weeks, and the weather along their way that summer was unusually cold and rainy. To judge from Keats's letters, their diet was limited to oatcakes, eggs, and whiskey. When Keats returned to London in August he visited his friends, the Dilkes. Mrs. Dilke described his appearance then in a letter: "As brown and shabby as you can imagine; scarcely any shoes left, his jacket all torn at back, a fur cap, a great plaid, and his knapsack."[86]

All along the way, their itinerary included places that were rich in Celtic history. Only about one of the six weeks was spent in England, as they headed toward Scotland. While still in England, Keats wrote to Tom that they "set forth about a mile & a half...to see the Druid temple [the Druid Circle near Keswick]. We had a fag up hill, rather too near dinner time, which was rendered void, by the gratification of seeing those aged stones."[87] The Druid Circle is an impressive site of 48 prehistoric megaliths. In the same letter, Keats wrote with enthusiasm of viewing the Highland Fling at his inn: "They kickit & jumpit with mettle extraordinary, & whiskit, & fleckit, & toe'd it, & go'd it, & twirld it, & wheel'd it, & stampt it, & sweated it, tattooing the floor like mad; The differenc[e] between our country dances & these scotch figures, is about the same as leisurely stirring a cup o' Tea & beating up a batter pudding....I never felt so near the glory of Patriotism, the glory of making by any means a country happier. This is what I like better than scenery."[88]

He wrote this early in their tour. But more and more as they went on, he noted in his letters the poverty of the people of these Celtic colonies. In his letter to Tom about his visit to Burns's tomb, he wrote: "Yesterday was an immense Horse fair at Dumfries, so that we met numbers of men & women on the road, the women nearly all barefoot, with their shoes & clean stockings in hand, ready to put on & look smart in the Towns. There are plenty of wretched Cottages, where smoke has no outlet but by the door." About this time, Brown wrote to Dilke that Keats "says the [Scottish] women have large splay feet, which is too true to be controverted, and . . . he thanks Providence he is not related to a Scot, nor in any way connected with them."[89] The splay feet, of course, would have come from continual hard rural work without shoes. Keats notes again and again that the women he passes along the road are barefoot.

They made a brief excursion to Belfast, but only stayed there a day because of the expense. Again, Keats wrote to Tom of the present state of the Irish people: "On our walk in Ireland we had too much opportunity to see the worse than nakedness, the rags, the dirt and misery of the poor common Irish — A Scotch cottage, though in that some times the Smoke has no exit but at the door, is a pallace to an irish one . . . We had the pleasure of finding our way through a Peat-Bog — three miles long at least — dreary, black, dank, flat and spongy: here and there were poor dirty creatures and a few strong men cutting or carting peat."[90]

The twentieth-century Irish critic Declan Kiberd considered Keats in his letters here to be showing the characteristically condescending British attitude toward the Irish, calling them "cunning blusterers and gallous fellows."[91] This misses Keats's keen observation that the Scots and the Irish he observes are role-playing for the paying English tourists; it misses Kiberd's own comment elsewhere about the "fawning duplicity" of the Irishmen acting such a role "which the Irishman could control and regulate at will."[92] For Keats actually writes: "A Scotchman will go wisely about to deceive you, an irishman cunningly — An Irishman would bluster out of any discovery to his disadvantage . . . An Irishman likes to be thought a gallous [fine] fellow. . . . It seems to me they are both sensible of the Character they hold in England and act accordingly to Englishmen — Thus the Scotchman will become over grave and over decent and the Irishman over-impetuous."[93] None of Keats's observations in his letters were those of the usual English tourist, whose sense of the justification of English rule tended to be reinforced by the sight of the misery and squalor of the natives.

Near the end of the tour Keats came to share the experience of the natives in a fateful way with the mysterious episode on the Isle of Mull. In late July they arrived at Oban, a town along the coast of Scotland in the West Highlands. They wanted to sail around the Isle of Mull to visit the islets of Iona and Staffa, the usual route for tourists. Both places were rich in Celtic and Gaelic history. Dating from the sixth century AD, the monastery at Iona was founded by Saint Columba who brought Christianity to Celtic Scotland. It became a major center of Celtic Christianity and many ancient Scottish kings were buried there. Staffa was the site of Fingal's Cave, another intersection with Ossianic myth for Keats as well as being, more recently, the stopping point for Bonnie Prince Charles when he landed on the Highland coast to rally the clans against the English. But Keats and Brown reluctantly gave up the idea because of the expense of the steamer ride. Keats wrote to Tom what happened next.

> In came one of the Men with whom we endeavored to agree about going to Staffa — he said what a pitty it was we should turn aside and not see the Curiosities. So we had a little talk and finally agreed that he should be our guide across the Isle of Mull — We set out, crossed two ferries, one to the isle of Kerrara of little distance, the other from Kerrara to Mull . . . The road through the Island, or rather the track is the most dreary you can think of — betwe[e]n dreary Mountains — over bog and rock and river with our Breeches tucked up and our Stockings in hand. . . . We arrived at a shepherd's Hut into w[h]ich we could scarcely get for the Smoke through a door lower than my shoulders. . . . Our Guide is I think a very obliging fellow — in the way this morning he sang us two Gaelic songs — one made by a Mrs. Brown on her husband's being drowned the other one a jacobin one on Charles Stuart. For some days Brown has been enquiring out his Genealogy here — he thinks his Grandfather came from long Island [the Island of Luing in the Inner Hebrides] . . . Well — we had a most wretched walk of 37 Miles across the Island of Mull . . .[94]

Who was that enticing "Guide" who suggested that they "turn aside to see the Curiosities" and then suggested the walking trip across Mull, a bleak place with mountains and bogs but no roads or inns? These "Curiosities" could have been those ahead at Iona and Staffa. They could also have been those back at Kilmartin, a few miles south of Oban. Kilmartin was the ancient capital of Dalriada; and burial cairns were to be seen there, as well as tumuli, carved stone graveslabs dating back to 1300, and several stone circles. Was the guide a native of that secluded town, with its eerie magical overtones, or of the more bustling Oban? Was he some impoverished Scot hoping to make a little money from these traveling Englishmen? But if Keats and Brown did not have enough money to spare for the steamer trip, journeying by foot with their "shabby...torn" clothes and knapsacks, then they could not have promised much to the guide. Brown himself was not an outsider, but spoke some Gaelic and had a Hebridean background.

The guide drew them on across Mull, over the long rock-strewn track that served as a road, through marshes and bogs. And what of those songs that he sang to them in the ancient tongue? The song of "Mrs. Brown" to her drowned husband was not a cheering one to sing to travelers going to visit islands, particularly when one was named Charles Brown. The other was "a jacobin one on Charles Stuart," or Bonnie Prince Charles leading on to Culloden. Both were songs of death.

In fact their guide acted curiously like one of the malevolent faeries likely to live under the hill-like tumuli such as those at Kilmartin,[95] or the water-spirits that haunted areas near rivers, lochs, and especially the sea.[96] Encounters with Scottish faeries were usually dangerous, more than with English ones.[97] Such shape-changing faeries delighted in leading unwary travelers astray, drawing them on and on until they were lost or exhausted. Faery singing was often an evil omen; and disease was often their lingering aftermath.[98] Whatever the nature of this guide, the sojourn on Mull proved to be the decisive event in Keats's breakdown of health that caused him to return prematurely to London. In October 1818, he wrote to his brother George of his "bad sore throat which came of bog trotting in the Island of Mull."[99] This "bad sore throat" never left him.[100]

From 1860 to 1891 J.G. Campbell collected folk-beliefs and legends of the Western Highlands and Islands of Scotland. The Isle of Mull was a rich source. Many of those legends were tales of faery encounters. Campbell's informants told him, "No wise man will desire either [faeries'] company or their kindness....to consort with them is disastrous in the extreme."[101] Campbell records nine such meetings on Mull; and many of those meetings were with spirits that foretold death.[102] He also notes several parts of Mull where there were faery hills or mounds, the realms of faery dwellings that mortals strictly avoided.[103] One was on Ross of Mull, the moorland through which Keats and Brown tramped after their stay at the shepherd's hut.[104] Several of the faery encounters that Campbell recorded were on Ross.[105] The sense of place about Mull was that of the faerie.

2
Romantic Celticism in Context

Of course, the real question to be answered is why Keats would share the antiquarians' enthusiasm for Celticism. Why would he be attracted to the history of the Celts in antiquity as well as their history on the British Isles, and from such an early age? Why would a primary source for his poetry from its very beginnings be, as termed by an early twentieth-century anthropologist of the British Isles, "the fairy-faith"?[1] His fascination was not solely aesthetic. Celticism in general implied defiance of the present political British status quo. Moreover, Celtic-derived folklore provided him with the quietly held means of resistance to the period's aristocratic literary establishment that privileged classical learning as an index of breeding and culture. The "fairy-faith" may also have been congenial to his own quicksilver sense of ambiguity and possibility.[2] Certainly, allusions to classical mythology run through Keats's poetry. But so do the closer native myths that, as Celtic scholars believed, were prior in their origins to classicism.

It was not that he was engaged in a systematic way with eighteenth-century British Celticism and its antiquarian debates about the relations between various ethnic groups and the relative antiquities of the European languages. (However, in a second-hand way he participated through his enthusiasm for Edward Davies.) But in his sympathies and his art, Keats was part of the movement that has been termed the Celtic Revival, more diffuse and less political than the Irish Celtic Revival a century later. The earlier Celtic Revival was a significant movement among British men of letters during the 1760s that continued well into the Romantic period.[3] This "revolution in literary taste"[4] dates from the 1750s and 1760s with the publication of Thomas Gray's long poem "The Bard" and then James Macpherson's Ossian poems. It led to a widespread public interest during the late eighteenth and early nineteenth centuries in archaic Britain, especially Druidism and bardism, and Celtic culture more generally. In a larger historical context, Celticism and the native British past it summoned up were increasingly subjects of antiquarian interest during this time.

For the English, it was a self-glorifying patriotism that made them search for what could be learned about the ancient Britons who were pre-Norman, pre-Saxon, and pre-Roman. But for many others, it was something else altogether more impelling. Romantic Celticism was needed for psychic survival by the Scots, Irish, and Welsh; and to an extent, it functioned that way for Keats too. Celticism was a way of dealing with *shame*, the shame of the declassed who were considered worthless by those in power. The Welsh, Scots, and Irish were reminded of what they had once been, a statement of personal worth in the face of the English negation of them as colonized subjects. The non-English Celtic scholars had this same ideological zeal in their pursuit of lore that otherwise seemed arcane and bloodless, but instead would help to prove their peoples' ancient identities. For Keats too, the Celticism and the folklore were ways of dealing with shame.

Shame is at once the most social of the emotions and also the most immediately, devastatingly internalized of them.[5] When one is shamed, one wants to hide from the sight of others. Shame is social in that it results from the painful sense that one's inferiority and weaknesses have been exposed to others; one's very self seems to be defective and disgusting to others. Since shame is primarily a social experience, it is also a highly successful method of enforcing control. Shaming may be used to "cut down to size," to stigmatize and thus exclude. However, there are strategies for coping with shame and defusing its burning pain. One may escape shame to a large extent by identifying with an idealized group, submerging the shamed individual self and finding instead a significance through belonging to the larger and honored collective body.[6]

In the case of Keats, there were possible reasons for shame almost everywhere, from his immediate personal circumstances to his art. His early poetry that gave him his most authenticating self-defense against the feeling of inferiority because of his social class also caused him the greatest public shaming.

To begin, we need to imagine hearing Keats. He was, literally, born a "cockney," for his birthplace at Moorgate was within the sound of Bow Bells.[7] During his early childhood, he lived above the Swan and Hoop stable at Moorgate, and he grew up on the East Side. He continued to live with his brothers in rooms off Cheapside until Tom died several years later. Perhaps we can't know the extent to which Keats's speech was accented by this notorious London dialect of several centuries' standing.[8] But he seems to have had a pronounced enough accent for his friend Richard Woodhouse, born in Bath, to write to John Taylor in 1819: "[Keats] then read to me Lamia . . . I was much pleased with it. I can use no other term for you know how badly he reads his own poetry: & you know how slow I am in Catching."[9]

Keats's choice of profession would have marked him as surely as his accent. Apothecaries often treated the poor as substitute doctors, and their profession carried the implications of social climbing.[10] Also, as all of his acquaintances knew, tuberculosis ran throughout his family. This was especially the disease of the poor in the city, those who lived at close quarters in the filthy parts of London. The city in general was unsanitary and dirty, which was why its wealthy escaped so often to their country houses. Contagion and dirt had class-based connotations, suggesting those who had to remain in town.[11]

Further, Keats was, famously, quite short. It was a rankling source of self-consciousness for him, though he attempted to use irony to deal with it in letters to friends: "Tom [Keats] is taken for a Madman and I being somewhat stunted am taken for nothing."[12] In an aside that hits at both his height and his class status: "I heard that Mr. L Said a thing I am not at all contented with — Says he 'O, he is quite the little Poet' now this is abominable — you might as well say Buonaparte is quite the little Soldier — You see what it is to be under six foot and not a lord."[13] To Fanny Brawne, he wrote directly and simply: "My Mind has been the most discontented and restless one that was ever put into a body too small for it."[14] His "stunted" height itself had class implications, for the typical heights for the poor and the working class of the early nineteenth century were considerably lower than that for the upper class.[15]

Keats carried this baggage with him as he entered the literary arena in late 1816 when he first met Leigh Hunt and others of the circle. He continued to carry it for Byron. He certainly did for John Lockhart. Later critics usually elevate Keats a notch by claiming that Lockhart termed him a "Cockney Poet." Lockhart termed Leigh Hunt's circle "the Cockney School of Poetry" in *Blackwood's Edinburgh Magazine*; however, he did not dignify Keats with the title of poet but designated him a "Cockney rhymster."[16] His review of Keats's "Cocknified" poetry was designed to control this creature from the social-climbing "mob" through shame, to squash and efface him. He wrote: "[Keats] was bound apprentice some years ago to a worthy apothecary in town. . . . But all has been undone by a sudden attack of [Metromanie]. Whether Mr. John had been sent home with a diuretic or composing draught to some patient far gone in the poetical mania, we have not heard. . . . The phrenzy of the 'Poems' was bad enough in its way; but did not alarm us half so seriously as the calm, settled, imperturbable drivelling idiocy of 'Endymion.'"[17]

The key metaphors used here about Keats imply his loss of control of bodily functions that others see with disgust. According to these metaphors, his poems are convulsions, urine, slaver. His friend John Reynolds wrote perceptively in October 1818, after Lockhart's attack on him as a "Cockney rhymster": "The overweening struggle to oppress you only shews the world that so much of endeavor cannot be directed to nothing. Men do not set their muscles, and strain their sinews to break a straw."[18] Indeed. Why would Lockhart aim his cannon of shame and destruction at a person such as the 22-year-old Keats? It was something more than Keats's association with Leigh Hunt and his circle.

Lockhart's designation of Keats as a "Cockney rhymster" suggested other associations peculiar to the times in which Keats lived, that related both to his working-class origins and his lower middle-class adult life. Of course, the label referred to London's East End, the rough working-class area that shaded into lower middle-class propriety. Critics have primarily fastened on the literary and political reasons why this term would be used for Keats and his early poetry, while generally ignoring class stereotyping.[19] There were other uglier implications about the term "Cockney" being applied to Keats. Emily Lorraine de Montluzin shows the extent to which the *Blackwood* reviews of Hunt, Hazlitt, and Keats used animal and insect imagery to suggest that these "Cockneys" were subhuman, a common demonization of the working and lower middle classes by the Tory upper class and aristocracy.[20] The lower social classes were typified as degenerate in their sexual appetites, promiscuous, and physical. This class stereotyping may be closer to why the term was used about Keats's early poetry than his involvement with the Hunt circle.

All of these contemporary associations and realities surrounding the Cockney Londoner help to explain Byron's well-known venomous estimation of Keats and his poetry. Byron left England for good in 1816 and, as Trelawney remarked, Byron's opinions and manners were those of the early Regency England he had left,[21] a kind of petrification of former social mores lingering on for him into the early 1820s. His views of Keats and Keats's poems seem largely drawn from the Tory literary establishment, and his comments on Keats all had class connotations. His particularly nasty, sexually slanted estimations of Keats's poetry drew on stereotypes of the working class as sexually deviant: "Johnny

Keats's *piss a bed* poetry"[22] (an allusion to Lockhart's "diuretic or composing draught"?), "the *Onanism* of [his] poetry,"[23] "mental masturbation — he is always frigging his *Imagination*" [all italics his].[24]

Byron wrote of Keats himself as "a tadpole of the Lakes," a "Mankin," "that little dirty blackguard Keates [*sic*]."[25] By "tadpole" Byron *could* have meant a minor version of the Lake Poets. All of these comments *could* have alluded to Keats's youth, *or* they could have summed up Keats as only a "stunted" Cockney. "Blackguard" in Byron's time had class connotations. By the late eighteenth century it meant "the dirty boys who ply Streets to clean shoes... to black the shoes of guards... one of the idle criminal class."[26] Byron left aside this personal invective after he learned that Keats had died, but his remarks still carried class implications. Keats "was spoilt by Cocknefying and Surburbing [*sic*]."[27]

The degree of shame called up in Keats by the designation "Cockney rhymster" and by the reception of *Endymion* may be seen in his comments about the contemporaneous *Isabella; or, The Pot of Basil.* Based on a story by Boccaccio, this long narrative poem was written at intervals in 1817 during the composition of *Endymion* but not published until his volume *1820.* He and John Reynolds had originally planned to collaborate on a volume of poems that retold some of the tales by Boccaccio, although after Keats finished *Isabella* Reynolds urged him to go on alone. Keats thought well enough of it to send fair copies to Reynolds and George Keats, and offered to read it to Bailey in Scotland. This was in May and June of 1818. Some of the negative reviews of *Endymion* had come out those same months, but not Lockhart's series of articles on the "Cockney School of Poetry." Lockhart's fourth article, with its shaming disposal of "good Johnny Keats," appeared in September.

Endymion proved to be contagious for *Isabella.* By 1819 Keats had written "Eve of St. Agnes" and *Lamia,* and was eager to redeem himself as quickly as possible by publishing them with his publishers Taylor and Hessey; but he withheld any mention of *Isabella.* As his friend Woodhouse wrote to Taylor, "I wondered why he said nothing of Isabella: & assured him it would please more [than] the Eve of St. Agnes — He said he could not bear the former now. It appeared to him mawkish."[28] A few weeks later Keats explained his dislike of the poem more fully: "I will give you a few reasons why I shall persist in not publishing The Pot of Basil — It is too smokeable — I can get it smoak'd at the Carpenters shaving chimney much more cheaply.... I intend to use more finesse with the Public. It is possible to write fine things which cannot be laugh'd at in any way. Isabella is what I should call were I a reviewer 'A weak-sided Poem' with an amusing sober-sadness about it."[29]

As Kelvin Everest points out, by "smokeable" Keats did not mean that the poem had faults that were easily exposed but that it was "too easily made fun of."[30] It was "weak-sided" or vulnerable to ridicule, and its "sober-sadness" was "amusing." "Mawkish" and "amusing" are odd words to use about this macabre tale of greed, death, gruesome fetishism, and madness. It is an indecorous and *extreme* tale. The audience that Keats seemed to be imagining for *Isabella* was one with a supercilious gaze, and a fastidious sense of what is fitting to be discussed. The ridicule that Keats seemed to be fearing for *Isabella* was meted out earlier by Lockhart to *Endymion*, sneering at the apothecary's apprentice who "knows Homer only from Chapman." For after all, Keats had only read Boccaccio in translation.

James Chandler suggests that much of the later density of Keats's poetry after 1817 is due to his sensitivity to being "smoked out" by the Tory reviewing establishment.[31] In other words, he dreaded another public shaming. Lockhart had jeered at him for "acquir[ing] a sort of vague idea, that the Greeks were a most tasteful people, and that no mythology can be so finely adapted for the purposes of poetry as theirs."[32] So Keats resolved to write with "more finesse" about "fine things which cannot be laughed at." What better way to do that than to draw on the history of the other far-flung people of antiquity and their continuity into modern times on the British Isles, and to work with the native folk-beliefs in addition to the culturally acceptable classical mythology? What better way to avoid the Tory literary establishment completely than to draw upon a tradition and history altogether closer to home — that of British Celticism?

From a wider perspective, Keats's situation as a "Cockney rhymster" scorned by the English upper-class establishment paralleled that of the Celtic periphery countries in his time, declassed much in the way that he was. This probably was why he was drawn to their history and past culture. Their signs of difference were also ridiculed and scorned by those who feared they might climb to power. As Murray Pittock remarks in his fine, acidly written dissection of the English dehumanizing portrayal of Scottish and Irish Celts from the eighteenth century to the present, "It is arguable that in the eighteenth century more xenophobia was directed internally in the British Isles than externally towards France and other rivals."[33] Shaming certainly was part of England's way of controlling these colonial subjects who persisted in being alien. Their poverty was held up as an identifying marker, although it mostly came from their economic exploitation by England. Like Keats and the Cockney Poets who were characterized by the Tory literary reviewers as subhuman and filth-ridden, the Irish had long been portrayed as apes, the Scots as savages, and the Welsh as stupid thieves.[34]

As with Cockney Keats, their native language was considered especially shame-worthy and a sign of backwardness. The English attempted to root out these linguistic markers of difference by prohibiting any language but English from being used in the schools or in the Anglican churches, also imposed on these non-Anglican countries. There was a relentless English effort to root out the speaking of Gaelic in Ireland from the time of the seventeenth-century Plantations until the mid-nineteenth century. In Scotland, the assimilation of the more prosperous and arable Lowlands after the 1707 Act of Union was eased by the fact that they spoke Scots, a dialect of English. But the Highlanders had always spoken Gaelic, then called "the Irish language" or Erse. After the 'Forty-Five, Gaelic was outlawed in all Scottish schools during the eighteenth century.

Of all the Celtic fringe countries, Wales had a population that was closest ethnically to the English, for a large minority were descendents of Anglo-Saxons or the Norse. Their own Celtic-based language was their primary mark of distinction from the English.[35] They were intensely proud of their unique native tongue, holding that it was similar to ancient Hebrew and of equal antiquity.[36] However, they also experienced the deliberate attempt by the English to efface their language so as to make them good British subjects. After the 1707 Act of Union, the Church of England with its mandatory tithing was imposed upon Wales with services conducted only in English. Their language that was incomprehensible to outsiders was generally derided by the English throughout the eighteenth and much of the nineteenth century as a sign of the country's "backwardness."

Celticism functioned for these countries much as it did for Keats, who faced a similar cultural imperialism from Lockhart and his confederates. A significant aspect of that imperialism was its absorption of ancient classical culture into the patrician values of present-day England.[37] A classical education carried class status for it suggested the wealth to attain it at public schools and universities, and the leisure to attain this non-professional knowledge. The study of the literature of the Roman Empire implied a patriotic allegiance to the more contemporary empire established by England, although, as the historian Linda Colley points out, the classical themes of war and sacrifice were safe from any subversive readings since the empires celebrated were dead.[38]

Celticism too had an extrahistorical significance in the eighteenth and early nineteenth centuries, with historical realities changed or conflated. Nationalists of the periphery countries considered their native cultures equally ancient to those of the classical civilizations, and Celticists pitted their culture against the foreign Roman one that was associated with classicism.[39] Patriotism also was implied, although with a rather different emphasis. Welsh, Irish, and Scottish scholars sought to counteract the colonizing experience by using their own Celtic or Gaelic heritages to demonstrate that their native civilizations had been the equal of those of classical antiquity.[40]

Both Ireland and Scotland possessed national myths that traced the lineage of their people back to ancient kingdoms on the Isles predating the Roman conquest; and both drew on these myths as a counteroffensive to English domination of their countries. In Ireland, the "Old Irish" were the legendary Milesians, descendents of the three sons of King Mileadh of northern Spain, who supposedly invaded Celtic Ireland and formed the kingdom of Milesia. From the time of the Plantations onward, Gaelic nationalists sought to create a Milesian identity with an ancient culture that rivalled those of classical antiquity.[41] Scotland also traced its history back to a primordial kingdom, Dalriada in the west Highlands. Unlike the Lowlands, the west Highlands had never been conquered by the Romans. So Scots could claim to derive from a kingdom with an ancient autonomy predating that of the English monarchy; and this Gaelic history became the cornerstone of the later demand for the independence of a Scotland that included both the Lowlands and the Highlands.[42]

But Celticism also provided a much more powerful defense against the experience of worthlessness than these histories specific to certain countries, a defense shaped by contemporary antiquarianism. During the eighteenth century, antiquarians laid the groundwork for the later disciplines of archaeology, comparative ethnology, and linguistics as they individually followed their enthusiasms for collecting and studying relics of archaic Britain. The survival of the Celtic-based Welsh and the closely related Gaelic language spoken in Ireland and the Scottish Highlands seemed a living link to ancient British times, and spurred a general scholarly focus on Celtic culture. Part of the antiquarians' fervor in exploring the ancient past was their curiosity about the place of the present ethnic nationalities within it. Which were the truly original, and which were hybrid stock?

Their investigation of this question (indeed, all of those about the past) had parameters that we may not imagine today. As the eminent British archaeologist Stuart Piggott reminds us of the pre-archaeological sixteenth through eighteenth centuries: "The world picture of educated men in these centuries was emphatically not ours, and the world picture was one which included the past as well as the present."[43] This world picture presumed the literal accuracy of Mosaic history. The past was believed to be known through the texts of the ancient written authorities and supremely through the Scriptures, with Moses as the author of the Pentateuch.

The Book of Genesis defined the boundaries of early history, providing a literal account from the Creation to the Flood, with the subsequent peopling of the postdiluvial world by the descendents of Noah's sons, Shem, Ham, and Japheth. It was generally held that the descendents of Japheth populated Europe; and various nationalities claimed their ancestral lineage from one or another of Japheth's offspring. There was considerable disagreement as to the date of the Creation, though by the eighteenth century the consensus was that it occurred in 4004 BC. More crucial for antiquarians and historians was the date of the Flood; and from the seventeenth century onward, the date was generally agreed to be between 2500 BC and 2000 BC.[44] This meant, of course, that all postdiluvial history had occurred within about 4000 years. It was not until the mid-nineteenth century that this was questioned, when evidence to the contrary began accumulating with a large-scale excavation of British barrows and an ensuing mass of archaeological evidence. Keats's fascination with "Kent's Cave at Babbicun" was that of the antiquarian.

Central to eighteenth-century Celticism was the Breton ethnological scholar and Abbé, Paul-Yves Pezron. His intent was to restore the continental Celts, in particular the Bretons, to their rightful place in Mosaic history; and his widely influential treatise *L'antiquité de la nation et de la langue des Celtes, autrement appellez Gaulois* glorified the ancient Gauls and Celts as direct descendents of Gomer, son of Japheth. Pezron's ideas passed into a general acceptance by Celtic scholars, who extended and elaborated his arguments. Pezron held that these Gomerian offspring, the major enemies of the ancient Greeks and Romans with an empire spread across ancient Europe, were linked to the myth of the Titans.

The association of the Celts with the Titans was not unique with him, but an old one. In *Paradise Lost*, Milton had followed this traditional connection when his Satan summons the dispersed Titans who as "the Celtic roamed the utmost isles" (I.510–20). This linking had significant implications for Keats's fragmentary epics about the Titans, *Hyperion* and *The Fall of Hyperion*. In Milton, the Titans and thus the Celts are associated with the fallen angels, but Pezron dwelt upon this tradition to the benefit of the Celts. Eighteenth-century Celticists usually thought the Celts of Wales also derived from Gomer, while the Gaels of the Scottish Highlands and Ireland often were connected with Magog, another of Japheth's sons.[45] One Celtic scholar declared that the people of the British Celtic periphery were "the only unmixed remains of the children of Japheth upon the globe."[46] The present-day British Celts had an impeccable pedigree.

Edward Davies ("curate of Olveston, Gloucestershire," he announced on the title page of *Celtic Researches*) entered this dialogue of Celtic scholars quite comfortably. His book was generally well known in his time, if not now. Blake, Wordsworth, Peacock, and even the American Emerson were familiar with Davies.[47] Keats was encountering in Davies commonly held ideas about the nature of ancient man, and not only in Davies's belief that the Celts derived from Japheth. He too connected the Titans with the Celts, although with his own twist that Keats was to follow.

For Davies as for many Celticists then, the Titans were the original giants sent wandering off from Nimrod's Babel. He describes how they became identified with the Celts. "All ancient nations acknowledge their acquaintance with such a race [Nimrod's giants]. They intruded into the recesses of their country, they lurked among their caves, their forests, their rocks and their desolate places, practicing sorcery and diabolical arts... fierce and savage.... These are the people who are described as *Exiles* and *Wanderers*, and at the same time are called the *Titans*.... These *Exiles* and *Wanderers* from Babel [were the]... rebellious and unvanquished giants [the historical Gauls], whose features are exactly recognized in the poetry of the Greeks and Romans, and in the tales and traditions of all primitive nations, *amongst whom* they were scattered abroad, as universal monuments of the punishment of pride and disobedience."[48] These Gauls were spread across ancient Europe and Asia Minor, and battled the classical Greeks and the Romans. They eventually settled in British Gaul to become the progenitors of the Celts. "... [T]he original *Celtae* of the *West*, who anciently possessed the whole of Gaul, the Islands of Britain, *part* of Germany, and *part* of Spain... were distinguished by the names of *Titans* [italics his throughout]."[49] And he refers to the "Titanian Celtae" throughout his book.

However, Davies's centerpiece was his long speculation on the true identity of the Druids. He definitely departed from the usual view of this learned priesthood whose actual history, with the Celts, went back to the classical world. The Druids were exclusively British, Davies maintained, and their original name was the Hyperboreans.[50] This identification of the British Isles with the mythic country "beyond the land of the north" from classical antiquity and the Druids with the Hyperboreans is startling but plausible given contemporary assumptions. Geographically, of course, the British Isles would have seemed like the "land beyond the North Wind" to the ancient Greeks. The Hyperboreans supposedly worshipped Apollo, from whom they got their advanced knowledge which they passed on to the ignorant Greeks. The Druids, held Davies, preserved the religion and sciences of Noah and his sons, and this accounted for their esoteric wisdom.[51] It was known in Davies's time that astronomy was central to the Druidical religion, and this was congruent with worship of the sun-god. Finally, if one believed like most educated scholars then (especially clerical ones) that the Flood occurred around 2000 BC, it would be possible for the Druids to have existed prior to the archaic Greeks.

Brown seems to have lent Keats his own copy of Davies's book and probably introduced him to it, for when he listed the books in Keats's library posthumously he noted "m" beside some, including *Celtic Researches*, which most probably meant "mine."[52] Keats and Brown first met in the summer of 1817 while Keats was in the middle of writing *Endymion*. Keats wrote Book II in August, Book III in September, and Book IV in November.[53] From internal evidence in this long poem we can deduce that he most probably began reading Davies's book about this time, and certainly by November when he finished *Endymion*. This will be addressed in greater detail in Chapter 3, but here it is sufficient to note that the first borrowing that possibly came from Davies occurs in the passage that opens Book II, with lines 19–21 an obscure, learned allusion to the Druids. The figure of Glaucus that dominates Book III has many characteristics of the Druids as described by Davies. The opening lines of Book IV that are addressed to the "Muse of my native land" and include allusions to "England" and "Druids" (1–7) quite clearly show the strong influence of Davies's ideas.

Celtic Researches, on the Origin, Traditions & Language, of the Ancient Britons was a seminal work for Keats at this particular point in his life, influencing his later works as well as *Endymion*. Davies's theories about connections between the Titans and the British Druids influenced *Hyperion* and *The Fall of Hyperion* in significant ways. However, Keats's interest in Davies was not solely that of the antiquarian. As with Spence's connection of the present-day reverence for Latin with the colonization of the Celtic Briton by the Romans, Davies's speculations about the "ancient Britons" had a contemporary relevance for Keats as an underclass-ranked English poet facing an upper-class literary establishment that seemed closed against him. As mentioned in Chapter 1, *Celtic Researches* would have focused Keats' reading about

Celts, Gauls, and Druids up to that time. It also would have advanced his understanding of the role of the poet.

Like other Celtic antiquarians, Davies knew the central position of Druids in Celtic society as priests, lawmakers, and adjudicators. However, he drew additional conclusions about them from his beliefs that Japheth and his descendents colonized Britain a century after the Flood, and that these descendents were Celts. The Druids represented the highest rank of these "ancient Britons" who were only a few generations away from Noah. Davies significantly held that "*their disciples were the 'Most Noble'*" [italics mine], and that "it was the immediate and selected province of those who were admitted into the order, to record and perpetuate the customs, traditions, and general history of the nation."[54] Like many of his contemporaries, Davies considered the Celtic bards to be Druidical disciples.[55]

Lemprière had simply stated that Druids were "ministers of religion among ancient Gaul and Britain," one of whose orders was the Bardi. This followed the usual division of the intellectual classes of Druids by classical Greek and Roman authors. Lemprière further noted of the Druids that their "office was open to every rank and station."[56] This last characteristic would have particularly caught Keats's attention, for it designated class as extrinsic to becoming either Druid or Bard. However, Davies went beyond the usual classification of the orders of Druids to elevate the position of the bard considerably. Where the bard had traditionally been considered the Celtic poet who praised the heroes of his people, Davies held that the role of the bard was "to inculcate several of [the Druids'] genuine doctrines" and to preserve the "arts, or traditions, of the Druids."[57] The bards immediately succeeded the Druids, and maintained their history and their secret knowledge in the poems recited to the people.[58] And, he stated confidently, "*Bardism*, or *Druidism*, originated in *Britain* — pure *Bardism* was never well understood in other countries — of whatever country they may be, they are entitled *Bards*, according to the rights and the institutes of the *Bards* of the *Island* of *Britain* [italics his]."[59]

The eighteenth- and early nineteenth-century fascination with British Druids and the mysteries of their esoteric wisdom is well known, and to an extent continues down to this day.[60] Davies's high praise for the Druids' antiquity, their primary authority in their society, and the extent of their learning was characteristic of his time, although with his own individual emphasis. He was particularly interested in connecting the Druidic order of bards with Welsh bards for the nationalistic purpose of demonstrating that the Celtic language of the Druids (Welsh) paralleled

Hebrew, Greek, and Latin in antiquity. The Druids, as understood by the early nineteenth century, had assumed definite characteristics that were not always historically accurate though some were culled from classical sources, particularly Pliny's *Natural History* and Caesar's *Gallic War*. But there was also a wealth of local legends and folk-beliefs about the Druids of ancient Britain.

They usually were portrayed as aged men with long floating hair and a waist-length beard, wearing cowls and white robes. The oak was their sacred tree, and they performed their secret rites in secluded oak groves. They held the mistletoe that grew on the oak to be sacred, and the mistletoe came to signify the Druids for eighteenth- and nineteenth-century artists and writers. Like many of these enthusiasts for the Druids, Davies failed to discuss or even acknowledge the feature of the Druids that was remarked by most Graeco-Roman historians — the human sacrifice that was part of their religious rituals. This was also a central feature of their prophesying, with auguries taken from the particular actions of the victims after the sacrificing. However, the latter-day Druidists including Davies *did* generally remark the Druids' belief in metempsychosis, which was the explanation given by most of these ancient historians for this human sacrifice. For the transmigration of the indestructible soul from one body to another after death meant that the particulars of an individual death, whether in sacrifice or in battle, were unimportant.

Druids also were assumed to be steeped in the knowledge of magic. One of the legends surrounding Merlin was that he was a Druid.[61] Both Davies and Lemprière considered Druids magicians. Following most of the classical sources, Lemprière noted that they foretold the future, knew the secrets of astrology, and believed in metempsychosis. He added that they "were acquainted with the art of magic."[62] This was the most familiar image of them through antiquity, and has survived from the eighteenth century on down to today. A significant element in the British fascination with Druids was the longstanding belief that somehow they were associated with the faeries through their knowledge of the native Celtic magic; and this belief was the basis for many folklore motifs relating to Druids. That Druids were prophets and magicians was assumed.[63] Some held that Druids directed the faeries, and that their magic could be more powerful than that of the faeries.[64] Some of the beliefs about Druids echoed similar ones about the faeries: the Druids caused illusions as did faeries; they could become magically invisible; and they too were sometimes turned to stone by saints like the malevolent faeries that were witches or trows (trolls).[65]

This eighteenth-century fascination with British Druids was part of a larger English interest in their own national identity and the nature of the ancient Britons. There was also a parallel, intense interest in the class of Druids who were the bards, though it was primarily held by the Britons who were Celtic rather than English. They too wished to determine their present national identities through evocation of the ancient Britons, those Celts who had faced the colonizing Romans and who were commemorated by their bards. The Celtic bard was an emblem of resistance, an explicit counterpoise to the distant and respectable Homeric bard of classical Greece favored by the English upper class.[66]

The figure of the Celtic bard prominent in the late eighteenth century was central to Romantic Celticism, for the historical reasons discussed earlier and also, appropriately, for literary ones — more specifically, Thomas Gray's 1757 poem "The Bard." One critic has pronounced it to be "a begetter of that interest in all things Celtic now known as the Celtic revival...the key text inaugurating the Celtic revival in the eighteenth century."[67] The Celtic bard who held such a central place in his ancient society particularly appealed to late eighteenth- and early nineteenth-century poets whose own position in society was increasingly dwindled and neglected, and Gray's own version inspired artists as well as writers during the Romantic period. Over and over, they portrayed the moment he celebrated of the bard with his lyre, his "hoary hair stream[ing], like a meteor, to the troubled air" (Gray, 19–20), about to leap from a high crag.

Thomas Gray may have inaugurated the Celtic Revival, but James Macpherson with his supposed translations of Ossian in 1765 created a sympathy for the Celtic bard among a whole generation of Romantic artists and writers. There is scarcely any literary interest in Ossian or his poem about the Gaelic hero "Fingal" today.[68] Few wish to make the effort to read this deliberately contrived six-book "epic" of a time that never existed. But present-day Celtic scholars and folklorists are coming to think that the literary worth or even authenticity of the poet Ossian is not his real significance.[69] They focus on the historical context in which Macpherson "translated" the works by this ancient Gaelic bard for an instantly admiring English and Lowlands literary audience.

Fiona Stafford's analysis of Macpherson's true worth as advocate for his vanishing Gaelic culture is particularly valuable. She considers that in a fundamental way Macpherson's creation of Ossian's voice was not truly fraudulent, for it expressed the experience of the contemporary Highlander. As she reminds us, Macpherson was a Highland clansman during the period of the 'Forty-Five and its grim aftermath. Ossian's constant lamenting for a distant heroic past was that of the Highlander who saw the traditional clan culture inexorably destroyed: "Blind, and tearful, and forlorn I now walk with little men. O Fingal, with thy race of battle I now behold thee not. The wild roes feed upon the green tomb of the mighty king of Morven" (*Fingal*, Book III, p. 79).

Macpherson traveled through the Highlands gathering old Gaelic manuscripts and attending oral recitals of Gaelic poems that he had transcribed by local speakers. He wove the resulting translations into an epic narrative, artistically embellished as a great national treasure should be, and presented it as Ossian's own. The resulting controversy is too well known to rehearse. The wide popularity of Ossian became a source of national pride, so that attacks on the veracity of Ossian's *Fingal* and *Temora* became, for many Scots, an attack on their national pride. However, Stafford argues, Macpherson's work was valuable whether or not he had indeed found and translated third-century Gaelic epics. His field trip through the Highlands had preserved Gaelic materials at just the point when they were in danger of extinction.[70]

He also created a receptive audience for the vanishing Gaelic culture and traditions with the poems, and this partisan sympathy went far beyond Scotland's borders.[71] At a time when the English were doing their best to extinguish all traces of the ancient Gaelic traditions and legally prohibited the language, dress, and music of the Highland clans, *Fingal* mounted the counter-attack. Fifty years later, Hazlitt proclaimed that the Gaelic bard ranked with Homer and Dante — the unimpeachable classical and Christian bards. "Ossianism" had come to mean a whole attitude toward the present diminished world that accorded with the Romantic sense of nostalgia and loss.

With Macpherson, we come full circle to Keats and Celticism. Whether or not Ossianism was part of Keats's intellectual atmosphere at age 14 when he began reading the Scottish histories of Robertson and Gilbert, it clearly was by the time that he was attending Hazlitt's public lectures in 1817. If anything, an early, basic knowledge of the history that made Ossian's Gaelic epic seem so significant would have heightened his zeal for Ossian. The Gaelic bard that Macpherson celebrated was close to the Celtic bard so revered by Davies. Beyond that, Macpherson's celebration of the ancient folk-myths of the native Highlanders had a motivation that was similar to Keats's emphasis on the Celts, Druids, and faerylore in his own poetry: it was a powerful defense against the depreciation of one's self and one's group by the patrician English ruling group in power.

3
Keats as Bard

At the other end of the century, Yeats also found Celtic lore and the "fairy-faith" a powerful defense against the English in the service of the more well-known Irish Celtic Revival. The early anthropologist W.Y. Evans-Wentz, whose book *The Fairy-Faith in Celtic Countries* is a classic in Celtic studies, considered this a living faith that "depends not so much upon ancient traditions, oral and recorded, as upon recent and contemporary psychic experiences."[1] For Yeats, the faery-faith was more or less synonymous with folklore, and he regarded it as such when he collected folklore materials in western Ireland during the 1880s. Yeats himself seemed to have believed that faeries did exist and spoke of this belief in several speeches of the late 1880s and 1890s, though he was prudent in admitting it.[2] Yet one wonders.

As Yeats collected the folklore, he felt that this private belief was a bond with the country folk whom he interviewed and he associated this belief with them. More than that, it also seemed to him his own experience of connection to the ancient Celt whom he wished to reach — quite important, given that he himself was middle-class Anglo-Irish and not a Catholic Irish peasant.[3] That is, the faery-faith for him was *useful*. It had the practical and ideological purpose of serving as the basis for a new Irish literature, sources whose existence seemed to oppose the commercialism and materialism of modern life.[4] Nor did he hesitate to systematize the inhabitants of the faery world in his 1888 *Fairy and Folk Tales of the Irish Peasantry* into those faeries who were solitary and those who were sociable or "trooping," with many subdivisions. But if he truly believed, then he would have known that such anatomizing was the sort of prying and spying that faeries traditionally punished severely.[5]

Yeats always saw Keats as a poet who was also drawn to faerylore and that Keats's faerylore was connected with folklore, not merely derivative from Spenser and Shakespeare. As Yeats wrote dismissively of the "fairy poetry of England": "The personages of English fairy literature are merely, in most cases, mortals beautifully masquerading. Nobody ever believed in such fairies. They are romantic bubbles from Provence. Nobody ever laid new milk on their doorstep for them."[6] That he did not count Keats among these English poets is clear from his earlier proclamation: "Folk-lore is at once the Bible, the Thirty-Nine Articles, and the Book of Common Prayer, and well-nigh all the great poets have lived by its light. Homer, Aeschylus, Sophocles, and even Dante, Goethe, and Keats, were little more than folk-lorists with musical tongues.... Shakespeare and Keats had the folk-lore of their own day, while Shelley had but mythology."[7]

In his early poetry with faery motifs, Yeats drew heavily upon Keats for atmosphere and imagery, particularly "La Belle Dame" and "The Eve of St. Agnes."[8] He also considered the late poem *Lamia* to be a work about a faery, not the creature from Greek mythology familiar to most Keats critics. He read the poem in 1889, and recognized her as one of the Irish fairies, or sidhe, familiar for their vanishing acts.[9] As he saw from his extensive study of Irish folklore, the world of the sidhe itself was lamian and, with the wonderful word he often used in describing the sidhe, poor mortals like Lycius who were dazzled and led off to faeryland were "glamoured" away.[10] This verb, meaning "to charm or enchant," was an eighteenth-century Scottish phrase that was later introduced into more general literary language by Scott in his studies of Scottish folklore; and it was an apt one indeed.[11] Oddly, when Yeats was spirit-writing much later with his wife George, he asked the spirits to inform him of Keats. He saw the ideas of Keats like wraiths floating about and accessible, still presences for Yeats.[12]

However, faerylore meant something rather different for Keats. His use of Celtic materials and folklore was less formulated and less programmatic than that of Yeats, although it was ideologically similar in its republicanism and implied resistance to the English status quo. Of course, Keats was writing during the earlier time when amateur and sometimes eccentric antiquarians dominated the field of folklore, while Yeats was a full-fledged Irish participant in the fairly well-developed discipline of British ethnography.[13] In many ways, Romantic Celticism anticipated the later Celticism of Yeats and the Irish Revival that was so much more focused as resistance against the English colonizer in their own country.

Yeats's reliance upon faerylore in his poetry was deliberately political. It also was that of the outsider to the Irish peasant world that held such beliefs. As many critics have noted, Yeats romanticized the peasants and their faery-faith, reading the folklore he gathered from them as proof for his imaginary construct of them.[14] But Keats was not drawing on this lore because of any such consciously held artistic agenda. He may have felt the sympathy of the political radical for the resisting Celt which Celticism implied. But the faerylore did not have the ideological utility for him that it did for Yeats, who saw it primarily as the possible source of materials upon which a national literature might be built.[15]

Instead, for the early Keats his interest in faerylore accompanied his general enthusiastic support of Celticism. His knowledge of these traditions was not simply gained through a familiarity with Shakespeare's literary version of Renaissance folk-traditions (or the antiquarian's notion of those traditions).[16] Rather it was supplemented to an important extent by Scott's popular four-volume *Minstrelsy of the Scottish Border*, and some of Burns's poems. This knowledge of British faerylore was part of a common ground of understanding that he shared with the liberal Hunt circle. It was a body of allusions that they sociably shared and one that did not require an aristocratic education. A good familiarity with Scott's *Minstrelsy* would have been sufficient. The real value of this collection of traditional Gaelic folk-ballads lay in the introductory essays relating the old folk-beliefs in faeries, witches, and spirits that Scott thought a necessary background for the ballads.[17] These beliefs that he notes are widespread motifs in folk-literature; and the motifs as a whole have been exhaustively catalogued by the twentieth-century folklorist Stith Thompson. The essays accompanying the ballads in *Minstrelsy* are full of local anecdotes, detailed in their accounts and thorough in their coverage of the faery-faith. The many folk-beliefs recorded there glimmer all the way through Keats's poetry, early to late.

Scott related many stories of faeries that he had collected from his Gaelic informants, as well as those he had gleaned from studying the Scottish witch-trials; and these faeries were not the comforting, diminutive ones familiar to readers of Spenser and Shakespeare. Scott noted that "the common people . . . dreaded even to think or speak about the Fairies,"[18] adding that the Scottish fairies were more malevolent than those of South Britain since they "retained more of their ancient and appropriate character."[19] One common account of the origin of the faeries was that they were originally the fallen angels, dwindled in form as they fell to earth and caught as spirits in a sort of limbo since they were not of heaven nor quite of hell.[20] In line with this was the belief that every seventh year the faery folk were bound to deliver one of them as a "teind," or tithe, to Satan, and that they much preferred to send along a mortal if they could.[21] They acquired these mortals by enveigling them into faeryland, or by exchanging one of their own children for that of a mortal child as a changeling.[22] In accordance with these beliefs, the queen of faeries was considered a generally vengeful figure of fateful beauty who glamoured away those mortal men unlucky enough to draw her desire, either to keep them forever with her in faeryland or to give them up to Satan as a teind.

Hills and caves were thought to be the dwelling places of faeries, and faeryland to be situated beneath them.[23] Scott noted that many believed that faeries "inhabit[ed] the ancient tumuli called *Barrows* [italics his]."[24] The faeries' timeless land was especially dreaded, for it trapped those mortals who wandered into it.[25] Eating or drinking faery food there doomed one to stay, as captives often surreptitiously warned newcomers who had followed the faeries' haunting music or simply stumbled onto faeryland, perhaps by sleeping on a faery hill after sunset.[26] If one did manage to leave, one discovered the penalty of entering this land beyond time: mortal life had cycled on, often by centuries, so that all those one had known were old or long dead.[27] Scott also noted many of the faeries' specific habits: green that was the color of their dress and always associated with them; the invisible processions of them riding horses; the entrance to Faeryland that was only found in the wilderness or sometimes under lakes or the sea.[28] The female faeries quite often were called by the euphemism "white nymphs" or "White Ladies," and they often rode white horses.[29]

To some extent, Keats's 1817 *Poems* gives us the faeries that are familiar from Spenser and Shakespeare. Such faeries were drawn from literary and classical sources, not folkloric ones, and conflated with classical nymphs and goddesses. Shakespeare's idea of faeries was new in literature, and influenced the way they were portrayed from then on. Tiny in size and wholly benevolent toward humans, they had the small objects of nature such as flowers, creeping plants, and insects in their special care.[30] The figures of the king and queen of the faeries also were literary in origin for these Renaissance writers. The character of Oberon, king of the faeries, derived from literary romance, in particular the French *Huon de Bordeaux*. The queen of the faeries Titania had more classical, and more august, origins. Her name itself was not the folk name for that queen, but Shakespeare's own invented name taken from Ovid's *Metamorphosis*.[31] It was one of Ovid's names for the goddess Diana (*Metamorphosis*, iii, 173), probably because her mother Leto was a daughter of the Titan Coeus. For Shakespeare, Titania was an emendation of Ovid's Diana, goddess of the moon with its bewitching light; she was the ancient made new.[32]

Ever after Shakespeare, however, the name came to signify the Queen of the Faeries for the cultivated and literate, though she usually wasn't given a name in the folktales about her.

This was the taming of a long, long folkloric tradition far different from the literary version of faeries, one that associated them with the realm of the dead and feared any contact with them.[33] The faeries of folklore were alluring, amoral, and dangerous. They were not those of Spenser and Shakespeare, or of what Yeats contemptuously called the "fairy poetry of England." Nor were they always the faeries of Keats's early 1817 *Poems*, which at times showed hints of these older natures. Four of the poems in this first volume relate to faeries in some way, and two recount the situation he later returns to again and again of the mortal who happens on faeryland or is enticed into it ("Imitation of Spenser" and "Calidore: A Fragment").[34] For the most part, the faeries here are diminutive, pliant to human wishes, and similar to classical nymphs; and the faeryland in "Calidore" is lusciously compliant to Calidore's wishes too, at least before this "fragment" ends.

In the poem that Charles Brown called Keats's "earliest attempt,"[35] "Imitation of Spenser," the miniature-sized "fay recline[s] voluptuously" (18) on the back of a swan sailing past, simply part of the scenery. Oberon himself is pictured in "On Receiving a Curious Shell, and a Copy of Verses, from the Same Ladies," crouching under the shell's "canopy" that is like "the work of a fay" (25) and playing on his lute "'mong the dewdrops of morning" (32).[36] The speaker doesn't seem to fear any alluring after-effects of this elfin music as he listens to it and "sink[s] to repose" (40).[37] In any case, the king of the faeries is trapped under the "curious shell."[38] The persona of "Had I a man's fair form," persuasively argued to be a faery by J. Burke Severs,[39] humbly wishes to be a shepherd so as to whisper in the ear of his mortal love and is tiny enough to collect "dew" for spells to bewitch her.

At 160 lines, "Calidore: A Fragment" is one of the longer poems in this volume and Keats's first extended rendition of faeries and their realm. Sir Calidore on his mysterious island encounters the "little bright-eyed things / That float about the air on azure wings" (73–4), as well as the "happy burthens" on the "steeds" that appear to him, all of which can only be faeries.[40] These "smiling ladies" with their "soft luxury" yearn over him with the "evening dew" on their hair, and "a dimpled hand, / Fair as some wonder out of fairy land" (93–4) embraces his shoulder. Dew, that appears in all these poems and three times in "Calidore," is associated by Shakespeare with fairies and their activities.[41]

The faeryland in "Imitation" and "Calidore" is also generally unthreatening, full of colors and flowers in the first and an uncomplicated hospitality in the second. When Calidore is greeted by Sir Clerimond and Sir Gondibert in the island's castle, all are led into a chamber where the three sit conversing like old war friends, with the ladies and their "enchanted isle" (151) quite ignored. No offer here by the ladies of fatally captivating food or drink, and no warnings either from the other knights to Calidore. But still . . . but still . . . Keats introduces folkloric touches in both poems not found in Spenser or Shakespeare, some faintly sinister.

The "verdant hill" in the opening lines of "Imitation of Spenser" is a faery hill, as we know a few lines later when the "fay" (the older word for faery) appears riding its swan on the lake at the foot of the hill. In some parts of the British Isles to this very day, hills are still viewed as the possible abode of faeries.[42] There were folktales reporting that sometimes faery cities could be dimly viewed beneath lakes.[43] Green has always been considered a sign that faeries are near, and to a lesser extent red also has these associations.[44] Both colors appear in this poem ("verdant," "emerald," "ruby," "rosy"). There's an ever-so-faint hint of faeryland's ability to lure the mortal away from the human world and its grief in lines 21–2, and even its association with the timeless world of death in the allusions to Dido and Lear.[45]

There are more such traditional allusions in "Calidore: A Fragment." The scene into which Calidore sails in the opening lines is green, with its "green tufted islands casting their soft shades" everywhere and the island with its "leafiness" where he lands.[46] The sun is setting and the liminal time of twilight, the time of enchantment, is approaching.[47] As he sails to these green islands, he leaves behind him on the shore the protection of a chapel with a cross (42). The plants he first encounters on the shore have faery associations: the dock or elecampane, also called "Elf Dock" because its roots attracted faeries; the foxglove which was called by the Welsh "faery's glove" and the Irish "faery-bells"; and the birch which traditionally was a tree associated with hauntings and faeries.[48] Shimmering among them also is "the glow / Of the wild cat's eyes" (49–50), and cats not only have been considered favorites of fairies but sometimes the forms assumed by them.[49] "White coursers pranc[e]" ahead of him, suggesting the white faery horses commonly ridden by the White Ladies.[50]

A staple element in the account of mortals entering faeryland is their encounter with a faery court that dazzles them.[51] Here, Calidore enters a castle where everything seems "delicious" (73). The floors of this castle are "oaken," a faery tree.[52] There are the little faeries floating above on their "azure wings" as he comes into the court, where there are more faery horses, the "two noble steeds" or "palfreys" that carry the ladies who greet Calidore. Why would horses be needed on an island but for the faery rade, the procession of faeries riding at night on their wild faery horses?[53] There is the chilling detail noted that Calidore passes beneath a "threat'ning portcullis" (79), with this sliding metal grill in the gateway suggesting the possibility of entrapment.[54]

He meets the other mortals here, who do not seem much like the familiar captives in faeryland who long to leave but cannot.[55] They are allowed to converse with one another, and indeed find each other more interesting than the "sweet-lipp'd ladies" on this "enchanted isle" (151). But one isn't sure what will happen as the night wears on. Those ladies are said to "greet" the plant with "purple stars, and bells of amber" that climbs round the castle window, which sounds very like belladonna or the deadly nightshade with its poisonous berries (that appears again in "Ode on Melancholy"). The moon shines while a "mysterious, wild" trumpet sounds, like faery music.[56] The "happy mortals" keep "convers[ing]" while "portals / Are closing in the west" (159–60). Is the portcullis descending in the enchanting moonlight?

We don't know, for here Keats abruptly ends the poem. But although this poem is named for Spenser's knight, it is not quite Shakespearean or Spenserian. As Robert Gleckner comments about "How many bards gild the lapses of time," another one of Keats's juvenilia from *Poems*: "the verbal echo . . . constitutes distinct evidence of the poet's ability to transmute the borrowed material into his own idiom."[57] In "Calidore," Keats may seem to borrow from Spenser's renowned presentation in *The Faerie Queene* of Sir Calidore, the knight of "Courtesie" who encounters faeries in their faeryland; and his knight too longs to hear stories of gallantry, rescued damsels, and "spurning of all unworthiness" (143–4). But Sir Calidore's encounter with faeries in Spenser's faeryland is quite different. In Canto Ten of Book VI, Calidore comes upon a faery hill with water at its foot and then an island where faeries are dancing in a ring. However, Spenser intersperses the faeries with nymphs, and the center of attention is the dancing three classical Graces. All are compared to figures from classical myth — Venus, Cytheron, Ariadne — and all vanish as soon as Calidore starts toward them.

Any allusions to classical nymphs, goddesses, or Graces are missing from Keats's version of "Calidore," and these White Ladies ("a dimpled hand, / Fair as some wonder out of fairy land, / . . . of whitest cassia" [93–6]) certainly don't disappear. They may be Shakespearean "little bright-eyed things" (73), but the flowers they tend include the nightshade. There is the strong implication that they travel at night with the faery rade. Like good hostesses, they let the "happy mortals" converse while they blow out "the taper's flame," "mysterious, wild" music sounds in the background, and the "portals clos[e] in the west." The last words of this unfinished poem, "sweet be their sleep," imply that faeryland's trance has begun for those mortals.[58]

There is another short faerie poem not included in the 1817 *Poems*, written about the same time that Keats began composing *Endymion*, which could be a short monologue spoken by Endymion just after leaving Cynthia. It foreshadows the faerie elements of that ambitiously longer poem. The situation is that of several other of these short poems, some epistolary and some left unpublished during Keats's lifetime. The persona of "Unfelt, unheard, unseen" has just left his "little queen" sleeping with her "faery lids" closed in "silver slumber" (2–7),[59] another White Lady. He seems to be a mortal captivated by the faerie queen, for he notes that her touch can be either "cruel or complying" and produce "madness" (6). Evidently he's caught in faeryland and can't leave, for he must "bend unto [her] laws," continue his "dalliance" with her, "and feel my heaven anew" (14–17). He is the mortal glamoured away by the faery queen for her sexual pleasure and possibly faery children.[60]

Keats's faeries and their realm often prove alien to the literary worlds of Shakespeare or Spenser. Similarly, the bards in his poems often are not the exalted traditional poets familiar to the cultivated reader of the eighteenth and early nineteenth centuries, the bards whom he celebrates in "Ode to Apollo." In that early poem Keats uses the word "bard" with its general meaning of a great national poet, as we can tell from his inclusion of Shakespeare and Tasso. This is also clearly his sense of the word in his sonnet from the 1817 *Poems*, "On First Looking into Chapman's Homer," with Homer designated as one of the "bards in fealty to Apollo" (4). Critics have usually seen his other 1817 poem "How many bards gild the lapses of time" similarly. Thus for Gleckner, its "verbal echo[es]" come from Spenser's *Faerie Queene* and Milton's *Il Penseroso* and *Paradise Lost*,[61] so Keats's "bards" must be Spenser and Milton. However, Keats is alluding here to a different bardic tradition, that of the Celtic bard who commemorates his nation's heroes and laments the passing of glory for his people.

The bards named in "Ode to Apollo" are singular in nature, lifted above the rest of their poetic contemporaries. But not here. Here, Keats is musing upon the great number of bards who "gild the lapses of time" and how these bards come to his mind "in throngs" as he writes his own poems. These are not distant and revered bards of the past who are far elevated above him in reputation, but poets who are all crowding behind their latest colleague. It's quite an early poem (1816) about his sense of place in the poetic tradition, as many have seen.[62] But which tradition?

The works from the 1817 *Poems* generally are characteristic of a major poet's juvenilia, and mostly worth reading primarily for their promise. However, there are two which show the sure grasp of poetic language and original thought of his mature works, and this is one of them. (The other is the sonnet on Chapman's Homer.) It is worth considering the precise contemporary meanings of the words he uses, for here he achieves his own individual voice for the first time. The word "throngs" has been frequently criticized as a "youthful infelicity."[63] However, it is a fairly precise word to use if one is thinking of the Celtic bards, which would include the domestic bards retained by the Irish and Welsh families and Scottish clans as well as the minstrels with their harps.

"Gild" and "lapses" are also words with meanings that could refer specifically to the tradition of the Celtic bards who lament their countries' lost unity and cultural subjugation.[64] "Gild" does not only mean to cover with a thin layer of gold, but also to tone down something unpleasant.[65] "Lapses" does not only have the present meaning of intervals elapsed, but in Keats's day equally implied the decline into a lower state or fall into ruin.[66] The octet of this sonnet gives us the image of these Celtic bards pressing together behind the present poet as he "sit[s]...down to rhyme." They sing and play their tragic songs of domestic massacre and defeat in battle, with the "confusion" and "disturbance" now mellowed by time so their harp-songs blend into a "chime" (5–8).

The sestet continues this image of the poet writing among the ghosts of these Celtic bards. This "chime" of the "throng" of bards around him becomes one of the "unnumber'd sounds" of evening; and the sounds of nature, the "leaves" and "waters," all sound that note of melancholy summoned up by Ossian as he grieved the past by the tombs of dead warriors. Here "the great bell / Heaves with solemn sound" (11–12) like a funeral bell. "Thousand others more" join the "few" bards of the opening lines, and their "distance of recognizance bereaves" (13). "Recognizance" then was not simply a synonym for "recognition" but, in a usage now rare but common then, could also mean the acknowledgement of a person who held a certain position.[67] "Bereave" too had a meaning that could allude to the tradition of the Celtic bard, especially the Welsh ones famously massacred by the English. It did not only mean "sadden," but more particularly to plunder or take away by force. Taken together — the "throng" of past bards who are no more, the "great bell" that mourns their passing, the note of nostalgia for all of this — Keats seems to be saying that he can make "pleasing music" in his "rhymes" out of the "wild uproar" of the bards' Celtic past and traditions. The atmosphere of this sonnet is Ossianic rather than Miltonic.

The Celticism that underlies the *Poems* of 1817 permeates *Endymion* as well, although at the surface level this "poetic romance" may seem to be an outstanding demonstration of Keats's classicism, or at least his knowledge of classicism. Displaying this familiarity with Greek and Roman mythology, with Homer, Ovid, and all the archaic legends from Lemprière and Tooke, may appear to be an important reason for Keats to compose it. The sources for the poem obviously indicate the strong influence of classical Greek and Roman mythology on Keats at this early time — with the central characters from Greek mythology, the details about Endymion and Cynthia/Diana from Lemprière and Tooke, and the subsidiary episodes from Ovid's *Metamorphoses*. We know that in his small library, Keats had two copies of Ovid's work.

Yet at the same time, within the poem there is a running Celtic counterpoint to this overtly displayed classical mythology which subverts the dominance of the classicism. Keats seems to have begun the composition of *Endymion* hoping that the finished poem would be proof that he too could enter the ranks of the bards, not only the great poets known from classical literature but the Celtic ones as well. He was reading Edward Davies's *Celtic Researches* as he composed the later books of *Endymion*, and within the poem are increasing echoes of Davies' ideas about the Druids and their disciples the Bards. Endymion himself as a native of Caria came from a Celtic region according to Edward Davies, who connected the Magi and Brahmins with the Druids since the ancient Celts came through Asia Minor.[68]

There is other, more internal evidence from *Endymion* that Keats thought that he might be similar to the ancient Celtic bards so closely associated with the Druids . . . a native bard of Britain, in other words. Each of the four Books is introduced by a first-person address by the poet insistently reminding the reader that Endymion's story is an artifice created by a contemporary, not a classical, poet. Taken as a whole, these four passages (I.1–62, II.1–43, III.1–21, and IV.1–29) show Keats' progressing realization of the situation of the British bard/minstrel/poet in the present-day dwindled world. The only viable role is that of the Celtic bard — and even there, as IV.1–29 suggests, the Celtic Muse may not be available now for inspiration.

The introductory passage to Book I gives us the poet happily anticipating the completion of "the story of Endymion" (I.35), with the specific work thus named and the immediate situation of its chronicler rendered for us too. He's evidently a city-dweller who's retreated to the nature found in the suburbs with its tamed luxuriance of plot gardens, paths, and fresh country air, for now he "cannot hear the city's din" and he notes the "daisies," "clover," and "sweet peas" blooming about him (I.40–52). Keats seems to be deliberately emphasizing here that he is not one of the landowning aristocracy familiar with the sublimity of mountains, waterfalls, and moors; nor is he one of the traditional bards celebrating this sublimity. This was not missed by Tory readers such as John Lockhart.[69]

The passage introducing Book II continues this musing upon the experience of writing a long poem today, stressing that the old themes of "pageant history" and "the death-day of empires" known from classical epics have been superseded by themes of romance. Like the other native bards he cites here — Chaucer, Shakespeare, Marlowe, Spenser — Keats is transforming classical myth into his own "poetic romance." However, unlike them, he "has dared to tread, / Without one muse's smile, or kind behest" (II.36–7), which seems to be another allusion to his class status.

Very different is the tone of Book III's opening 21 lines. Where the opening to Book II had been fairly traditional in its metrics and literary allusions (with *only* literary allusions), lines 1–18 here are a biting radical attack upon the present Tory political establishment which also, of course, is the literary establishment. The passage has little to do with the narrative at this point, for Endymion has just left Alpheus and Arethusa. But then Keats in lines III.19–21 pushes back this immediate reality as simply an "uproar past and gone," resolving to act as did the "old Chaldeans" who ignored the "thunder clouds that spake to Babylon." The Chaldeans, known as ancient astronomers and magicians, ruled Babylon; and Davies held that the Babylonians visited Stonehenge,[70] thus connecting them somehow with the ancient Druids as well. So Keats here implies that his own role in continuing to write in such corrupt present times is like that of the Druids, or their disciples the Chaldeans, functioning in the exoteric world.

This smallness of the present times, of "our dull, uninspired, snail-paced lives," is the backdrop of lines 1–29 of Book IV; and this Book opens with the invocation of a Muse that is Celtic, not classical. We know that Keats was reading Edward Davies in 1817, about the time that Book IV was composed; and Davies clearly is the source here, with his fervent belief that the ancient Greeks received their learning from the Druidical

Hyperboreans. It is not a familiar classical Muse that is summoned here. The portrayal of her is significant, for she will re-appear in Book III of *Hyperion* and then indirectly throughout most of his major works.

> Muse of my native land! loftiest Muse!
> O first-born on the mountains! by the hues
> Of heaven on the spiritual air begot:
> Long didst thou sit alone in northern grot,
> While yet our England was a wolfish den;
> Before our forests heard the talk of men;
> Before the first of Druids was a child;—
> Long didst thou sit amid our regions wild
> Rapt in a deep prophetic solitude...
> Yet wast thou patient. Then sang forth the Nine
> Apollo's garland:—yet didst thou divine
> Such home-bred glory, that they cry'd in vain,
> "Come hither, Sister of the Island!"...
> ...still didst thou betake
> Thee to thy native hopes. (1–17)

Keats thus establishes the priority of Celtic Britain to classical Greece. The classical Muses were begot by Zeus upon Mnemosyne after his war with the Titans so they could entertain the assembled Olympians at their victory celebration. This earlier Celtic Muse seems to have sprung unassisted from England's "spiritual air," purified of any connection with warfare or utilitarian purpose. Her "home-bred glory" eclipses the latter-day "Nine," and she remains where she is "in northern grot" to inspire different bards. This latter-day English bard who has invoked his Muse goes on to quite describe the present times of "despondency" and "scorn" that are once again "wolfish." He adds revealingly, "Long have I said, how happy he who shrives / To thee!" (26–7). So his devotion to this Celtic Muse predates this present occasion of her invocation. However, he then thinks of "poets gone," like Ossian or like Scott's "Last Minstrel"; and he proceeds to the last Book of his own ambitiously long poem "in lowliness of heart" (29).

But Keats is right to summon the "Muse of [his] native land" to assist him as he composes his long work, for he recasts Endymion's story into one that was long familiar to Celtic bards. In a general way, Endymion's meeting with Cynthia and his continual quest for reunion with her echo the traditional folktales of men who encountered the Queen of Faeries, and forever after found the mortal realm dull and pedestrian.[71]

Variations on the tale of the mortal who is glamoured away to faeryland appear throughout the poem; and again and again the source of the images or situations in *Endymion*'s phantasmagorically shifting scenes that seem so odd proves to be Scott's essays on folk-beliefs in *Minstrelsy*. More conclusively Celticist than this, however, is Keats's retelling of the classical story of Endymion as the old Gaelic story of Thomas the Rhymer, the subject of one of the ballads included by Scott in *Minstrelsy*. Indeed, the inspiration for *Endymion* probably came from Scott's comment in his extended essay accompanying this ballad: "We find the elves occasionally arrayed in the costume of Greece and Rome, and the Fairy Queen and her attendants transformed into Diana and her nymphs, and invested with their attributes and appropriate insignia."[72]

The tale of Thomas the Rhymer is very definitely an atypical one of a mortal's encounter with the Queen of Faeries, both because of its conclusion and because Thomas was an actual historical Scottish poet whose "memory," states Scott, "even after the lapse of five hundred years, is regarded with veneration by his countrymen."[73] For usually mortals only escaped faeryland through trickery or with the aid of loved ones still in the human realm, and returned with relief to the living.[74] Not so Thomas the Rhymer. He was allowed to leave faeryland by its Queen; but she bound him to return to her when she wished. Safely back in the village of Ercildoune, Thomas made the prophecies about Scottish history to be consulted in later centuries by his countrymen.[75] When he learned that the Queen had summoned him to rejoin her in "Elfland," he left the mortal realm of his own volition and never was seen again. Later Scottish legends held that Thomas continued to live there in faeryland, which was located under the local Eildon Hills, waiting to return when his countrymen would especially need him and his powers.[76]

Scott separates his ballad into three parts. "Part First ancient" is the traditional version of the ballad, beginning with Thomas's encounter with the faerie queen and ending with his first, seven-year sojourn in Elfland. Scott himself composed, or "reconstructed," the other two parts: "Part Second altered from ancient prophecies," that related Thomas's prophecies after returning from "Elfland"; and "Third Part — Modern," that dramatized Thomas's abandonment of Ercildoune for Elfland. All three parts of Scott's ballad are sources for *Endymion*.

It is significant that Keats chose Thomas the Rhymer as the source for his hero rather than some generalized character from the countless folktales involving the faerie queen, because of the particulars surrounding this figure. Thomas the Rhymer had existed in historical fact, living in the village of Ercildoune in the Scottish Borders during the thirteenth century whether or not his encounter was equally verifiable, and still venerated by his countrymen now at the present time.[77] His prophecies became legendary with Scots who regularly consulted his predictions for centuries, even down to the Jacobites in preparation for their Uprisings in both 1715 and 1745. Because of his supposed contact with spirits and his powers as seer he was considered to have ties with the ancient Druids, even to be a Druid himself. He became generally known again after a lapse of several centuries when Scott included "Thomas the Rhymer" in *Minstrelsy*, with an extended introduction that summarized the facts and legends surrounding "this ancient bard."[78]

The possible association of Endymion with Thomas the Rhymer has been noted before. In her brief essay on the role of women in Keats's romance poems, Nancy Moore Goslee comments that the situation of *Endymion* is similar to "Celtic myths of the elfin queen," such as that of the ballad of Thomas the Rhymer.[79] Her focus is on the types of visionary women in Keats's romances, so she does not develop this idea further. However, the similarities are more than passing, and the significance of this "elfin queen" should not be dismissed by considering her to be merely a literary stereotype from old romances, a "wilderness enchantress, an elfin queen who...bewitch[es] the male quester into dalliance."[80] There were also many accounts of women who met faeries or the faeries' Queen and were stolen away to Faeryland for a time before they returned, and the results were more tragic than "dalliance." Scott recounted the witch-trials of some of these women.[81]

Scott's remark that "we find the elves occasionally arrayed in the costume of Greece and Rome, and the Fairy Queen and her attendants transformed into Diana and her nymphs"[82] proved particularly prescient for Keats. For in Ovid's *Metamorphoses* one name for Diana is Titania (III.176), the name famously adapted by Shakespeare for his own Queen of Faeries who appears on a moonlit summer's night. Throughout *Endymion* Keats retells many of the stories from *Metamorphosis*, most obviously Ovid's story of Diana and Acteon as Cynthia and Endymion, but also his tales of Venus and Adonis, Alpheus and Arethusa, and Glaucus and Scylla. However, Keats's narratives conclude with all of these characters left in faeryland, a faeryland with details often taken from Scott's descriptions of that realm in *Minstrelsy*. At the very end of the poem, Endymion like Thomas "vanish'd far away" (IV.1002) with his restored Cynthia. The word "fairy" or "faery" keeps re-appearing in Keats's descriptions of Endymion's journey; and myriad details of both his original encounter with Cynthia and his ensuing quest for her contain motifs about the faerie common in folk-literature.

Keats's general story of Endymion's encounter with Cynthia and subsequent quest echoes Scott's ballad at key points. Like Endymion on his mountain side, Thomas is lying on a "grassy bank" when he is visited by the Queen of the Faeries who has spied him from afar. He first mistakes her for "the Queen of Heaven," the Virgin Mary in Scott's ballad and Cynthia the Moon in Keats's romance. They unite erotically (she says to Thomas, "and if ye dare to kiss my lips, / Sure of your bodie I will be" ["Thomas," I.19–20])[83] as do Endymion and Cynthia. This union is the cause of his enchantment for Endymion.[84] Then they begin their journey to "Elfland" on her steed. Like Endymion in Book II who rushes "into the earth's deep maw" (II.899) and then passes through an underground cavern until he sees "the giant sea above his head" (II.1023), Thomas "wade[s] through rivers aboon the knee" and "heard the roaring of the sea" ("Thomas," XV, 57–60). At the very end Endymion leaves his sister Peona and rejoins Cynthia, and "they vanish'd far away!" (IV.1002) as does Thomas when he leaves his village for Elfland and its Queen.

Endymion follows the outlines of this old Celtic tale, as it does the more familiar Greek myths recounted by Lemprière and Tooke. Keats also retells Ovid's stories of shape-shifting, but altered into tales of mortals who lost their human forms because they entered faeryland or became involved with a faery or the Queen of Faeries herself.[85] He changes the endings of Ovid's grim accounts of hapless men and women who lose their human forms forever because they have unwillingly attracted the attention of an immortal, so that these humans have some hope of disenchantment or their tales conclude with the union of human and faery as does the legend of Thomas the Rhymer.

The foremost example of this is the central story of Cynthia and Endymion that is so like that of Diana and Acteon related in Ovid, the moon-goddess approached by the mortal man. Ovid's episode is full of what the later, more Celtic-inclined readers would consider faery overtones. It takes place upon an isolated mountainside in a woodland, so like a faery hill, and beneath it "Titania" is in a grotto bathing with her attendant nymphs or fays. Faeries have been famed from early times for being secretive, desiring neither to be watched nor even thanked, and wishing their transactions with humans to be kept private.[86] Poor Acteon has lost his way and comes upon Diana at the end of the day's hunt as the sun is setting, the mortal straying into the faery's realm at that time when enchantment is near and infringing upon the faery's privacy with the usual terrible result.

Endymion's similar story lacks this sinister conclusion, for his moon-goddess is the one who ventures upon him accidentally. However, his narrative is also full of faery elements. His situation as Book I opens is very like that of the mortal who has just left faeryland, dazed and indifferent to the flatter, more prosaic cycles of human life.[87] We don't see him for the first 400 lines, for Keats is building up the everyday reality of his surrounding society of friends and companions who are worshipping Pan on the mountainside. The word "fairy" is sprinkled casually throughout the poem, so that this comes to seem the context for the scenes and events. Here, Pan's altar is bedewed with "fairy phantasies" (I.92). Everyone is dancing, singing, and moving save Endymion. He sits apart, eyes shut with "his senses... swoon'd off," eaten by a "cankering venom" at being thrust back into natural life, "in the self-same fixed trance," "dead-still," and "frozen" (I.396–406).

His sister Peona leads him away from the crowd to a river, and they sail off in a little boat to her favorite isle where they can speak. (Did Keats know that little bags of peony seeds were hung around the necks of children to protect them from faeries?) Endymion describes what he was like before "the change wrought suddenly" (I.520–1). As both Tooke and Lemprière noted, Endymion was thought to be an astronomer. Here, he tells Peona how he spent his time tracking the course of the sun until the time when he fell asleep at the close of day — twilight, again — in a "magic bed / Of sacred ditamy [dittany] and poppies red" (I.554–5). From here on, we share this experience with him. Dittany is another faery flower, and both flowers are ancient opiates.[88] Poppies also had classical associations with the underworld, as the flower worn by Demeter when she rejoined the abducted Persephone. Here, those poppies cast their own spell with a breeze through them that causes "visions... / Of colours, wings, and bursts of spangly lights" so that he falls asleep into an "enchantment" (I.568–73).

And then Cynthia comes to him.[89] Faeries often were called "the White Ladies"; and Cynthia who descends in this "enchantment" appears to Endymion with "her pearl round ears, white neck" and "hovering feet... whitely sweet" (I.616–25).[90] They ascend together into the sky, but then head back to earth and enter "huge dens and caverns in a mountain's side: / There hollow sounds arous'd [him]" (I.648–51).[91] Endymion embraces her, and then feels "a warmer air: a moment more/[Their] feet were soft in flowers / ... Sometimes / A scent of violets, and blossoming limes." Above their "nest," "an arch face peep'd — an Oread as [he] guess'd ... sleep o'er-power'd [him]" (I.664–72). Flowers blooming in a cave beneath a hill? A mountain nymph spying on them? A trance-like sleep overcoming him at a time when he surely would prefer to be awake and active? Clearly this is faeryland.[92]

When he awakes alone, his reaction is that of the mortal who was glamoured away to this timeless realm and then returned to the human world that seems glamourless indeed. "Shades" seem "dungeons," "rills seem'd sooty" and full of dying fish, the rose blooms in "frightful scarlet," a bird seems like a "demon," and life itself seems "weary" (I.693–710). He goes on to tell Peona what he's learned that seems to wither any joy in ordinary life for him:

> Wherein lies happiness? In that which becks
> Our ready minds to fellowship divine,
> A fellowship with essence: till we shine,
> Full alchemiz'd, and free of space. Behold
> The clear religion of heaven! (I.777–81)

If we consider the nineteenth-century meanings of some of the key words here, we can see that this is the longtime wish to leave the mortal world behind for the faerie and that Keats expresses reservations about this "happiness" that's rather like faery gold. "Becks" is an ambiguous word, a signal to approach what remains out of reach. So the will-o'-the-wisp "becks" the traveler onward. "Essence" now predominantly means the intrinsic nature of a thing, but it had the older meaning of a "spiritual or immaterial entity" such as a spirit, from the seventeenth through the nineteenth centuries.[93] "Divine" too had the additional meaning then of "celestial" or "heavenly," as well as "sacred."[94] And an old meaning of "alchemize" was to transform with the implication of being counterfeit, rather like the faery trick of creating illusions.[95] Of course, the phrases "free of space" and "clear religion of heaven" also conjure up the image of Cynthia the moon who is "becking" Endymion to join her far out of the mortal realm.

This kind of "happiness" is beyond space and time, a vision of faery love with all of the flaws of "men-slugs and human serpentry" (I.821) removed. And Endymion begins his long quest through the poem for his White Lady, as he and Peona set sail on the river.[96] However, mysteriously, for the rest of the poem he seems to journey by himself since Peona disappears until the last lines of the poem.

Book II opens with him wandering on through "woods of mossed oaks" (II.49), that faery tree, led on by a golden butterfly like the flickering light of the ignis fatuus that appears to travelers.[97] It's twilight again, a "green evening," and he is led to the entrance of another hill, a "cavern's mouth," by the butterfly which disappears "so fairy-quick" (II.93). Another faery-spirit, a Naiad, appears briefly to him as his guide and then leaves for her own "hollow cell" (II.130). And on he goes, searching for Cynthia (II.170) or "Dian" (II.300): Endymion the "exil'd mortal" (II.316) on "his fairy journey" (II.352).

Before he meets her again he happens on Adonis, another of Ovid's creatures who was changed out of his human shape. In Ovid's tale, Adonis is gored with a bloody finality and turned by Venus into an anemone. Keats instead preserves him hidden away in his "chamber," always sleeping save when Venus comes to wake him once a year. There are many touches to suggest that he is caught in faeryland. As Endymion comes upon Adonis at sunset, he hears "sleepy music" like a "faint charm" or spell (II.356–8).[98] Adonis is under an "enchantment" (II.428), slumbering away in his nested place surrounded by a flower garden very like the garden of "Elfland" in the "prophesia" by Thomas the Rhymer that Scott produces in his note.[99] Here, Adonis is surrounded by little spirit-like "Cupids" who term Adonis "fond elf" (II.461). As these "winged listeners" (II.493) flutter around, they hear Venus approach and threaten to pinch one another with "the blue-bell pinch" (II.505). Faeries were notorious for pinching sleepers, and blue-bells long were taken as a sign of the presence of faeries.[100] Adonis wakens to meet Venus, and Endymion leaves them.

He proceeds on his "fairy journey" into the "twilight" (II.587), down through caves to another faeryland under a hill. Its fantastic "palaces" are made of precious stones and metals.[101] There are a thousand silvery fountains (II.603–4) and streams whose "changed magic" (II.613) makes the waters assume shifting shapes and colors, now "spangled" with peacocks and naiads, now "mimick[ing] the oaken beams" of cathedrals (II.623–6).[102] This ability to create deceptive illusions of grandeur is characteristic of faeryland's glamouring that makes the humble object seem transfigured, like the gold coins of folktales that later turn into brown leaves when the mortal returns to earth.[103]

Endymion hurries on down through "gulphs" and "dells" to lower levels, falling until beneath "little caves" he lands in "a jasmine bower" that is an extension of the earlier faeryland he passed through.[104] And here he at last meets his "enchantress" again (II.756). This long passage (II.707–853) describing the lovers' reunion is an explicit rendering of the brief account of Thomas the Rhymer's lovemaking with his own Queen of Elfland ("...he has kissed her rosy lips, all underneath the Eildon Tree" [Part First, 26–7]). Its eroticism is characteristic of the folktales relating the sexual demands of the Queen upon the mortal man whom she has chosen, often because she wishes children from him.[105] The blood-vitality of humans seems to attract faeries to them, whether as children to be abducted or as lovers to be tricked away. Cynthia shows the intense desire for privacy that is typically shown by the faery who has taken a mortal lover (II.777–81). Indeed, in such situations any tale-telling by the mortal is usually punished by the disappearance forever of the faery, or worse.[106] Here, she leaves as he is sleeping, with the implicit promise of return, much as the Queen of Elfland leaves Thomas back on earth after seven years with her in Elfland.

Throughout the rest of Endymion's search he passes through caves, grottos, and caverns beneath hills and mountains, and through underground vaults to rivers, streams, and the sea. These kinds of places all were common faery haunts, as Scott noted: "Wells, or pits, on the top of high hills, were likewise supposed to lead to the subterranean habitations of the Fairies.... They inhabit the interior of green hills, chiefly those of a conical form.... Fays frequent streams and fountains."[107]

Here Keats turns again to Ovid for the tales of Alpheus and Arethusa and of Glaucus and Scylla that occupy the rest of Book II and Book III, two more variants on the story of the mortal glamoured away by faeries. Again, he changes Ovid's endings. Both stories involve spirits of water and the sea. Endymion encounters the first pair after he awakes to find himself in a "grotto" (II.878) with pearls, shells, "fish-semblances" (II.884) or more illusive appearances, and streams of water that spray over him.[108] It is a seductive replay of his recent union with Cynthia, this yearning song of the river-god Alpheus termed "enchanter" (II.965). Alpheus follows after Arethusa, the nymph who has been turned into a stream by "Dian" whom she serves. But whereas in Ovid she fled from him in horror and was turned into a stream as protection, here she longs for union with him in her "huntress" (II.1008) form again; and Endymion too prays to the "Goddess" to join the two "in some happy plains" (II.1017) beneath the "dark gulph." And he turns and finds himself in a land beneath the sea.

When "Thomas [the Rhymer] was carried off, at an early age, to the Fairy Land...he acquired all the knowledge, which made him afterwards so famous," noted Scott;[109] and this sojourn in the land of faerie with the acquisition of hidden knowledge is the subject of Book III of *Endymion*. The story continues with Cynthia in her "green or silvery bower" (III.73), like the moon in its beginning phases, weakened and searching for Endymion in his "deep, deep water-world" (III.101). He in his turn continues his quest below the sea, his search recalling legends of the land of faerie beneath the sea with its water-spirits and faery palaces dimly seen beneath the waves.[110] He addresses Cynthia as the Moon whom he has loved since his childhood — caught in faeryland "at an early age" indeed — because of the folk magic associated with her: the moonlight that bewitched the humans it fell upon (III.149–52), the moon-phases that affected planting times (III.153–5), the night music of the "passing spright" which "solemnize[d] thy reign" (III.158–9).[111]

It's at this point that Endymion looks up to see Glaucus "in the concave green of the sea" (III.191). Glaucus is, in fact, the first other mortal met in the poem aside from Peona. In Ovid, Glaucus was a fisherman who loved the sea-nymph Scylla and thus incurred the wrath of the spurned witch Circe, who turned him into a sea-god with a blue fish's form and Scylla into a monster.[112] Keats changes Glaucus into a faery who was once a mortal but is now caught in faeryland, Scylla into another such captive, and Circe into the faery that has inveigled them there.[113]

Glaucus's fate was a possible one for mortal men, as we know from "The Young Tamlane" (or the modernized version "Young Tam Lin"). This famous ballad also was included by Scott in *Minstrelsy*, and the occasion for his long essay on "fairies of popular superstition." In fact, Glaucus's story is not unlike Tamlane's, and much more typical of those who met the Queen of Faeries than that of Thomas the Rhymer. Tamlane had caught the Queen's fancy as a boy of nine and was carried off to become "a fairy, lyth and limb" ("Tamlane," 123). As a grown faery in the ballad, he feared she had stolen him to be their teind and so he maneuvered with his mortal lover, whom he had haunted in his faery form and impregnated, to win him back to human form during the faeries' Hallowe'en Rade. The woman succeeded; and the angry Queen chillingly wished that she had blinded him, taken out his human heart, and "paid my kane [coin] seven times to hell" ("Tamlane," 267) before she let him ride at Hallowe'en.

Keats's Glaucus is an old man sitting on a rock in the sea, and he has many Druidic associations. He is wrapped in "a cloak of blue... / O'erwrought with symbols by the deepest groans / Of ambitious magic" (III.197–9), and these symbols of "every ocean-form" continually change shapes. This "dark blue cloak" is mentioned again much later when he wraps it around Endymion (III.751–2). While Ovid describes Glaucus's fish-form as blue, it also is a color associated both with the ancient Britons and with the robes worn by some orders of Druids. Faeries also were sometimes dressed in blue, and their connections with Druids should be remembered.[114] Glaucus looks like the conventional portrayals of Druids too, with his long white hair and "snow-white brows" (III.221), the "pearly wand" (III.213) he carries, and the book he keeps studying. When he sees Endymion, he twice proclaims, "Thou art the man!" much to Endymion's alarm. Like those who fear to draw the attention of the faeries, of the "good people," Endymion fears that this magician-like figure will sear him with his touch or feed him to "his magian fish" (III.265). However, then he wonders if Glaucus is simply an old man or a sage or, in fact, a mortal caught in a magical state. And as Glaucus tells his story, it becomes apparent that he is.

He was a fisherman a thousand years ago . . . the old, old story of the mortal taken out of time. He loved Scylla, a nereid or sea-nymph in Ovid but here simply a woman who fled his advances. Fatally, he went to the "enchantress" (III.413) Circe for assistance, who decided that she wanted him for herself. And we're in faeryland once more with him, stolen away "in a twilight bower" (III.418) while he was only a "tranced vassal" in "a golden clime" (III.455–60). However, her true faery nature emerged. Looking for her one day in the forest he accidentally caught her unawares, a fatal thing to happen with faeries.[115] She was working as faeries do, transforming human shapes into beasts with "a branch of mistletoe" (III.514), a sign of her faery connection to Druids. Not only was he the mortal who saw through the "glamour" of faerie, always punished in folktales, sometimes with blindness. Worse, he unmasked her by naming her (III.544).[116]

Her curse was that he would live in "the watery vast" (III.593) as an old man for a thousand years, that is, stay caught in faeryland while human time cycled on without him.[117] Scylla too was cursed. Keats changes the classical punishment of Scylla that Ovid provides as well, the snarling pack of dogs that Scylla's legs became. Instead, Glaucus found her floating dead upon the sea and "clung about her waist" (III.626), and then brought her to a castle beneath the sea where he stashed her away in a niche, thus also caught in a timeless realm and preserved.

He remained on his rock in the sea until the day he saw a shipwreck in a sudden storm that seemed raised by "hell-born Circe" (III.665).[118] Witches, demons, and evil faeries always were considered to have this power (which caused many Scottish and English women to be accused of whistling up storms and condemned as witches by their neighbors).[119] The one survivor gave Glaucus a scroll and a wand, and sank back beneath the sea . . . at which point the storm stopped and the sun emerged, underlining its supernatural cause. This scroll contained predictions that were exactly suited to Glaucus's situation, and the "magic" that he must "explore" if he wished to live after Circe's spell is ended (III.697–700).[120] He must gather all the lovers lost at sea while he has been under Circe's spell and rejoin them "side by side," and then he will encounter a youth "whom he shall direct / How to consummate all" (III.709–10). To both, Endymion clearly is the predicted youth.

Glaucus has already managed to fulfill his part of the prediction and has placed these lovers in Scylla's "crystal palace" beneath the sea, all caught out of time and laid in rows like bewitched captives in faeryland with their "shut eyes," ruddy lips, and hands crossing their hearts. Now, as the two approach these lovers, Glaucus more than ever takes on the demeanor of an aged Druid passing on his secret knowledge to the adept as he began to "tear his scroll in pieces small, / Uttering the while some mumblings funeral," wrapping his "dark blue cloak" around Endymion, and striking "his wand against the empty air times nine" (III.747–53). He instructs Endymion to take his wand and break it against the lyre on the pedestal nearby (the lyre recalling Lemprière's classification of bards as an order of "Druidae"), and then to scatter the scroll fragments on him. As Thomas the Rhymer gained supernatural knowledge while in Elfland, so does Endymion here. For when he follows the instructions, the spell drops off and the youthful Glaucus appears to take his place by the awakened Scylla.[121]

Endymion strews more scroll fragments on the sleeping lovers, who all awake, and there follows another long re-creation of faeryland. The poem is full of these. "Enchantment" showers light over everything, and Glaucus and Scylla taste a "wine / Of happiness from fairy-press ooz'd out" (III.796–802).[122] Along with Endymion and the other re-united lovers, they enter the spacious "emerald" hall of Neptune.[123] It should be recalled that there are many tales of faeryland seen under rivers or the sea.[124] The marvels of this glamoured realm sound very like the one in Book II, 590–626. Here, the gold doors open "swift as fairy thought" (III.856) to an "emerald," a "gold-green" palace.[125] Water-faeries dance, the "Nereids," "Syrens," and "sea-nymphs" (III.889, 896); and the banquet begins which is such a common feature recorded by mortals who managed to leave faeryland, the endless "Nectar" for all, the "dance and song" (III.925–33).[126] Oceanus, the king of this realm, enters with his White Ladies, "Amphitrite, queen of pearls/And Thetis pearly too" (III.1004–5). However, Endymion longs for his own "white Queen of Beauty" (III.976); the palace whirls around him as he sinks asleep; and the Nereids carry him out to a lake and "forest green" in this trance, with Glaucus and Scylla happily left behind in faeryland.[127] There Book III ends.

So far, Endymion's adventures are fairly easy to follow, and loosely parallel those of Thomas the Rhymer. Endymion encountered the Queen of the Faeries and was taken with her to faeryland, entranced away from his own mortal realm which seems mundane by comparison as he sought to meet the Queen again. During his magical quest, he met other mortals in faeryland and heard their own tales of capture, and gained an esoteric knowledge of spells and "enchantment." At the end of Book III, faeries returned him to the mortal realm, back to the "forest green" that's "cooler than all the wonders he had seen" (IV.1030). He's back in Ercildoune.

With the final Book IV, *Endymion* breaks down into confusion. To be sure, Keats ends it with Cynthia at last revealing herself to Endymion in the last 20 lines and then "they vanish'd far away" (IV.1002), just as Scott had concluded, "But ne'er in haunts of living men / Again was Thomas seen" ("Thomas," Part Third, 159–60). However, the preceding 980 lines seem jumbled and arbitrary. There often doesn't seem to be a reason or motivation for the narrative events, and Endymion's psychology is ineptly portrayed.

The narrative action of Book IV after faeries deposit Endymion on his "grassy nest" back in the ordinary human realm may be summarized fairly quickly. It opens with an Indian maid calling from the forest for someone to help her return to India. Endymion hears her, declares his undying passion, and asks for her story. She responds with a long tale of seeing Bacchus and Silenus riding along in India[128] and following them to the present glade. Mercury suddenly appears with two winged horses which they mount.[129] Endymion and the Indian maid fall asleep as they fly; Endymion dreams of Cynthia, awakes and looks up at the moon; and then the Indian maid disappears. Endymion flies on alone dreaming of Cynthia's wedding banquet;[130] and then the horse flies him back to earth, where he rejoins the Indian maid. He proclaims his love for her again and asks her to live with him forever, which she declines to do. He wanders along, dejected . . . and Peona is back! So he proposes that the Indian maid and Peona live together as sisters, and they agree — the Indian maid suddenly transmogrifies into Cynthia and reunites with Endymion — and off the two vanish for good, while Peona "went / Home through the gloomy wood in wonderment" (IV.1002–3).

The general critical reading of Book IV has been that Endymion learns the superiority of the actual, human realm of experience to the transcendent, immortal one, and this makes possible his final re-union with Cynthia. For when he rejoins the Indian maid, he speaks of leaving the "caverns lone," the "air of visions," and the "visionary seas" of Books I through III, foreswearing any "airy voices" that might call him to "tangled wonder." He bids a final farewell to his coyly withholding White Lady (which this dark-skinned Indian maid is certainly not): "Adieu, my daintiest Dream! although so vast / My love is still for thee . . . / On earth I may not love thee" (IV.656–9). He turns instead to life with his maid: "one human kiss! / One sigh of real breath — one gentle squeeze... / ... warm with dew at ooze from living blood" (IV.664–7). Their pictured life is firmly on earth, with apple orchards, bee-hives, and fishing streams. He chooses the Indian maid who seems to be of this world, and is rewarded by getting Cynthia after all.

Yet there are insoluble contradictions in Book IV. For in the very last line of the poem, Peona is left by herself to go "home through the gloomy wood in wonderment." She really is the only one who exists in the human realm at the end. Cynthia has promised that all three will meet in the forest soon, but "vanish'd far away" with Endymion before he can even finish giving her three kisses. Further, everything about the Indian maid suggests that she is not really human. Her story is very strange. She says that she has followed Bacchus's procession of tigers, leopards, elephants, zebras, alligators, and crocodiles (so like a faery rade) all the way from India to the present forest full of "crisped oaks" (IV.295).[131] "Crisped" may mean crumbling and brittle, and the two words call to mind the old adage that "faery folks / live in old oaks." Her voyage, moreover, was "a three days' journey in a moment done" (IV.253).[132] She concludes by lamenting that "bewitch'd I sure must be" (IV.277). The world of faerie often was located in India according to Celtic lore.[133] This Indian maid comes and goes as faeries do. Endymion himself seems glamoured away by her as surely and rapidly as he was by Cynthia, so that in the end it is hard to see that he has much of a will at all.

Keats seems aware of this problem with Endymion, for he writes near the beginning of Book IV: "He surely cannot now/Thirst for another love: O impious, / That he can even dream upon it thus!" (IV.86–8). Indeed. This plot-switch nullifies any sympathy for Endymion that has been created in Books I through III. Supposedly, Cynthia's love for him only increases since he evidently is able to love her in any guise. However, this runs quite counter to the logic of either classical mythology or traditional faerylore, not to mention human psychology. Diana/Cynthia was among the least likely of the Greek goddesses to be lenient in this regard, for she punished her votaries who broke their vows of chastity to her with exile or death. While shape-shifting was certainly common to the faery nature and there were many tales of the faeries testing humans, the faery queen's reaction to the apostasy of her mortal lover was far more likely to be the fury she showed to Young Tamlane.[134] With Book IV, Keats's artistic control in *Endymion* breaks down.

No matter how sympathetic a partisan of Keats, few of his readers have expressed a fervent appreciation of *Endymion* taken as a whole. It may illustrate his ambitious attempt to revivify a Greek myth he had known since he was a school-boy, or, alternately, an old Celtic legend surrounding an historical native figure; but it is a difficult work to read through with consistent pleasure. Too often, it is diffuse with long repetitive passages that are a muddle of classical allusions. There are the peculiar turns of the plot. If Endymion steps into the small boat with Peona at the end of Book I, where is she while he sails along on his quest (evidently alone) for the next two and three-quarters Books? How can Endymion forget Cynthia so quickly and thoroughly in the beginning of Book IV? Even if one argues as a Celticist that he is glamoured away by the faery Indian maid, he's already been glamoured away by Cynthia and thus, so to speak, has been pre-empted by the Queen. Occasionally, there are incongruous words and phrases that create an unintentionally humorous effect, worth remarking since this is not true for Keats's subsequent poems.[135]

All of these problems point to an undeniably forced quality about the poem. We know that it was the result of another timed "poetry contest" with Hunt and Shelley. These exercises in poetic machismo were harmless enough when the purpose was to see who could compose a sonnet within fifteen minutes. However, the announced goal this time was to finish a 4000-line poem by the end of 1817.[136] All shared the familiar eighteenth-century idea that the long poem, preferably epic, was the superior one; and that the writer who could produce it was superior too. By the end of 1816 Shelley and Hunt had already proved themselves with long poems, Shelley with *Queen Mab* and Hunt with *The Story of Rimini*; and they soon abandoned the project now. Predictably enough Keats kept on, considering that such a long poem would be a general measure of his worth as poet. "A long Poem is a test of Invention which I take to be the Polar Star of Poetry, as Fancy is the Sails, and Imagination the Rudder," Keats wrote firmly to Bailey while in the middle of composing *Endymion*. "Did our great Poets ever write short Pieces?"[137]

To judge from the opening lines of *Endymion* (I.41–57), Keats evidently expected to complete it within five to six months in a fireworks display of virtuosity; but the effort soon began to tell on him. A month after he began it in April, he wrote to Taylor and Hessey: "I went day by day at my Poem for a Month at the end of which time the other day I found my Brain so over-wrought that I had neither Rhyme nor reason in it — so was obliged to give up for a few days."[138] The finished line-length desired was as onerous as the time-limit. He wrote to various friends: "I am getting on famous with my third Book — have written 800 lines thereof, and hope to finish it next week"[139]; "within these last three weeks

I have written 1000 lines — which are the third Book of my Poem";[140] and "you must forgive although I have only written 300 Lines — they would have been five but I have been obliged to go to town."[141] He expressed the mechanical quality of the operation quite well near the end when he wrote to Bailey: "I must make 4000 Lines of one bare circumstance and fill them with Poetry; and... this is a great task."[142]

In these early faerie poems, his subsequent motifs of faeries and faeryland appear but with only a hint of the later menace. There are many motifs in the *Motif-Index* about the benevolent, gift-giving and grateful faeries that were termed the "Seelie" (or "blessed" from the Old English *selig*) Host, as there also are about the "Unseelie" Host or the malicious, vengeful ones. In Keats's early works, motifs about the Seelie faeries generally predominate, although he shows some ambiguity. The "queen" of the short little effort, "Unfelt, unheard, unseen," gives "heaven" to the captivated speaker, but also "madness." It's not clear what the intentions of the faeries that Calidore meets will prove to be, although they seem friendly enough. Circe of *Endymion* may seem witch-like but only because she is provoked by her human lover Glaucus who dares to prefer a mortal woman, a familiar faery motif. However, the other faeries met by the various mortals in this poem are well-meaning (even if the mortals do wind up as captives in the faerie realm), including, most obviously, Cynthia. And in all these early faerie poems Keats glories in imagining faeryland as it is experienced by the humans who are captives there: the feasts, the lights, the flowers, the sinuous eroticism. Again and again in *Endymion* as Keats's "great task" of composing 4000 lines progressed, he returned to the experience of leaving the dull mortal world behind and entering faeryland.

4
The Native Muse

The short poems that were unpublished during Keats's lifetime, many of them epistolary, usually are not considered worthy of critical attention. There have been few studies of them. The best known of these poems is "Old Meg she was a gipsey," generally seen as a footnote to Scott's character Meg Merrilies in *Guy Mannering* and often relegated to children's anthologies of poetry. Yet the unpublished poems that he wrote after the 1817 *Poems* number more than seventy. He copied out many and sent them to friends and relatives in letters. Most of the unpublished poems about the faerie were epistolary: the early "Unfelt, unheard, unseen," and "Dear Reynolds, as last night I lay in bed"; "Old Meg she was a gipsey" that was written on the 1818 walking tour; and "When they were come unto the Faery's court," and "Song of Four Fairies" that were written in 1819, the year of his great faerie poems.

The epistolary context affects these poems, for they were written for a sympathetic audience who shared a common context of knowledge and supported whatever he wrote. They have the mercurial nature of the letters, also sliding from mood to mood, allusion to allusion, as they foray into the subject of the faerie. Often the faerie here has an eerie touch of the unearthly that is untrammeled by human moral codes, sometimes even an intimation of the sinister. "Old Meg" contains motifs of the benevolent, gift-giving faery, but also a few that link her to the dead. The faerie poem to Reynolds is his first to explore the aspect of the faerie that conveys away humans to a sorrowful captivity, and is connected with the world of the dead; and its motifs relate solely to this malevolent side.

These "minor" poems complement his published major works dealing with the faerie — *Endymion*, "Eve of St. Agnes," "La Belle Dame," "Ode to a Nightingale," *Lamia*, and *The Fall of Hyperion* — for they suggest the lure and then entrapment of the faerie world. This lure that glamours us away to the Otherworld is presented clearly enough in *Endymion*, though not with the accompanying menace so common to lore of the faerie. But an epistolary poem that he sent to Reynolds about four months after he finished *Endymion* suggests this clearly enough. "Dear Reynolds, as last night I lay in bed" is a fantastical, at times humorous, and ultimately chilling portrayal of faeryland.

The poem was evidently composed to entertain the ill Reynolds as he also lay in bed, and it opens with Keats describing the "visitings" he dreamed "last night," evidently occasioned by the picture *The Enchanted Castle* by Claude that both had seen.[1] In that liminal state as he drifts to sleep, "things all disjointed come from north and south" (5), a jumble of incongruous images beginning with "two witch's eyes above a cherub's mouth." It's worth noting that the direction of North is often mentioned in Keats's poetry, nearly always associated with the sinister unknown. This accords with the old tradition that Satan dwells in the North, as well as the widely spread belief that the presence of evil spirits is accompanied by cold.[2] For Keats, this association of the North with magic could well be connected also with Davies's idea that the ancient Druids were the Hyperboreans, those literally "beyond the North wind."

Among the "visitings" is a replay of Sir Calidore sailing on the lake to a strange "little island" ("Calidore," 24), but the castle that these "mariners" reach is more clearly termed "the Enchanted Castle" ("Reynolds," 26).[3] There aren't the earlier "delicious sounds" and the "little bright-eyed things" floating about, or the "sweet-lipp'd ladies" like docile hostesses leading Sir Calidore to the other knights. Here, the "Enchanted Castle" is "a Merlin's hall," not a re-assuring predecessor; and the "mossy place" where it is located "seem[s] a lifted mound / Above some giant, pulsing underground" (34–40).[4]

The castle itself is a blend of Christian and demonic elements, implying the ineffectiveness of Christian belief against the faerie.[5] Part of the castle is a "see," or bishopric seat, built by a "banished" holyman of "Chaldee," seat of ancient magic; and part was built "two thousand years" later by "Cuthbert de Saint Aldebrim." One wing was built by a "Lapland witch turned maudlin nun" (the North again), and others by "mason-devils." The doors open by themselves, and the windows seem "latch'd by fays and elves." There are flashes of light mysteriously coming from within like gleams from the eyes of a beautiful woman "gone mad through olden songs and poesies" (54), which sounds as if the castle may have a bewitched inhabitant.[6]

From the distance appears another ship, very different from that of the mariners.[7] This "golden galley all in silken trim" comes in silence then disappears, rather like the faery ship that came for Arthur when he died.[8] As the galley approaches the castle, a clarion sounds (like the trumpet Sir Calidore heard when he approached his castle) and then "an echo of sweet music." It's the music of faeryland; and Keats describes its effects on humans who happen to approach this place: the music "doth create / A fear in the poor herdsman who doth bring / His beasts to trouble the enchanted spring" (62–4).[9] Keats has not acknowledged this "fear" as a possible, even reasonable human reaction to the presence of faeryland before.

This new sense that the faerie may include the sinister extends to a wider possibility that "the dark void of night" is a constant "shadow" of the "soul" and that the "imagination . . . / Cannot refer to any standard law / Of either earth or heaven" (70–82). It is a variation of his insight written a few months earlier to George and Tom Keats that "Negative Capability . . . is when man is capable of being in uncertainties, Mysteries, doubts, without any irritable reaching after fact & reason,"[10] but here with distress at this state. Rather than giving the comforting sense of being "a Man of Achievement especially in Literature" like Shakespeare, this essential lawlessness of the imagination, seemingly a rejection of the "standard law . . . of heaven" that includes Christianity, produces a vertiginous glimpse "into the core / Of an eternal fierce destruction" (96–7). It's an early version of Tennyson's "Nature, red in tooth and claw" (*In Memoriam.* LVI, 15), with Keats seeing the shark, then the hawk, then the "gentle robin" that pursues the worm. These are the culminating "moods" (105–11) of these "visitings," which all began with his dream of the Enchanted Castle enclosed in the "lifted mound" so like a tumulus.[11]

Another such epistolary poem was written several months later during the walking tour, as Keats made his way with Brown up along the Scottish coast and through the western Highlands. He sent back travel letters along with poems to his siblings and friends. One, "Old Meg she was a gipsey," draws on Highland faerie beliefs. As Joan Coldwell has noted in one of the few critical readings of the poem, Keats may term Meg a gypsy but she really does not seem to be one. This Meg is essentially solitary, whereas actual gypsies are clannish and travel in groups.[12] She is obviously modeled upon Meg Merrilies, the character who is a witch in *Guy Mannering,* for as Keats noted in the accompanying letter to Tom Keats: ". . . Brown is coppying [*sic*] a song about Meg Merrilies which I have just written for her."[13] And Scott's Meg was certainly a witch, chanting spells, predicting the future, and suddenly materializing out of thin air, which was a large part of her popular appeal. But Keats's Meg isn't really a witch either, muttering curses and malevolent as witches are in folklore. She doesn't conjure up faerie food for herself, and her main activity seems to be altruistic weaving for the local poor people.

However, Keats gives her faintly uncanny, supernatural touches. This Meg inhabits the pathless moors as spirits do. Her only food includes "pods o' broom," and Keats was likely to know that the fruit of broom is toxic from his medical training at Guy's Hospital.[14] She reads tombstones ("her book a churchyard tomb").[15] She weaves her "chip hat" — such hats are woven from wooden strips — from the poisonous "dark glen yew" that has old associations with magic and Druidic rites, a tree that also is common in the churchyard's realm of the dead.[16] And she's a creature of legend, for we find out in the last line that "she died full long agone!" with that exclamation point further suggesting her mythic quality.

Not quite a gypsy or a witch, she's clearly a faery of some sort. It's noteworthy that "Old Meg" is written as a ballad, for Keats's only other ballad is "La Belle Dame," also a poem about a faery. This literary form suggests the folk-ballads in Scott's *Minstrelsy*, with their heavy overlay of the supernatural. In fact, this Meg seems to blend many Highland legends about helpful faeries. She wears "an old red blanket cloak," and faeries throughout the Isles were as fond of wearing red as green, to judge from the folktales about them.[17] Keats's Meg spends most of her time weaving "garlanding" from woodbine, and "plait[ing] mats o' rushes" to give to the "cottagers" she happens to meet in the wild, "among the bushes."[18] Cottagers would have been among the poorest of the poor in the Highlands, being the cotters. These also were the people from whom a great many of the tales about faery encounters came, though the faery-faith certainly was spread throughout the classes.

Keats had intended his walking tour with Brown through Scotland "to make a sort of Prologue to the Life I intend to pursue.... I will get such an accumulation of stupendous recollolections that as I walk through the suburbs of London I may not see them."[19] Scottish history had drawn his imagination from his earliest school days, as did, more recently, the Scottish writers Scott, Burns, and the supposed Gaelic epic bard Ossian. His walking tour proved to be much more than a prologue. It consolidated Keats's growing interest in Celticism, especially in Ossian and the bardic tradition he represented. This in turn accorded with Edward Davies's ideas about the "Titanian Celtae," Druidism, and bardism in *Celtic Researches* that Keats read about a year before he set out for Scotland.

More immediately, Keats's immersion in his experience of the Highlands and Islands helped to generate the epic that was beginning to form in his mind as he left for the tour. He had hinted in his "Preface" to *Endymion* dated 10 April 1818, that he had in mind another attempt at a similarly long poem based on Greek mythology: "I hope I have not in too late a day touched the beautiful mythology of Greece, and dulled its brightness: for I wish to try once more, before I bid it farewel [*sic*]." A month later he left on his walking tour. *Hyperion* is influenced by that tour through Northern England, and especially Scotland, in important ways. He began writing it soon after he got back in London; and although he dropped it about three months later, he took it up again near the end of his life as *The Fall of Hyperion*. On one level both epic attempts were based on "the beautiful mythology of Greece" that was culturally so familiar and so respectable. But on a deeper level, both works conflated the familiar narrative of the defeat of the Titans by the Olympians with the defeat of the British Celts by the Romans. Keats was attempting to write the epic of the Celts.

There are several hints that he was thinking of *Hyperion* as he progressed through northern England and then Scotland. He referred to the Titans in his letter to Tom Keats after visiting Fingal's Cave on Staffa off the Isle of Mull. This popular tourist site itself had Celtic associations, of course, since Fingal was the ancient Gaelic hero of myth celebrated later by Macpherson in the most well-known epic by "Ossian." More recently, Bonnie Prince Charles had landed there when he summoned the clan chieftains to fight with him against the British. Keats wrote: "The finest thing is Fingal's Cave — it is entirely a hollowing out of Basalt Pillars. Suppose now the Giants who rebelled against Jove had taken a whole Mass of black Columns and bound them together like bunches of matches — and then with immense Axes had made a cavern in the body of these columns... such is fingal's Cave."[20] He repeated the allusion in the accompanying epistolary poem when he described the cave: "This was architected thus / By the great Oceanus" ("Not Aladdin magian," 27–8). The Titan Oceanus would have a major role in the second book of *Hyperion*; and, as Stafford notes, his name has "a striking resemblance to Macpherson's Celtic bard."[21]

One should also consider the epistolary poem "There is a joy in footing slow across a silent plain," which he wrote while crossing Mull on the way to Staffa. The importance of its Scottish setting is clearer in its original title, "Lines written in the highlands after a visit to Burns's country." There's nothing about the Titans or their battle with Jove here. But there was the long-standing tradition that connected the mythical Titans with the historical Celts that was familiar to Milton, and eighteenth- and early nineteenth-century Celticists generally, including Davies and Scott. Keats's epistolary poem makes it plain that in walking through the Highlands he was re-living the historical time when "Druids old" existed (3); and at two key points in *Hyperion* the Titans are compared to the Druids. In the first, Saturn is termed a Druid (I.137); and in the second, the other fallen Titans are said to be "like a dismal cirque / Of Druid stones, upon a forlorn moor" (II.34–5).

This last reference draws upon his earlier experiences on the tour. In Northern England Keats and Brown had gone out of their way to visit the stone circle called the Druid Circle near Keswick. Mysterious circles of the large stones called menhirs are found all over the British Isles, apparently built by the early prehistoric Celts. Like many of his contemporary antiquarians, Davies held in *Celtic Researches* that Britain's prehistoric stone monuments were constructed by the Druids.[22] There were many other general legends about the stones, some still in circulation today. One of the most widespread is that they are petrified Druids, turned to stone by the early Christian missionaries when the Druids would not convert.[23] This was the reason for the name of the circle near Keswick. It is also likely that Keats and Brown passed another such stone circle on Mull, the Loch Buie Stone Circle that is nearly perfectly preserved. They evidently crossed the extended boggy moorland of the southern part called the Ross rather than the mountainous northern coast, since that led to the departure point for Iona at Fionnphort. The Loch Buie Stone Circle is located near the beginning of the Ross on the only flat part of this southern coast, which would have been an added attraction for the weary Keats and Brown.[24]

This fascination with the time of the "Druids old" and the end of Celtic domination in Britain runs through Keats's major works, from *Hyperion* to *Lamia* to *The Fall of Hyperion*. It is first expressed in "There is a joy in footing slow across the silent plain." The opening line of this epistolary poem brings us to a "plain" that is "silent" because the present doesn't seem to exist. What the poet hears instead is the "patriot battle . . . when glory had the gain," in the time of "Druids old . . . / Where mantles grey have rustled by" (3–4). This then is the time of the Druids, more specifically the first century AD when the "patriot" Celts were fiercely struggling to repel the Roman invaders. "Glory had the gain" in Scotland at least since they succeeded in keeping the Highlands free of the Romans, with Hadrian's Wall keeping the Romans out of Scotland as well as keeping the Scots out of the conquered England.

But an even "deeper joy...more solemn in the heart" comes from sensing that the voyager also may be near the birthplace of one who "died of fame unshorn," and "find a bard's low cradle place about the silent north" (28). This knowledge makes the vivid reality of the present quite fade away, with its sound of "woodlarks" and streams, its sight of the "blood-red" sun setting, and the eagles and "ring doves" flying upward. That word "bard" is richly allusive. On one level, it may seem to refer to the "bardie" himself, the Burns of the original title. However, Burns was not really born in the "silent north" of the Highlands but near the southwestern Ayr. Such a bard may be more accurately identified as Ossian, supposedly discovered by the earlier traveler Macpherson, who found evidence of this "Scottish Homer" in the Highlands. For Macpherson had made the same journey through the Highlands about sixty years earlier when he collected first the Gaelic manuscripts later published as *Fragments of Ancient Poetry, collected in the Highlands of Scotland* (1760), and then the fragments of Ossian's epics *Fingal* and *Temora*. As it happened, this second journey included a brief sojourn on Mull. (His stay was more propitious than that of Keats, being a Highland clansman related to the clan's chief and familiar with Gaelic.) "Bard" may refer as well back beyond the Gaelic Ossian, to the bardic disciples of the "Druids old" cited in the opening lines.

The presence of this ancient Celtic past lures the poet in a familiar enough way. For Keats uses here the metaphor of the mortal glamoured away by faeryland to express the powerful desire to feel that one is living in the time of Druids and Celtic bards.[25] Here in the Highlands, in the eerie north again, one who re-enters its ancient past feels "beyond the bourn of care, / Beyond the sweet and bitter world" (29–30). Staying longer "would bar return and make a man forget his mortal way," forget the "well-remember'd face, / Of brother's eyes, of sister's face," and "lose his mind on mountains bleak and bare" (31–46).[26] The poem ends with "a prayer" to keep his "vision clear" so that he will be able to leave for home. In many ways, "There is a joy in footing slow across a silent plain" is an introduction to the world of *Hyperion*.

Keats began this epic several months after returning to London from the walking tour, and a month or so after Lockhart's notorious article about the "Cockney School of Poetry" and its "new star...the good Johnny Keats." We know that the review stung enough to cause him to withhold publication of what he feared was the similarly "smokeable" *Isabella; or, The Pot of Basil*. We also know his explanation a year later to Richard Woodhouse as to why he did not wish to publish *Isabella*: "I intend to use more finesse with the Public. It is possible to write fine things which cannot be laugh'd at in any way."[27] Modeling this long poem that followed *Endymion* on the irreproachable *Paradise Lost*, that he admired so greatly before Lockhart ever wrote his reviews, is one way to prevent further shaming; and *Hyperion* obviously does this.

However, this work is also an almost defiant reaction to Lockhart's comment in his review of *Endymion* that "John Keats has acquired a sort of vague idea, that the Greeks were a most tasteful people, and that no mythology can be so finely adapted for the purposes of poetry as theirs."[28] *Hyperion* uses a British frame of reference that just underlies the classical Greek one. As most readers of it have seen, the model for its first two Books are the first two books of *Paradise Lost* that open with Satan speaking to the congress of fallen angels.[29] But the particular sections of Milton's first Book that seem to have inspired Keats were the two passages that included the Titans among the fallen angels summoned by Satan, and identified the Titans with the Celts.

We know that both passages struck him as significant in Milton's original, because they were among those that he underlined in his marginalia to his copy of *Paradise Lost*. In his copies both of Shakespeare's plays and of Milton, he underscored passages with striking imagery or poetic techniques that he very often drew upon for his own poetry.[30] Keats seemed to have written his marginalia to Milton's work in early 1818, which would have been several months before the walking tour.[31] On that tour, Brown brought a copy of Milton's poems. The first such passage in *Paradise Lost* occurs when Satan summons the pagan deities to join him. Among them are the Titans:

> ... who with Saturn old
> Fled over Adria to th' Hesperian fields,
> And o'er the Celtic roamed the utmost isles. (*PL*. I.519–21)

Here "the utmost isles" signifies the British Isles. The second passage returns to a description of the Titans who have joined Satan, and they are compared to Celtic faeries:

> Earth's giant sons,
> Now less than smallest dwarfs ...
> Like ... fairy elves,
> Whose midnight revels by a forest side
> Or fountain some belated peasant sees,

Or dreams he sees, while overhead the moon
Sits arbitress, and nearer to the earth
Wheels her pale course; they, on their mirth and dance
Intent, with jocond music charm his ear;
At once with joy and fear his heart rebounds. (*PL*. I.778–88)

As Scott notes, there's an old association between the faeries and devils, or fallen angels.[32]

In addition, the atmosphere of the portrayals of Keats's Titans is closer to Ossian's doomed Celtic heroes than to the giants of Greek mythology. Here too, Milton influences Keats's Titans. As his marginalia shows, Keats's favorite passages in the poem prefigure Ossian's melancholy laments for a lost dominion. Among the most heavily marked passages in Keats's *Paradise Lost* are lines relating to the fallen angels, where he notes that Milton "is godlike in the sublime pathetic. In Demons, fallen Angels, and Monsters the delicacies of passion living in and from their immortality is of the most softening and dissolving nature.... Another instance [of this] is *'pensive I sat* alone We need not mention *'Tears such as Angels weep.'*" This last quoted line is the most heavily marked in Keats's entire copy.[33]

Hyperion is a native work. In it Keats is attempting the vastly ambitious project of composing an epic that captures the downfall of the Celtic Empire that had dated from antiquity, with its final decline seen in the defeat of the Celtic Druids by the Roman invaders in Britain. To understand this traditional connection between the mythic Titans and the historical Celts we should remember, as discussed in Chapter 2, the parameters of belief during the seventeenth through the nineteenth centuries about the past as predicated upon the literal accuracy of Mosaic history. If one believed that the date of the Flood was between 2500 and 2000 BC, as Biblical scholars and many others did, then it would be plausible to link the offspring of Gomer — held then to be the Celts (or Gauls) who were the great opponents of classical Greece and Rome — with the mythic Titans who rebelled against the Olympians and fell from power as the Celts ultimately did. The defeat of the Titans by the Olympians was conflated with the passing of the Celts from the world stage.

Thus the end of the wide-flung Celtic world of antiquity began with the Gauls' defeat by the Romans at Telamon in the second century BC. Their decline continued during the Gallic Wars as their realm dwindled to Gaul. Then when Rome conquered Gaul in the first century BC, the only Celtic lands left were the British Isles. The Druids that had been the

Celtic priestly class in Gaul and Britain finally gave way in Britain to the Romans and then the Christians. But the Romantic Celticist preserved the memory of what the Celts had been, in antiquity and in Britain.

Hyperion re-creates the end of the dominance of the Celts. So Saturn's fall in *Hyperion* that began the Titans' defeat could allude to the first defeat of the Gauls by the Romans that signaled the beginning breakup of the Celtic Empire. The imminent defeat of Hyperion as the last of the Titans to be conquered would complete the end of the process, as the British Druids were massacred and driven out by the Romans during the first few centuries AD. Hyperion as the sun-god is a particularly appropriate Titan to represent the Druids here, for their cult of the sun, solar rituals, and astronomical knowledge were well known since antiquity. Davies, of course, identified them with the ancient Hyperboreans who worshipped the sun-god.

Classical sources focus on the drama of the explosive war between the Titans and Olympians, but do not specify which Titan is the last to be overcome. This is Keats's invention. His account takes place during a hiatus with only Hyperion left in his heavenly realm; and the implication is that when Apollo inevitably defeats him, he will join his fellow Titans in their fallen state. It has often been noted that Keats's doomed Titans engage the reader's sympathies as the classical Olympians do not, especially as represented by the adolescent Apollo of the abruptly truncated Book III. This is understandable if Keats is also writing here of the ancient Britons. They are considerably closer to home.

Recent critics of the last few decades have read *Hyperion* anew as they have turned to look at the social and political dimensions of Keats's works. It has long been remarked that Keats's very choice of Milton as his literary model here assured that a similar republicanism would underlie this unfinished epic. Recent critics have looked more closely at the period in which it was composed. Daniel Watkins places it in the context of Romantic Hellenism and its politics of revolutionary liberalism. He considers the battle here to illustrate in a veiled way the collapse of social hierarchies in post-Napoleonic Europe.[34] Others place *Hyperion* more specifically within the time frame in which it was written, namely the post-Napoleonic era in England when it seemed that the goals of the French Revolution had failed and the old European monarchies were being re-established through the machinations of the Holy Alliance.[35]

The historical relevance of *Hyperion* goes deeper than its being commentary on post-Napoleonic Europe, however. It is permeated with contemporary Ossianism and its powerful nostalgia for the ancient times when the Celts prevailed on the British Isles. Fiona Stafford was the first to note the strong imprint of Ossianism on *Hyperion*, with Saturn mourning for the fallen Titans very like Ossian lamenting his fallen battle comrades who are now remembered only by him. Stafford considers Keats's walking tour north through Scotland as the generating cause of the poem, and his exploration of the myth of the Titans to be strongly influenced by the idea of possible connections between the Titans and the Celts.[36] She thinks it significant that one of the books in Keats's small library was Davies's *Celtic Researches*.[37]

The sources ascribed for *Hyperion* usually are limited to Greek mythology, particularly of course those handbooks found in his library. Watkins argues that our interpretation of the coming of the Olympians depends upon Keats's understanding of the Greek myth of the war between the Titans and the Olympians, which in turn was related to the ways in which his sources viewed the battle. He considers these sources to be Lemprière, Tooke, Hesiod's *Theogony*, and William Godwin's *The Pantheon*, a popular handbook of mythology similar to Tooke's.[38] However, there are additional sources that extend the impact of *Hyperion* beyond the immediate historical circumstances of post-Napoleonic England in 1818–1819.

Edward Davies was another source that influenced Keats's epic; and Macpherson's Ossian did so more intimately than Davies. It's not only that, as Stafford remarks, "[Keats's] portrayal of 'grey-haired Saturn' with his 'Druid locks' (I.4) seems closer to Ossian than to [Milton's] Satan."[39] More importantly, Books I and II of *Hyperion* are filled with the famed Ossianic melancholy that the mighty heroes of the past have fallen and the dwindled present-day approaches. This can be seen in the hushed sadness of Thea who doesn't even try to comfort the immobilized Saturn. It's implied with the as-yet unfallen Hyperion when "instead of sweets, his ample palate took / Savour of poisonous brass and metal sick" (I.188–9), which hints forward not only to the coming Age of Brass but beyond that to Keats's own time with its industrial pollution. It fills all the "bruised Titans" who "each one kept shroud, nor to his neighbor gave / Or word, or look, or action of despair" (II.39–40). As Oceanus says in a revealing choice of words when trying to rally them, they were "once chiefs" (II.207), which sounds more like Gaelic chieftains than Greek primordial gods.

Beyond this general tone of Books I and II, there are more specific parallels. There are distinct echoes in the opening scene of *Hyperion* of Macpherson's *Fragments of Ancient Poetry*.[40] He published these "fragments" with the anticipation, expediently expressed in its Preface for possible patrons, that he would find the complete epics in the Highlands: "There is ground to believe that most of [the 'fragments'] were originally episodes of a greater work which related to the wars of Fingal" (5). These sixteen fragments all relate to the narrative of Ossian, son of Fingal and bard, who alone is left to remember old battles. Each fragment laments a lost warrior. Fragments II, III, and VIII all give us the same memorable scene between Saturn and Thea that begins Keats's own epic.

In Fragment II the immobilized, aged hero is accompanied by a woman who mourns with him. He says: "I sit by the mossy fountain.... It is mid-day: but all is silent. Sad are my thoughts alone" (9). In Fragment IX, Ossian addresses a "fair daughter of the isles" with a long listing of the fallen "whose memory is preserved in these tombs" (19). Fragment III again evokes Saturn. "Evening is grey on the hills.... Sad, by a hollow rock, the grey-hair'd Carryl sat" and remembers the warrior Malcolm, "gone, like a dream of the night." This hoary survivor vows, "I will sit by the stream of the plain. Ye rocks! hang over my head. Hear my voice, ye trees! as ye bend on the shaggy hill" (10).

More than any of the others, Fragment VIII seems to portray Saturn as he sits in the opening scene of *Hyperion*, "still as the silence round about his lair,/ Forest on forest hung above his head," with "his realmless eyes... closed" (*Hyp.* I.5–19). Here in Ossian, "by the side of a rock on the hill, beneath the aged trees, old Oscian [*sic*] sat on the moss; the last of the race of Fingal. Sightless are his aged eyes; his beard is waving in the wind." At the end we are left with the image of the solitary bard: "I hear the wind in the wood; but no more I hear my friends. The cry of the hunter is over. The voice of war is ceased" (18).

There are echoes of *Fingal* in *Hyperion* as well. *Fingal* is primarily a narrative account of the heroic efforts by King Cuchullin of Ireland and King Fingal of Scotland to repel King Swaran of Lochlin (the Gaelic name for Scandinavia) who has invaded Ireland. Since Fingal's son Ossian is relating this narrative, we read it knowing that eventually he will be the only one left to mourn all these heroes. Here, the similarities seem even stronger between Ossian and Saturn. Ossian says: "Often have I fought, and often won in battles of the spear. But blind, and tearful, and forlorn I now walk with little men. O Fingal, with thy race of battle I now behold thee not" (79). *Fingal* ends on the same note: "Battles! where I often fought; but now I fight no more. The fame of my former actions is ceased; and I sit forlorn at the tombs of my friends" (104). All of this is echoed by Saturn's tormented speech to Thea before he joins the other fallen Titans (I.95–134).

But beyond this similarity between the heroes Fingal and Hyperion is the ultimate outcome that waits for them; and this produces the particularly Ossianic quality of both epics. In both *Fingal* and *Hyperion*, the poet and the listener / reader know the historical dimension that the ancient characters do not. Ossian knows what is to come, which gives the special edge to his sadness. Fingal wins and sends Swaran back to Lochlin; but soon in the future his son Ossian will lament alone over the tombs of the Gaels. Hyperion still reigns in the heavens, but he is about to succumb to the Olympian Apollo like the other fallen Titans.

Keats's portrayal of the fallen Titans takes little from Tooke, Lemprière, or Hesiod beyond the general outlines of the Titans' doomed battle with the Olympians. Tooke only notes that the Titans "were beaten; and afterwards cast down into Hell."[41] Lemprière does detail the war to some extent; and Hesiod supplies a vivid account of the "wondrous conflagration" and "unbearable din" (700, 709).[42] For both Lemprière and Hesiod, the war is full of action and fireworks without any cessation until the end. Lemprière states that then some Titans were crushed under mountains and others buried in the sea. Only Hesiod describes the war's aftermath according to Greek tradition, relating that in Tartarus "the divine Titans have been hidden in the misty gloom / in a rank realm at the utmost limits of giant earth. / . . . grim and dank and loathed even by the gods — / this chasm is so great that, once past the gates, / one does not reach the bottom in a full year's course" (729–41). As one commentator notes, it's a dank, stagnant wasteland.[43]

Keats's account is strikingly different. Those Titans who have fallen seem to have landed in an autumnal British countryside. Saturn is sitting deep in a forest vale with a marshy stream flowing nearby. When he finally rises with Thea to join the other fallen Titans, he makes his way "through aged boughs" of the "forest on forest [that] hung above his head" in the opening lines of this scene. These other Titans lie in a "den" without light that is part of a landscape remarkably like that of the Scottish Highlands, as Stafford has remarked.[44] Surrounded by "thunderous waterfalls" and "torrents hoarse," amid "crags," "rocks" of "hard flint," and "slaty ridge / Stubborn'd with iron," they are like "a dismal cirque / Of Druid stones, upon a forlorn moor, / When the chill rain begins at shut of eve, / In dull November" (II.8–37). This does not sound like the dank, enclosed realm envisioned by Hesiod; nor do the Titans seem to be existing in a region of hell.

In fact, they sound remarkably like displaced British Druids as envisioned during the early nineteenth century, both by the general educated public and more specifically by Edward Davies. Antiquarian enthusiasts shared a general understanding of what they had been like. As all knew, they had conducted their mysterious rites deep in the seclusion of forests, particularly in glades of their sacred tree, the oak; and the ceremony most identified with them from Pliny onward was held at the beginning of winter, when they gathered to harvest the mistletoe growing on oaks. For his part, in "the Institution of Druidism" Davies included a description of British Druids when they faced the invading Romans during the first century BC. He considered the interior forests to be the Druids' last preserves. As the Romans advanced, the Druids gradually retired into the forest and mountain recesses of the Isles: "Into that sequestered scene, the Druids, who detested warfare, had gradually retired after the irruption of the Belgae, and the further incroachment of the Romans. They had retired from their ancient, magnificent seat at A[ve]bury, and from their *Circular, Uncovered* Temple on Salisbury Plain.... an order cautiously withdrawing itself, into the bosom of its primitive nation" [italics his].[45]

There are allusions to Druidism throughout *Hyperion*. Keats is not merely using the word "Druid" as a synonym for aged or long-haired when he refers to Saturn's "Druid locks" (I.137); nor is he drawing upon a random recollection from his walking tour when he compares the other fallen Titans to "Druid stones, upon a forlorn moor" (II.35). We first meet Saturn at the beginning of Book I in a pose very like the stereotypical Druid or like Macpherson's Celtic bard Ossian, and Bards were closely linked with Druids. He is "gray-hair'd" and old ("his old right hand lay nerveless" [I.18] and "wherefore, poor old King?" [I.52]), with a long beard ("his beard / Shook horrid with such aspen-malady" [I.93–4]). Saturn's stillness is compared by Thea to that of "tall oaks, branch-charmed by the earnest stars" (I.74). Evidently the time is near the beginning of winter, for as he sits in silence "where the dead leaf fell, there did it rest" (I.10), and there's the reference to November in the description cited above of the other Titans.

The powers lost by Saturn since he fell are those of the Druid priest who had adjudicated his society, and ruled the heavens through his mastery of astronomy. Now Saturn is "unsceptred" (I.19) and "buried from all godlike exercise / Of influence benign on planets pale / Of admonitions to the winds and seas" (I.107–9). He has lost the Druidic power to prophesy and cannot foretell the future, for he has to ask Thea what is to come. "Search, Thea! Search! and tell me, if thou seest / A certain shape or shadow, making way / With wings or chariot fierce to repossess / A heaven he lost erewhile / ... Thea! Thea! Thea! Where is Saturn?" (I.121–34). He doesn't even know where the other Titans have fallen, for Thea must lead him to the place where she left them.

At this point, Keats moves to Hyperion in his heavens, still unfallen and possessing his Druidic ability to foretell the future from auguries and visions. Like mortals, he "shudder[s]" at "omens" and "prophesyings," but unlike mortals he doesn't mistake the ordinary "dog's howl" or owl's "screech" for these (I.169–74). Rather the "horrors" that make him "ache" are the signs that the realm he will inhabit is about to change from the heavens to the earth: the shadow of an eagle that has ascended too far, the unfamiliar sound of horses neighing, the fragrance of ceremonial incense that is mixed with the smell of "poisonous brass and metal sick" (I.175–89). Striding with anger through his sun-palace, he asks the meaning of the "forms," "effigies," and "Phantoms" he has seen in his "dreams of night and day." He inquires: "Why do I know ye? why have I seen ye? Why / Is my eternal essence thus distraught / To see and to behold these horrors new? / Saturn is fallen, am I too to fall?" (I.231–4). The "shady vision" that he thus "sees" is not his present blazing palace of light, but future "darkness, death and darkness" (I.242).

He decides to descend and rally Saturn to fight against the "rebel Jove," but not by means of his chariot. This chariot itself signifies the esoteric magic of the Druids. Covered with "hieroglyophics old" that "sages and keen-eyed astrologers" read with "labouring thought," it is shaped like an "orb" with two wings (I.277–84). The winged sun-disk is an ancient magical symbol from Assyria and Egypt. Davies argues at length that when the Celts came through Asia Minor they learned the magic of the Magi, Chaldeans, and Egyptian priests, with this knowledge passed on later in Gaul and Britain through their own priestly class, the Druids.[46]

On his descent, Hyperion meets Coelus, another Ossianic figure in *Hyperion*. Coelus hovers indefinitely on a "dismal" drift of clouds somewhere between day and night, "in grief" as the heaven looks down on him "with pity" (I.302–6). He has lost the power to see the future that Hyperion still has, and can only see the past. Like Ossian recalling the death of his son Oscar in battle, Coelus remembers his son Saturn's recent defeat; and he laments in an Ossianic way: "I am but a voice; / My life is but the life of winds and tides, / No more than winds and tides can I avail" (I.340–2). He urges Hyperion to join the other Titans on earth, while he keeps watch for Hyperion on the sun before dawn.

Thus Book II begins with all the Titans rejoined. The other fallen Titans seem like the defeated Druids left after the Roman invaders had massacred their companions and cut down their sacred oak groves. As Goellnicht has noted, Keats seems to have drawn here upon his observations as a medical student of the operations that were held at that time without anesthesia.[47] For among these Titans, "their clenched teeth [are] still clench'd, and all their limbs / Lock'd up like veins of metal, crampt and screw'd; / Without a motion, save of their big hearts / Heaving in pain, and horribly convuls'd / With sanguine feverous boiling gurge of pulse" (II.24–8). One "upon the flint / . . . ground severe his skull, with open mouth / And eyes at horrid working" (II.50–2). Another is sobbing. These descriptions also echo Roman accounts of the Druids' victims, sometimes Druid lawbreakers, whose death agonies were scrutinized for auguries.

Saturn addresses them as one Druid to another, speaking out of a common context of esoteric lore and practices. He has searched fruitlessly for the reasons for their present state, consulting the "legends of the first of days" in Uranus's primeval "spirit-leaved book," looking there for some "sign, symbol, or portent" and "tak[ing] strange lore, and read[ing] it deep" (II.132–48). But he can't "unriddle, though I search, / And pore on Nature's universal scroll" (II.150–1), for he's lost his ability to interpret the "portents" and "lore." He asks the other Titans for "counsel." Oceanus and his daughter Clymene answer, and their replies are infused with the ancient Druidic belief in metempsychosis.

This tenet has been considered fundamental to Druidism since antiquity. Classical authors explained the Druids' human sacrifices and their indifference to death in battle by the Druid belief in the transmigration of souls from one body to another. Keats would have been familiar with this Druidic belief from Davies if nowhere else, for Davies expounded upon it in his long chapter on Druidism. He noted of the Druids that "some of their most prominent features were — the intercourse they held with souls, after death . . . and the inference they drew, from their lives, respecting the changes they would undergo, and the mode of their ultimate renovation."[48] Elsewhere, he added that "most of [the Druids'] philosophy respected the . . . changes and revolutions to which nature and man were exposed. That *circle of existence* embraced their famous doctrine of *Metempsychosis*. . . . The circle . . . was that, in which man, with all the works of nature, began in the *Great Deep*, of the *lower* state of existence" [italics his].[49]

Oceanus reminds the present Titans of the inevitability of cyclical change ("Nature's law"), and that though they were the earliest of the gods, "on our heels a fresh perfection treads, / A power more strong in beauty, born of us / And fated to excel us" (II.212–14). Historicist critics usually read this as evidence of Keats's political republicanism and his comment on the changes of political regimes in post-Napoleonic Europe. Yet Oceanus's speech in II.173–243 is couched in such fundamentally religious or at least philosophic terms that this localized reading seems counter to its spirit. This "law," Oceanus says, is part of "eternal truth" that has been present from the creation of "Light" out of "Chaos and parental darkness" when "the Heavens and the Earth, were manifest" (II.187–99). As that "fresh perfection" excels them and they pass into "Darkness," it is an impersonal fulfillment of that "law" and not a personal defeat.

He amplifies his meaning with similes implying that the spirit can pass from one form to another after death: the earth feeding the forests that grow "more comely than itself," the rooted tree that harbors the dove able to fly away. Strikingly, he terms the young Poseidon he has seen riding along the sea as "my dispossessor" (II.233). Evidently the spirit of the Sea will next possess this new creature in his chariot. Clymene underscores his words with a similar vision she has had of a younger god. She dreamt she was on a seashore with a land nearby full of fragrance, warmth, and flowers — we know from Book III that this proves to be the young Apollo's nursery — but she only wished to express her own "grief." Then she heard drifting over the sea a melody of joy, and a voice crying the name of Apollo.

Metempsychosis is not necessarily an easy belief to accept when the passage of one's soul to another form is imminent, as the victims of the Druids' sacrifices must have known. Nor is it an easy process to experience, as we will see from Apollo's transformation in Book III. The bodies of the Titans cannot physically die; but their spirits can leave their forms for other forms, which is happening here. Already their Druidic powers have left all of them save Hyperion. Enceladus expresses a resistance to this process, shared by many of the others. Trying to rouse the others to continue fighting, he "scorn[s] Oceanus's lore," but never explains how indeed it is that the Titans could be "smitten by a youngling arm" and Poseidon "scald[ed] in the sea" (II.318–20). Instead, he proclaims the coming of Hyperion, "our brightest brother, [who] still is undisgraced" (II.344). We last saw Hyperion at the end of Book I, "in the van / Of circumstance" (I.343–4). But now, he appears among the other Titans, "dejected" and almost as demoralized as they are when he sees their "misery" in his "most hateful seeing." He gives "mournful . . . sighs," and stands in silence with "his hands contemplative . . . press'd together" (II.368–80). At this sight, "despondence" fills the other Titans.

Hyperion began his flight downward with such energy and resolve that it seems he has already been dispossessed of his spirit, and Clymene's vision is becoming an immediate reality. Nor does he rally them with a call for Saturn although that would seem his role if he is still unfallen. That call comes instead from Enceladus and three of the Titans we first met convulsed in their suffering. It's an anticlimactic entrance for a character first seen striding through his palace full of wrath, and we wonder how Keats will ever return us to the former Hyperion. But we pass to Book III, and the Apollo destined to replace him.

This Book opens with Keats again invoking a native Muse who is evidently prior to the familiar classical Muses. For according to tradition, the Greek Muses were born of the Titaness Mnemosyne and Zeus after the Olympians' war with the Titans was over. We meet Mnemosyne here before she bears these classical Muses, obviously, for the war is still underway. Further, she encounters the young Apollo just before he becomes a god able to usurp Hyperion, when Jupiter is still an "infant thunderer" (I.249). Like the inspiring Muse of *Endymion* who sat alone in England until Apollo's Nine appeared, this Muse of *Hyperion* has been singing to Keats of an earlier time before the dominance of classical culture. She briefly appeared in Book II.82–6 to "chaunt" to Keats of Saturn and Thea. Here Keats suggests, "O leave them, Muse! O leave them to their woes," for she is "weak to sing such tumults dire." Instead, for this prior Muse "a solitary sorrow best befits / Thy lips, and antheming a lonely grief" (III.3–9).

This Muse is distinctly unlike her classical counterpart Calliope, who sang of wars and such imperialistic ventures. Calliope inspired her bards to tell of epic heroes who were the victors or, if defeated, went on to found future empires. Keats's Muse in *Hyperion* is sad and solitary, "antheming" (which means more than a general singing, but, specifically, singing a hymn of loyalty or praise) a "grief" that is "lonely," without many to share it. She sounds exactly like a Celtic Muse, always mourning through her bards for those who have lost, for their countries that have been conquered.

Indeed, *Hyperion* is afflicted with a pervading sadness, and its atmosphere is saturated with an Ossianic melancholy. Its contemporary readers would have seen the underlying parallels between Saturn and Ossian, and heard the echoes of Macpherson's *Fragments of Ancient Poetry* and *Fingal*. Book I opens with a tableau of utter depression as Saturn sits unable even to speak his grief at first, as Book II does with the fallen Titans sprawled around in despair. Nor does the mood change when finally the one unconquered Titan appears . . . and he too who had seemed so fiery and bold turns mournful and dejected, with his hands pressed together in what seems like a prayer of resignation.

Even Apollo in Book III is saddened. This is unexpected. Clymene had seen him "morning-bright," but we first see him on his lush island, wading through lilies-of-the-valley while thrushes sing, and weeping.

His tears trickle down, and he doesn't know why. The Titaness Mnemosyne has been searching for him, for she knows that the time has come for the passing of Hyperion's spirit to Apollo's form. We already have seen this at the end of Book II with Hyperion's doomed appearance. She too cannot quite understand Apollo's "griefs," since he has been sheltered on the island for all of his life so far. His answer shows that the Titans' spirit has began to pass into his form, for he states that "a melancholy numbs my limbs; / And then upon the grass I sit, and moan, / Like one who once had wings" (III.89–91). This was Saturn's opening posture and state of mind. Apollo receives the transforming knowledge that Mnemosyne gives him in a particularly graphic illustration of metempsychosis.

Metempsychosis must involve metamorphosis, as Apollo dramatically shows in the final 13 lines of this poem that concludes just as the process is about to be completed. Here, his "enkindled eyes . . . stedfast kept / Trembling with light upon Mnemosyne" and he's shaken by "wild commotions" that "flush" all his limbs, like someone dying who is "hot" and "with fierce convulse / Die[s] into life." As he "anguish'd," his hair "kept undulations round his eager neck" until finally he "shriek'd" . . . and then "from all his limbs/Celestial —" . . . and the poem ends in midline. Does its final word "celestial" refer to his "limbs," or to something like light about to come from them?[50] It's perhaps the most curious ending to a major poem in English literature.

This change in Apollo has provoked quite varying critical readings. Some consider it more or less transparently orgasmic, although it is difficult to see why Keats would wish to risk the reader responding with a snicker to the deification of Apollo.[51] Others more plausibly relate it to Keats's experiences in seeing patients dying, or even Tom dying as he did during the poem's composition.[52] The process as described, however, is similar to the biological process of metamorphosis in which an organism changes from one life-form into another. This process may be either gradual in stages or suddenly accomplished. Either kind of metamorphosis restructures the entire organism — the nervous, digestive, and reproductive systems — and not just its form. Insect metamorphosis involves molting, a sudden and dramatic transfiguration; and this seems the case here. It's as close to the literal experience of metempsychosis as Keats could render.

The sadness of *Hyperion* is not really explained by its mythological subject matter. The fall of the Titans was familiar enough from classical mythology; and their successors the Olympians were usually celebrated as harbingers of classical culture and, ultimately, the British Empire.

A sympathetic regret that the sacrifice of the early Titans was necessary for this to happen would have been sufficient. However, if one reads the Celtic subtext that historically the Titans were the Celts, then *Hyperion* becomes emotionally valid. The Celts, wanderers throughout history, have fallen save for their outpost on the British Isles; and now even there, the Celtic Druids are about to disappear from history altogether. This subtext may also explain why Keats abandons *Hyperion* so abruptly. The Druids and their society have been vanquished, and he found he had no heart to write of their successors.

5
Faery Lands Forlorn

The only vestige of Celtic Druidism by the early nineteenth century, aside from the historical ruins and megaliths then believed to be Druidical in origin, was the old regional folklore of magic and the faerie. Druidism does not figure again in Keats's poetry until *The Fall of Hyperion: A Dream* but this traditional folklore certainly does, in his great faerie poems of 1819: "The Eve of St. Agnes," "La Belle Dame sans Merci: A Ballad," "Ode to a Nightingale," and *Lamia*. Several of his epistolary works of this period also involve the faerie, and throw a revealing complementary light upon these major works as does his very last poem, *Cap and Bells; Or, The Jealousies: A Faery Tale*. In all of them, we can see what attracted Keats so much to the faerie and its lore. This fascination ran deeper for him than merely being a part of his ideological commitment to Celticism.

Traditionally the faery plays the role of the trickster, and so it does for Keats. This is not to claim that the faery is simply a psychological projection. But often its role for the human observer is that of the trickster. The archetypal function of the trickster figure is to disrupt an overly civilized and stratified social order or to invert a repressive morality. Such a figure acts in unpredictable ways, a kind of irruption of raw energy into an ossified situation or even culture. In his seminal essay on the trickster figure, Jung notes: "... it is not surprising to find certain phenomena in the field of parapsychology which remind us of the trickster. These are the phenomena associated with poltergeists. The malicious tricks played by the poltergeist are well-known.... Ability to change his shape seems also to be one of his characteristics."[1] Faeries were liminal figures that passed back and forth between their own realm and the human one, not bound by human morality or time. They could be capricious, hurtful, and even malicious from the human perspective. Certainly they were, as Blake said of his own trickster figure Orc, "hater of Dignities" (*America: A Prophecy*. 7.5).

And in Keats's poetry, the faeries seem to despise the fixed order of rank that will not give the faerie its due. Elevated social class is ineffectual against the world of the faerie; and their victims in the 1819 faerie poems are the highborn: a princess, a lady from a long line of nobility, a knight, princes, and kings. Traditional Christianity is no more effective, at least in its showy established form that has been "written and revised by Men interested in the pious frauds of Religion."[2] Wearing the prophylactic cross does not work for Madeline, nor does saying the rosary work for the Beadsman. St. Agnes does not help her devotee at all and, more significantly, neither does the Virgin Mary, invoked by that Beadsman with his prayer at the beginning of St. Agnes's Eve and his "thousand aves" at its end. If the knight is "at arms" when he encounters the "fairy child," then he is a Christian knight sworn to defend his realm that must be in danger but, like the other kings and warriors who appear at the end, he has left his post to join the faerie world.

In his poetry, Keats returns again and again to well-known portrayals of the faerie in literature as he bases his own poem upon a famous work that substantiates the faerie. This was true of his "earliest attempt," "Imitation of Spenser."[3] Increasingly, he goes beyond mere echoing to a more structural adaptation that at first alludes to the situation of the original, and then incorporates narrative details, even words. The originals are either revered classics in the English literary tradition, or those by Scott that were popular and widely read. Keats thus suggests that the native lore of the faerie is as legitimate a subject for serious poetry as classical mythology, with an unquestionable literary precedence. His first poem, termed an "imitation" of the author of the famous English epic set in faeryland, includes knowledgeable references to Dido and "aged Lear" (21–2) but its focus is on a swan-riding "fay" and the surrounding emerald isle.

In that first poem, the only references to the literary original lie in the title and scattered bits of general lore about the "fays." Somewhat later in "Calidore: A Fragment," he again includes a deliberate reference to his source *The Faerie Queene* in the title; and he also names his protagonist after a character in the original and derives the narrative situation from the incident in which that character stumbles on a ring of dancing faeries. However, Spenser's faeries are gamboling with the Greek nymphs and three Graces, and all vanish at once. Keats's White Ladies are distinctly local, and only lure Calidore and his friend Sir Clerimonde further away into their realm. This work is another of those "fragments" which Keats breaks off in midline, possibly because of this rather sinister difference from the original. Spenser's Calidore represents Courtesy, a virtue that is rewarded at the end of Book VI; and the Book concludes what we have of the epic. But Keats's Calidore seems destined to be one of those unwilling captives of the faeries forever.

Endymion is a vastly more ambitious adaptation of one of Scott's best known ballads that presents the hero caught in faeryland, namely "Thomas the Rhymer." The central situation of *Endymion* parallels that of "True Thomas": the human who is pursued by the Queen of Faeries and brought to faeryland for awhile only to be released back into human society, but who chooses to return to her in faeryland. Further, specific details of Endymion's encounter with Cynthia echo those of Thomas with the "queen of fair Elfland," and his search for her afterward parallels that of Thomas after he has returned to Ercildoune yet still longs for the "queen of fair Elfland."

Several of the faerie poems of 1819 incorporate not only the general plot of their original model about the faerie, but also narrative details and even words. More and more insistently, Keats includes these textual clues to point us back to the original work. The reality of the faerie in the original is like the initial premise that's posited to be true, to be amplified by Keats's poem; and he seems to mean us to think of this original as we read his own work about the faerie. The original not only is a source for his later poem, but it resonates just below the surface of his own poem as part of its meaning. This is true for "The Eve of St. Agnes" and "La Belle Dame sans Merci" that employ so many details of plot and character from Scott's ballads in *Minstrelsy of the Scottish Border*. It is true as well for "Ode to a Nightingale," Keats's own *Midsummer Night's Dream*.

Several of the little poems that Keats wrote around the same time as the more familiar canonized works of 1819 are either written with faery personae or from the faery's perspective, giving us the faery's world with its own funerals, loves, and intrigues. (There are some folk accounts of witnessing faery funerals.)[4] This world is chill, mercurial, but alluring, remote, and far from the human world and its concerns. One such is "Ah! woe is me! poor Silver-wing," originally titled "Faery Song" in Brown's transcript. This account of the imminent death of a faery queen by an onlooker who's presumably also a faery is addressed to the queen's page "Silver-wing," this color itself telling us that he is an attendant to a White Lady.[5] What's odd to the human eavesdropper/reader is that her dying is taken so easily by all concerned, including the queen. Death is apparently a familiar realm to all.

The speaker will "chaunt" her "dirge and death" — no wild laments of grief here — in her haunting place of flowery river-banks, and watch the flowers fall upon her coffin. But most of the poem renders the experience of death for a faery, and it's a smooth passage. Evidently, she doesn't know she's dying, but must be told by Silver-wing that "the hour is near" and she will have a "calm favonian burial." Favonius was the Roman name for Zephyrus, god of the west wind that was considered light and gentle (as Lemprière notes).[6] There were also the old beliefs that the land of dead and the land of faerie both were in the west.[7] This faery queen will be wafted away like the "blossoms" that will fall "upon her closed eyes, / That now in vain are weeping their last tears" because she is leaving "these arbours green" (15–17). And the last line suggests the moderate quality of sorrow in the world of faerie: "Alas! poor queen!"

It's not an especially memorable poem...but usually what is celebrated about the faery is not its ease in dying and the mildness of its death. Similarly, the faery figures remain indifferent to death in all of Keats's major faerie poems of this period, while the humans experience death in a very different way. It's a well-known world for the faeries.[8] At the end of "The Eve of St. Agnes," the Beadsman freezes to death unnoticed by anyone and Madeline seems to be heading into peril in the January sleet-storm on the moors. Porphyro, who lures her away onto those moors, is probably a demon-lover. And are those "death pale" kings and princes with their "starv'd lips...gaped wide" who appear to the knight at the end of "La Belle Dame" still alive? The "fairy's child" certainly is. The human world that the nightingale, that "deceiving elf," does not comprehend in the "Ode to a Nightingale" includes "fever" and "palsy" for the old, and death even for the young and for "Beauty" with "her lustrous eyes." Lycius dies at the conclusion of *Lamia*, horribly wound in his "marriage robe" like a mummy, while Lamia "vanishe[s]."

"When they were come unto the Faery's court" is another such poem that takes us into the faery's realm where humans really do not belong. Here Keats is also satirizing the pretensions of social rank among those humans, as he will do in *Cap and Bells*. He termed "The Faery's court" as "a little extemporare" when he included it in a letter to George and Georgiana Keats,[9] but this offhandedness is misleading. Its tone is whimsical, even mischievous as he describes the spoiled human Princess with her servants the Ape, the Dwarf, and the Fool, who underestimates the powers of the faerie as she wanders into "the Faery's court" and finds "no one at home — all gone to sport" (2). The joke is that she is about to discover the reality. But this unfinished literary effort is not really extemporare, for it has as its reference point the "Fairy Ballad" of Alice Brand in Scott's *The Lady of the Lake.*[10] Scott's ballads prove a significant source for many of the 1819 faerie poems, as his long essay "On the Fairies of Popular Superstition" and scattered notes on the faery-faith throughout *Minstrelsy of the Scottish Border* are for the poems generally.

Like Scott's "Fairy Ballad," Keats's work is written in cantos, although we find ourself after the first 75 lines of Keats's poem strangely at the "End of Canto xii." The three servants of Keats's Princess are humans who have been "faery-struck," and turned into an Ape, a Dwarf, and a Fool.[11] Likewise, the Dwarf and the Ape also appear in Scott's ballad as examples of the faerie glamour that there changes the ugly reality into the apparently beautiful. The Fool by its very nature is the human who has become something non-human, a frequent result of faery contact in folktales. Furthermore, the narrative situation of Keats's poem is close to that of these stanzas:

> 'T is merry, 't is merry, in Fairy-land
> When fairy birds are singing,
> When the court doth ride by their monarch's side,
> With bit and bridle ringing:
>
> 'And gaily shines the Fairy-land —
> But all is glistening show,
> Like the idle gleam that December's beam
> Can dart on ice and snow.
>
> 'And fading, like that varied gleam,
> Is our inconstant shape,
> Who now like knight and lady seem,
> And now like dwarf and ape.' (Canto IV, xv, 1–12)

Scott is alluding to a Faery Rade; and his general tale of Alice Brand is piously Christian.[12] Her lover is a faery captive, and his only chance of rescue is when he rides with them on a Faery Rade on Hallowe'en. She saves him by facing his guardian "grisly elf," and crossing the elf three times. Keats's version considers what happens back at the vacant faery court while the faeries are off on their Rade. His trickster tone is in the spirit of the faeries themselves, for he's playing with quite a bit of faery lore in this poem. The four humans (or at least the one still human and the other three faery-struck humans) have come to the "Faery court" and "rang — no one at home" (2).

The Princess doesn't question how they're able to see the court and she casually rings for entrance, although faeryland is usually hidden from view and dangerous even to approach.[13] So it is here although she doesn't notice it, for the woods are "lone and wild," even "the robin feels himself exil'd," and the brooks hurry to get away from this "magic shade" (5–8). Robin redbreasts were thought to be maltreated by faeries because of their legendary associations, for many believed that the robin's breast was red because it plucked out one of Christ's thorns at the Crucifixion.[14] Spirits couldn't cross running water, as was generally known.[15] Although the faeries' envy of a human should be avoided since it usually results in the human's comeuppance, the Princess wants to show them her "diamond cross," exotic servants, and "Otaheitan mule" (11–14). She may be wearing a cross but it won't protect her against magic, as the rest of the poem implies. "Otaheite" was the name given to Tahiti by Captain Cook in his journal, published in 1773 and the main source of late eighteenth-century ideas about Tahiti. The late eighteenth- and nineteenth-century literati associated the South Sea islands he explored with Prospero's island of magic in *The Tempest.*

The Princess decides to burst into the "Faery's court" since no one answers the bell, to the terror of her servants who know the faerie world quite well. The Dwarf speaks to dissuade her, and mentions "the three 'great crimes' in faery land": making "a whipstock of a faery's wand... snoring in their company... making free when they are not at home" (26–9). These "faery crimes" have their roots in faerie lore. Stealing faery treasures was usually punished severely, especially when it was for human gain.[16] Many of the stories of people who were inveigled away by the faeries began with the person unwittingly falling asleep in places where the faeries held their revels.[17] Finally, the faeries' hatred of human prying into their privacy was well known.[18]

The many euphemistic names for them, such as the "Good People," the "Men (or Women) of Peace," and so on, were really protective and came from the general belief in their malevolent, touchy nature that caused them to take offense easily. One can see this casually cruel nature of the faeries in the case of the Dwarf. He was "a baby prince" when he used a faery's wand as the handle of a little whip to make his top spin around,[19] and was taken off with his toys into faeryland (30–3). As the Dwarf speaks, the Princess peels a "hazel twig" to use on these three recalcitrant servants who balk at advancing; and hazel was long considered a faerie tree.[20]

As Keats relates the stories of these faery-struck servants, it becomes clear that all of those who are tricked by the faeries in this little poem are of noble birth. The Dwarf who was a prince relates the stories of the Fool and the Ape, one a prince and the other a king who committed these faerie crimes. And of course there is the Princess herself. The last we see of her is that she touches the "wards," or locks, of the court door with the Ape's picklock, the door "full courteously" opens with a welcome that should be alarming, and she enters with her servants.[21] The door closes — how? — and all that's left is the tethered Mule grazing outside. Even that Mule is a faery-struck king of Otaheite, as it turns out. Mules, of course, are anomalies, being neither horse nor donkey... rather faery-like themselves. The Mule finds his freedom through the agency of curious monkey-men (also from Otaheite and transformed along with their king?) who descend from a nearby "old pollard tree." Pollarding trees was an old British practice of cutting off the tree's lower branches to allow the grazing of animals below, which often produced a hollow core and led to a centuries-old longevity. These were exactly the kind of trees in which faeries traditionally lived.[22] Here the poem trails off.

This seemingly inconsequential and nonsensical "little extemporare" throws light on the canonical faerie poems to follow. It shows how much faerie lore Keats knew, to play with it so easily and confidently. In addition, we can see how much Keats apparently enjoyed creating the world of "the Faery's court" since we see it again and again in his poems. The faerie world could be shifting and prankish as well as sober-serious and ominous, but in either case it set up the social status and class pretensions of mankind as targets to be mocked. This is also the world of "The Eve of St. Agnes" and "La Belle Dame sans Merci," in which everything that seems so familiar has unfamiliar faerie overtones and is increasingly an alien place for human beings where they venture at their peril.

These two well-known faerie poems are linked internally as well as externally. The ballad that Porphyro sings to Madeline as he attempts to wake her in "The Eve of St. Agnes" is "La belle dame sans mercy" ("Eve," 292).[23] This is not necessarily a comment on Madeline's resistance, but could allude rather to Porphyro's origins. Externally too "La Belle Dame" seems an extension of "The Eve of St. Agnes," for alone of Keats's major works these two are overtly about the faerie. Further, like "the Faery's court," both have ballads by Sir Walter Scott as their originating source, here, several from *Minstrelsy*. "La Belle Dame" seems to be based directly upon "Thomas the Rhymer," and we are told in its title that it is a ballad. "The Eve of St. Agnes" has distinct parallels with Scott's "The Eve of St. John" and "The Daemon-Lover," although this has gone unremarked. It should be noted that Scott's two ballads do not seem themselves to be

"Imitations" that he composed, but rather his translations from the Gaelic.[24] Like most of the ballads that Scott included in *Minstrelsy*, Keats's two poems are set in medieval times when the faery-faith was prevalent and are also written in the genre of the romance. "The Eve of St. Agnes" is replete with archaic words and phrases.

It was not a simple matter of Keats trying to approximate his illustrious literary predecessors such as Spenser. This familiar critical explanation of "The Eve of St. Agnes" is somewhat in the spirit of Francis Jeffrey in 1820 who, meaning to praise Keats in the wake of Lockhart's attacks, wrote: "Mr. Keats has unquestionably a very beautiful imagination, and a great familiarity with the finest diction of English poetry; but he must learn not to misuse or misapply these advantages."[25] The medievalisms here may seem contrived — "amort," "perchance," "forsooth," "mickle," "amain," "beldame," "espial," "cates," "for aye," and all the "thous." However, Keats had a very good artistic, even ideological precedent for this in his models here.

Scott was well known for his revising and "improving" the old ballads; and Burns too used the Gaelic folksongs that he collected as the basis for his own poetic creations. Scott divided the old Gaelic Border ballads that he had collected into historical ballads and "the tales of romance," and termed his own rewritings of them "Imitations of these compositions by Modern Authors." He defended this by holding that these "Imitations" were "founded upon such traditions, as we may suppose in the elder times would have employed the harps of the minstrels.... uniting the vigorous numbers and wild fiction, which occasionally charm us in the ancient ballad, with a greater equality of versification, and elegance of sentiment, than we can expect to find in the works of a rude age."[26] He added that in attempting to give his ballads "an appearance of more indisputable antiquity... the utmost care has been taken, never to reject a word or phrase, used by a reciter, however uncouth or antiquated."[27]

For both Burns and Scott, these "Modern Imitations of the Ancient style of composition" were an expression of their nationalism as they saw the old Scottish ways fast usurped by English traditions, and the Gaelic language and ancient oral ballads forgotten. As Scott proclaimed of his rewritten ballads, "by such efforts, feeble as they are, I may contribute somewhat to the history of my native country; the peculiar features of whose manners and character are daily melting and dissolving into those of her sister and ally." And then he added some lines of verse that are also relevant to Keats's own general adherence to Celticism, and in particular his 1819 faerie poems: "Hail, land of spearmen! seed of those who scorn'd / To stoop the proud crest to Imperial Rome!"[28]

Scott was alluding to the old days of Caledonia; but Celticism for Keats had other, more immediate implications. He always retained his old love for classical mythology and culture, but the British Celtic past, the traditions of Druidism and of the faerie, all were for him his *native* traditions that seemed equally relevant. "The Eve of St. Agnes" and "La Belle Dame" have Scott's ballads as their Celtic sources, and allude again and again to folktales of the faerie. These two poems seem directly inspired by the "Muse of my native land" in her "home-bred glory," as Keats called her in *Endymion*.

"The Eve of St. Agnes" is strongly influenced by Scott's ballads "The Daemon-Lover" and "The Eve of St. John," that appear in Volume I of *Minstrelsy*. "The Eve of St. Agnes" shares a similar background of folk-superstitions with "The Eve of St. John." St. John's Eve is perhaps better known as Midsummer Eve, taking place at the summer solstice and widely celebrated throughout Europe since the Middle Ages. It's long been associated with weddings and fertility generally, accompanied by many rites to enable young women to foresee their future husband's face. Midsummer Eve is also universally believed to be a time when the faeries and spirits come out.[29] These beliefs were so familiar that Keats must have known them. The superstitions surrounding the eve of the feast of St. Agnes were less well known, but similar. It also was marked by rites which allowed the young virgin to envision her future husband. And in Keats's own ballad about this eve, it too is a time when faeries emerge.

The central situation of both of Scott's ballads is the damned spirit who comes back to claim his earthly love married to another. Similarly, Keats's Madeline in her way is married to the sisterhood of St. Agnes, which causes her to ignore both the cavaliers and Porphyro. She is ultimately seduced like Scott's ladies in the two ballads also. The outcome of Keats's poem is famously uncertain and so is the true nature of Porphyro, with much of the criticism focusing upon this ambiguity and proposing answers. But accumulating allusions to the faerie within the poem suggest the conclusion just beyond the frame of the narrative, as well as Porphyro's real identity. This implied conclusion echoes that of Scott's ballads too, although here it may be a voyage to some Otherworld besides Hell.

Beyond these general similarities between Scott's two ballads and Keats's poem, specifics of the ballads are quite close to those of "The Eve of St. Agnes."[30] In the narrative of "The Eve of St. John," the "Baron of Smaylho'me" returns covered with blood from a conflict, although not the Battle of Ancrum Moor which is the background for this ballad. He questions his page to find out what his lady has done in his three days' absence, which has fallen on the "eve of St. John." The page replies that he saw the lady with a knight on the moors, and heard them speak.

The lady asked the knight to visit her chamber, but he replied that he could not as it was the Eve of St. John. She implored him, and he answered that he feared that although the bloodhound was silent and the warder (porter) would not sound the alarm, he would be heard by the priest who slept nearby; but she replied that the priest was gone. The knight promised to come at midnight on St. John's Eve "when bad spirits have power." As it turns out, the knight is really the wandering, damned spirit of her lover whom the Baron has just killed; and this discovery sends her to the convent and the Baron to the monastery for the rest of their lives.

The details of these stanzas appear throughout "The Eve of St. Agnes," from the beliefs surrounding St. Agnes's Eve that cause Madeline to refuse any suitors and retreat alone to her chamber in the "honey'd middle of the night," to the appearance of Porphyro in her chamber at the time when "St. Agnes' moon has set," to the hurried flight of the two lovers at the end past the drunken "Porter" and the quiet bloodhound. Among those they flee are "the Baron" and the sleeping Beadsman with his rosary. There are other touches in Keats's poem that recall Scott's ballad. Angela comments that "St. Agnes! Ah! it is St. Agnes' Eve — / Yet men will murder upon holy days" (118–19), and tells Porphyro that Madeline is his "conjuror." Scott's lady also plays the role of conjuror, as her ghostly lover knows: "I had not had power to come to thy bower, / Had'st thou not conjured me so" (XLIII). Finally, Porphyro comes to Madeline "across the moors" (74), and then disappears with her at the end "o'er the southern moors" (351). Scott's ballad is set on Ancrum Moor.

Scott's "The Daemon-Lover" is a shorter ballad, but equally relevant to "The Eve of St. Agnes." The story is more straightforward: the protagonist who has been gone for seven years persuades his now-married love to sail away with him, and when she does he reveals that they have set sail for hell. As they approach their final destination, they see a mountain before them "all so dreary wi' frost and snow" which is "the mountain of hell" (XVI) — hell thus associated with intense cold, it should be noted — and then they sink in the stormy sea.[31] Here again, the lady at first is reluctant because of her religious vows, but is persuaded by the faery lover. The snow-storm in the last lines of Scott's ballad is paralleled by the sleet-storm that begins as soon as Keats's Porphyro has joined Madeline in her bed, and the ominous "elfin-storm" (343) into which they finally disappear. But in terms of complexity, Keats goes far beyond Scott's "Imitations of the Ancient style" as he creates the sense of a supernatural power that will overwhelm the humans who would resist it.

For just how should we regard his Porphyro, who is more than Scott's villainous demon-lover or damned spirit here? Keats provides some sympathetic touches in his portrayal, for in the beginning Porphyro seems an impetuous suitor with "heart on fire / For Madeline" (75–6), and when he urges Angela to bring him to her he is "woful" with "deep sorrowing" (160). On the surface level, we feel that he may be liberating Madeline from old wives' tales. His name is an oddly insistent clue, an unusual name for a supposedly medieval character in a romance. Marcia Gilbreath has considered the etymology of this name, and concludes that Keats could have derived the name from the Greek anti-Christian philosopher Porphyrius who is mentioned in Lemprière's *Bibliotheca Classica* or from Porphyrion, one of the classical giants who attacked Jupiter. In both cases, the figure broke a religious taboo.[32] As she also notes, Keats includes Porphyrion as one of the Titans in *Hyperion*. II.20. There is another, more significant aspect of this Porphyrion than his rebellious nature.

As a Titan, Porphyrion had long associations with the Celts and also indirectly with the faeries. Both associations were old, well-known folk-beliefs that Keats would have encountered in Milton as well as Scott. The connections between the mythic Titans and the historical Celts have already been discussed. When Milton designated the Titans as the classical Celts and included them among the bands of rebellious angels who followed Satan into hell (*PL*. I.510–21), he drew on this tradition. Somewhat later in the same Book, he also terms these Titans who are in hell as "fairy elves" (*PL*. I.777–88). This obviously refers to the shape-shifting powers of the faeries shown by "Earth's giant sons" who now as devils are "less than smallest dwarfs" (778–9). It also alludes to the longstanding belief that the fallen angels became the faery folk.[33] Scott records this as a common belief held about "the Fairies of Popular Superstition."[34] As Stafford has more recently noted, in Highland folklore the faeries who lived under the hills were the fallen angels.[35] Being angelic in origin, they could not reside in hell but dwelt in the "Middle Kingdom" instead.[36]

The word "faery" or sometimes "fairy," as well as allusions to enchantments, charms, and spells, fill Keats's poem. Usually critics consider this to be only part of the medieval atmosphere that he was trying to create, along with the archaisms, evocative details of dress, feudal architecture, and so on. "Faery" is taken as a metaphor for an extravagantly imaginary world, for the visionary, beautiful, unsubstantial, and unreal; and the *Oxford English Dictionary*, that august lexical source, cites line 70 ("hoodwink'd with faery fancy") as an illustration of that meaning of the word.[37] But it is a valuable strategy while reading "The Eve of St. Agnes" *to take Keats at his word*. Why not read "fairily," "faery fancy," "wand," "ghost," "witch's sieve," "Elves," "Fays," "conjuror," "crone," "enchantments cold," "legion'd fairies," "pale enchantment," "charmed maid," "mission'd spirit" ("mission'd" means sent on some duty or work, which implies magical control), "midnight charm," "stedfast spell," "elfin-storm," "faery land," "haggard seeming," "dragons," "phantoms," "witch," and "demon" as referents to specific entities or states? Again and again here, what seems to be merely a picturesque flourish has a meaning that, if taken literally, insinuates that a disguised power is gathering strength for the conclusion.

In 1945, Herbert G. Wright argued in a short article that some "agency hostile to mankind [is] actively at work" in the poem, and its elves and fairies are not the harmless beings of *A Midsummer Night's Dream*.[38] Critics have not really followed up this lead since. However, nearly every detail in the poem has supernatural associations or is related in some way to the faery-beliefs of "popular superstition." The stanzas contain so many allusions to these folk-beliefs, sometimes several within a stanza, that there is an accumulated faerie presence that seems real. If we heed Keats's portents, we realize that Madeline is surrounded by the inhabitants of faeryland who want her to join them there. The atmosphere grows increasingly sinister because the ancient force seeking her is so pervasive and no one human around her seems to understand what's happening, whether the Beadsman, her kinsmen, or the Baron with his "warrior-guests." It's simply outside their ken. They seem to be conventionally Christian, for they have their own chapel with an angel roof and a family burial ground as well as a Beadsman saying endless "aves" for their sins. If their resistance to the faerie is ineffectual, it's because they ignore or disbelieve in it.

The first sign that things are not what they seem is the unobtrusive person of the narrator, present from the opening lines but not really apparent until the last, distancing stanza. There we see unexpectedly that an objective third-person narrator has been recounting this seemingly immediate, vividly embroidered tale of characters actually long past and events whose final outcome is unknown.[39] This is the strategy of storytelling, and more specifically, of relating an old folktale. Its audience may or may not have heard it before; it doesn't really matter. A good teller of folktales embellishes them with particulars that create atmosphere and the conviction that the tale really happened; and this is especially important with folktales about the supernatural. So "The Eve of St. Agnes" begins with several stanzas that recount details about the setting that seem to have little to do with the plot except to make us feel as cold as if we could never be warmed; and cold is a significant supernatural element in this story. Beyond that, there are allusions to the folk-beliefs about the faerie throughout these opening lines.

From the very beginning, there are speech-signs signaling that someone is relating this tale to a present audience. The first two lines have a spoken quality ("St. Agnes' Eve — Ah, bitter chill it was! / The owl, for all his feathers, was a-cold") with the dramatic interjection, the inverted word order, the vernacular a-prefixing. The interjection is used again with a common evaluative adjective in line 91, "Ah, happy chance!" The dramatic last stanza that reveals the far-distant past of all of the preceding actions makes this vernacular speech-pattern plain in its first line, "And they are gone: ay, ages long ago" (370), with the discourse marker "and," the interjection "ay," and the vague phrase "ages long ago" that is itself a common storytelling phrase. The strategy of this final stanza is that of the storyteller too. The uncertainty of the outcome is stated in its opening two lines as a fixed element in the tale, not to be resolved by any reader or listener. The last seven lines follow with the supernatural details about those left behind, in a final grotesque flourish.

There also are lapses where this objective narrator addresses the audience directly, only one place in the published poem but several in the first draft. In the final version, the narrator addresses us as a storyteller would: "These let us wish away, / And turn, sole-thoughted, to one Lady there" (41–2). Originally, Keats added stanzas with lines that performed a similar function. Thus he shifted attention from the cold Beadsman in the opening to the "revelry" in progress: "Follow, then follow to the illumined halls, / Follow me youth — and leave the Eremite — / Give him a tear..." When he turned from the party to Madeline: "let me tell of one sweet lady there..." And he began the famous deleted stanza making it plain that Porphyro did more than melt into her dream: "See, while she speaks his arms encroaching slow...."[40] That directive "see" itself is an interactive sign of conversation.

There are additional marks of the storyteller's strategy. One of the eeriest qualities of the work is the disparity between the ugly reality of what is happening — pandering, voyeurism, betrayal, rape — and the dream-like tone in which it is related. Stillinger was the first to direct the reader's attention to the poem's unvarnished subject matter that had been ignored for so long.[41] This is a characteristic of a well-told faery story, for its immediate pain is removed although the horror of what is happening is retained. And tales of the human and the faerie worlds intersecting do usually involve some sort of horror from the human perspective. The faery king abducts the bride under the eyes of her new husband.[42] The faeries blind the human serving as midwife to the faeries, so she won't see them later when she returns to her own world.[43] The faery changeling replaces the newborn taken from the mother at her lying-in.[44]

This particular faery story begins and ends with a cold that gets increasingly numbing. There is an old tradition that connects cold with Satan, and considers it a sign of the presence of evil spirits.[45] Witches at their trials from the Middle Ages onward usually described intercourse with the devil as being penetrated by extreme cold with his organ feeling like ice. Scott was drawing on this old belief in "The Daemon-Lover." Even present-day accounts of encounters with poltergeists or ghosts note the unusual areas of cold surrounding the places where they linger. Keats alludes to the gathering cold throughout the action of the poem, from the Beadsman with his stiff fingers trying to say his rosary, to the freezing sculptures in the chapel, to the undressed Madeline getting into her warm bed, to Porphyro emerging from his unheated closet "pallid" as "stone," to the sleet-storm (so much more bone-chilling than a snow-storm), to the Beadsman in the last line dead "among his ashes cold."

There are other signs that supernatural forces are present. In the opening lines, the owl is cold "for all his feathers" and the hare "limp'd trembling through the frozen grass." Both of these creatures thus associated with the cold were often believed to be wer-animals, or shape-shifting spirits who had turned into beasts for disguise.[46] Owls also were often considered the familiars of witches, probably because they were the bird of Hecate, the Greek goddess of witches.

The Christian figures are inadequate as any guard. There is the ineffectual Beadsman. The ancestral spirits that might protect their latter-day kinswoman Madeline are confined to the icy statues of the "sculptur'd dead" of the family knights and ladies of the family behind their "black, purgatorial rails" (14–15). "Purgatorial" could allude to the state of their souls as well as the unpleasant quality of this wintry chapel, and if so they are not in a spiritual state to assist anyone. The Beadsman steps just beyond a door leading from the chapel to the castle as the guests enter for the revels. Like many medieval churches this chapel has an angel roof, which usually had spread-winged angels carved along the roof-beams of the nave to accompany the worshippers. But these "carved angels" watch the revelers from the open door with their wings furled or "put cross-wise on their breasts" (36). These angels can't fly anywhere.

Madeline appears amid the revelers as though bewitched, with her eyes unfocused, her breathing shallow, and her movements uncontrolled ("she danc'd along" [64]). And so she is. Those tales of St. Agnes and her rites that will produce visions were told to Madeline by "old dames" (45) who could be witches; and Angela, transparently a witch, is also termed an "old beldame" (90). These rites are later termed "enchantments cold" (134). It is curious that these "old dames" would tell their stories on the one night when Madeline is most likely to meet a real-life lover, as "many a tiptoe, amorous cavalier" (60) throng her castle.[47] It is also the night when Porphyro is coming. We last see her in this scene "hoodwink'd with faery fancy" (70). "Hoodwink" has another meaning than blindfolded or blinkered, which is the way in which this word is usually taken. It can also mean deceived or prevented from seeing the truth.[48] This is the faery act of glamouring.

"Meantime," as the narrator urges us with the familiar storytelling device, we turn to Porphyro. Here it is especially useful to take Keats at his word in order to understand the nature of this character. Superficially, the situation vaguely echoes Shakespeare's Romeo–Juliet situation, with the lovers kept apart by their warring families and only Juliet's Nurse to bring them together. Porphyro may seem another Romeo. But the narrator tells this story with so many unearthly details that it takes on quite another meaning. Porphyro stands outside the castle doors, "buttress'd from moonlight" (77). "Buttressed" means to be sustained or supported, and moonlight traditionally accompanies the appearance of faeries and signals the time of enchantment.[49] He's a great enemy of Madeline's family, and if his presence here were known the "very dogs would execrations howl / Against his lineage" (87–8). Animals notoriously sense the presence of spirits and shy away, with dogs howling in resistance.[50] "Execrations" can mean curses, and that "lineage" may well be the rebellious angelic one that opposed mankind. Somewhat later, Angela tells him to "flit like a ghost away" (105) and leads him off to "a little moonlight room" (112) as his hat's plume "brush[ed] the cobwebs" (110–12). Cobwebs were usually associated with magic and the faeries' spinning, one of their favorite crafts.[51] The full moon is the phase most conducive to magic;[52] and the light of the full moon (217) accompanies his progress with Madeline throughout. Again and again, objects are described as "silvered."

His deceptive nature is revealed here, as well as his lot as a damned or at least lost spirit. He asks "all saints" to let him see Madeline "but for one moment" so he can merely look at her and "worship all unseen" (78–80). Here, as when he speaks later with Angela, he pledges to suffer eternal divine punishment if he transgresses; but we realize that he can easily swear this if in fact he's already doomed. For he goes on to specify this worship, and it's obviously seduction ("speak, kneel, touch, kiss" [81]). Equally obviously, he does not fear retribution from those saints. Keats thus informs us from the beginning of Porphyro's intent to seduce Madeline, and we're meant to keep this in mind as he speaks to Angela.

Angela seems like a witch from the moment we see her, aged and shuffling along with her "wand" (92) like "an aged crone" (129). This last word sometimes means a witch. Her palsy is described throughout, with her "palsied hand" (97) as she grasps Porphyro's fingers here, her self-characterization as "palsy-stricken" (155), her "agues in her brain" (189), and her final "palsy-twitch'd" death (376). Paralysis was traditionally considered an illness associated with the faeries, a sign of being faery-struck. The word "stroke" comes from the belief in an afflicting faery-stroke or elf-bolt.[53] She might also be said to suffer from rheumatism, with her "shuffling" (92) and "hobbled" (181) gait; and this illness too was long suspected to be a sign of the witch.[54]

Porphyro and Angela clearly know each other very well, oddly since she seems to be an old family retainer. If he is an ancient family enemy, then how does she know him and why would she welcome him? Yet she at once addresses him by name and warns him that "they" are present, with the pronoun telling us that Madeline's family is their common enemy. She tells him that "dwarfish Hildebrand" has just cursed him (100–3). Hildebrand was the given name of the early medieval Pope Gregory VII, who was in fact squat in appearance, known in church history for his reforming zeal. As Porphyro relates his scheme to Angela, her witch-like response is to laugh "feebly" in the moonlight (127) at the idea that Madeline's belief in the "good angels" surrounding St. Agnes will lead to her loss of virginity, a spiteful cackling indeed.[55]

She exclaims, "Thou must hold water in a witch's sieve, / And be liege-lord of all the Elves and Fays, / To venture so" (120–2). Since he *is* venturing so, she must be stating the reality rather than indulging in rhetorical exaggeration. Holding water in a sieve is an obvious impossibility, but the reference to a "witch's sieve" has an element of malice that is relevant here. There were folktales in many regions of England about a faery cow that generously gave abundant milk to local villagers during a famine, until a witch milked it into a sieve and it vanished.[56]

This desire to see that starving humans are unable to get sustenance when one doesn't need it oneself, is rather what Porphyro is doing if he is indeed such a "liege-lord of all the Elves and Fays," for he is stealing away the human Madeline so none of those "amorous cavaliers" can get her.

Angela's response to him when he proposes his "strategem" is an enticing picture of Madeline in her solitary bed as she tells him to leave the "sweet lady" to "dream alone" (141–2). He pledges his abstinence in a way that is meaningless if he is a demon, swearing "O may I ne'er find grace / When my weak voice shall whisper its last prayer" (146–7), and then threatens to alarm the entire house if she does not cooperate. She may seem to beg for pity as a weak old woman, but considering her words closely we see how accurate they are if she's a witch. She terms herself a "feeble soul ... a churchyard thing, / Whose passing-bell may ere the midnight toll, / Whose prayers for thee ... / Were never miss'd" (154–8). This could be a reference to her attendance at the witches' Sabbath held in churchyards.[57] In any case, if she's a witch her prayers would certainly go unheeded by God.

Porphyro's rejoinder that he will "perhaps that night win a peerless bride, / While legion'd fairies pac[e] the coverlet" (167–8) reveals that his real goal is to glamour her away. "Legion'd" has vaguely military associations and so does the idea of pacing faeries surrounding her as she sleeps in "pale enchantment" (169).[58] At this point, the narrator suddenly interjects a brief commentary that should make it plain that this is not the usual romance of star-crossed lovers. It is like the storyteller's warning to his audience of the dire events to come that the characters cannot know: "Never on such a night have lovers met, / Since Merlin paid his Demon all the monstrous debt" (170–1). There is not a critical consensus about the meaning of this allusion, although most sense that it is important to the poem for it tells us how to regard these present lovers, one of them a woman of noble lineage.

Many consider that the "Demon" is Vivien, who finally ensnared Merlin to his doom;[59] and others think it a reference to Merlin's demon-father and the evils that Merlin performed during his life.[60] Yet while Vivien may be an enchantress or even a faery, she does not have the evil quality of a demon. The word "debt" seems too specific for something as general as Merlin's evil actions. Keats seems instead to have had something quite definite in mind. And indeed, it is remarkable how the central situation of "The Eve of St. Agnes" parallels key events in Merlin's life. Merlin's father was an incubus who visited a devoutly Christian princess; and Merlin arranged a similar meeting by deception that led to the birth of Arthur. Merlin's patron King Uther Pendragon desired the beautiful Igraine, the wife of Duke Gorles, who refused him. While Gorles was away in battle, Merlin through magic caused Uther to appear to her one night as Gorles, with Arthur as the result. Gorles died fighting, and Uther won Igraine as his own "peerless bride." Thus it may be argued that Merlin repaid the "monstrous debt" of life he owed to his demonic father by arranging for another such deception through magical shape-shifting to be played on a virtuous noblewoman.

These two lines are a turning point in the poem. Subsequent events turn darker and darker, and any resemblances to Shakespeare's lovers are left far behind. Angela agrees to do more than bring him to Madeline's closet. She will "quickly" supply the closet with delicacies and Madeline's lute; and she does to good effect, as we see. But how does she get all of this there so swiftly, especially since her lameness is stressed throughout?[61] She leaves the scene with a final exclamation: "Ah! thou must needs the lady wed, / Or may I never leave my grave among the dead" (179–80). This has the same kind of ambiguity as Porphyro's vows, if in fact she is already doomed. It also signals that she expects Madeline's eventual betrayal.

Madeline enters her chamber in "pallid moonshine" (200) and pauses before a stained glass casement there to pray. In many covert ways, this casement in her bedroom hints at her future. The first details described have faery associations. The only plant specified among its carved fruits and flowers is knot-grass (210), mentioned by Shakespeare in *Midsummer Night's Dream* as "hindering Knotgrass" (*MND*. III.2), and believed to thwart the growth of the young as part of a hostile faery's spell.[62] The stained panes of "quaint device...'mong thousand heraldries" (211–14) are compared to the wings of the tiger-moth (213). Butterflies and moths both have been traditionally associated with faeries because of their transformative metamorphosis, moths in particular since they emerge during the nighttime.[63] By Keats's time, faeries had been portrayed for centuries with insect wings (angels, with the wings of birds). This particular moth has the associated folk-superstition that its caterpillar, known as the wooly-bear, can predict the severity of a coming winter... a portent of the sleet-storm ahead?

All of these tiger-moth colors come from the panes of "quaint device," a heraldic term meaning the emblem adopted by a particular noble family. Since there are a "thousand heraldries," Madeline must come from myriad noble families. Among these "heraldries" are portrayed "twilight saints," with "twilight" implying their dubious sanctity as did the furled wings of the carved angels in the chapel earlier. Similarly, the "shielded scutcheon" of her family that "blush'd with blood of queen and kings" (216) may simply employ the heraldic color red; or it may include a bend sinister, sign of illegitimacy, as "blush'd" subtly implies, and predict Madeline's imminent rape and possibly its outcome.

The full moon shines through the window on Madeline (217) as she prays and the moonlight falls on the cross she wears, a significant detail. In Scott's introduction to "The Daemon-Lover," he notes another ballad with a happier ending in which "a fiend" was discouraged in his suit of a beautiful maiden by the "holy herbs which she wore in her bosom."[64] Here, we realize that Madeline has been wearing her cross all along. Now, she is termed "akin / To spirits of the air" (201–2), a "saint," an "angel" headed for "heaven" (222–4). As Porphyro watches her he "gr[o]w[s] faint," as Scott's fiend did. However, unlike Scott's knowing maiden, Madeline removes the cross as she undresses for bed as just one more "warmed jewel," and Porphyro's "heart revives." He can proceed.

With Madeline's cross gone, the faerie presence intensifies. Now when she disrobes she is "a mermaid in sea-weed" (231), an erotic image but also an allusion to a faery who appears part-human. When she sinks into her bed she is drugged by the "poppied warmth of sleep," with the poppy a classical emblem of Hecate and the underworld. Sleeping and closed to the world, she is like a "missal where swart Paynims [pagans] pray" (241). The "faded moon" (253) is still throwing its light over her when Porphyro emerges from her closet; and sleeping in moonlight has long been considered a dangerous invitation to supernatural presences generally.[65]

Here the presence of the faerie becomes most pronounced, for the feast that Angela has supplied for him clearly is a faerie banquet. Faery food always appears abundant and enticingly delicious, but turns out to be insubstantial or even poisonous.[66] Partaking of such food should be avoided, for it keeps one captive in faeryland forever; and there are many folktales of newcomers to faeryland who are surreptitiously warned by captives there against eating or drinking anything.[67] Porphyro brings from the closet gold and silver baskets of exotic sweets folded in white linen, with this luxurious presentation itself characteristic of the dishes at a faery feast; and their fragrance fills the room.[68] The foods are sugared fruits, spiced jellies, dates, and the mythical "manna," all "in argosy transferr'd . . . every one" from Fez, Samarcand, and Lebanon.[69] These highly flavored foods are not nourishing, and come from the Mideastern lands of ancient magic by means of that "argosy," the "legion'd fairies" who are pacing Madeline's coverlet.[70] And how could Angela take such valuable baskets and foods from the feast below without being noticed?

Madeline still sleeps as one bewitched, in a "midnight charm" as the moonlight shines on her, caught in a "spell" and "woofed [woven] phantasies," or deceptive appearances (282–8). Porphyro plays the song that proves to be about faeryland, "La belle dame sans mercy"; and the faeries were well known too for luring away humans with their music. Here, he plays it "close to her ear" (293), yet she still is caught in her spell.[71] She opens her eyes but is entranced with "the vision of her sleep," and speaks "witless words" (299–303). We should remember that the "spell" or "charm" that holds her was the work of those "old dames" mentioned near the beginning, and that it is to the benefit of Porphyro that she does not wake up. For now he is able to sink into her bed and her dream without resistance. He does so "beyond a mortal man impassion'd far" (316), a description which could be simply an exaggeration of his aroused state or rather a statement of fact that he is not a "mortal man." And the immediate result is the sudden storm as the full moon sets.

It is certainly very odd that the sky has been cloudless enough to allow the silver moonlight to shine through her chamber casement, and then suddenly a sleet-storm arises with "iced gusts" that "rave and beat" the "window-panes" (322–7). But this is a magical storm that has been conjured up.[72] Conjuring sudden storms was one of the most common charges against witches and warlocks in medieval witch-trials, and Porphyro tells Madeline plainly enough what it really is: "'tis an elfin-storm from faery land / Of haggard seeming, but a boon indeed" (343–4). One meaning of "haggard" is a witch, and the sudden convenience of its "boon" shows that it *is* "an elfin-storm" that has been raised. He urges her to come with him to his home "o'er the southern moors," and they leave her chamber.

The narrator's distancing begins with the last stanzas that follow, as the characters increasingly become figures in a related tale and the supernatural elements become more and more overt. Porphyro and Madeline pass "sleeping dragons," and in the house "no human sound" is heard. In the few minutes' time since they left her chamber the "frost-wind" has become the "besieging wind's uproar." Twice the narrator compares them to "phantoms." When they approach the door, the bolts "full easy slide" and the chains fall "silent" on the pavement while the key turns. All of this implies a supernatural agency at work.[73]

The final events of the last stanza let us know that the faerie dominates in the world left behind and presumably in the one to which Madeline and Porphyro have fled, although, as folktales typically conclude, we cannot know that. The Baron and his guests dream of those we have just seen, for they dream "of witch, and demon, and large coffin-worm" (374).

The "coffin-worm" could allude to spirits, or to dragons which in many of the old regional folktales were called "worms."[74] They could also predict Angela's final destination in the churchyard. The seeming anti-climax of the last lines is that of the storyteller whose folktale has come to an end.

"La belle dame sans mercy" is briefly mentioned in "The Eve of St. Agnes" (291–2). He may not have written "La Belle Dame sans Merci: A Ballad" until a month later, but surely he had in mind its characters and narrative as a point of reference. Again there is the highborn figure who is glamoured away from the human context by the faery being. In "The Eve of St. Agnes," the ending seems to be in doubt although Keats strongly suggests that the human Madeline has been captured into faeryland. And it should not be forgotten that such captivity always entailed the danger for the human of being the faery tithe to Hell, which makes the powerlessness of the Virgin Mary, the "sculptured dead," the "carved angels," and the Beadsman with his rosary even more sinister. The ending may seem less unclear here, for the knight has left the faery's "elfin grot" for his own world again, but it also seems ambiguous. Again there is the storytelling narrator who assumes a shared ground of faery-faith with the audience.

This seems to be an elusive poem, for we cannot be sure about the nature of the lady beyond the fact that she's a faery since we don't know how reliable the warning is at the conclusion.[75] The puzzle begins with the title. Why is it in French rather than English? It seems to be literally true, without any French idiom necessary to provide some shade of untranslatable meaning. The beautiful lady does seem to act without any mercy, to judge from the testimonials of the unhappy kings and princes at the end. And why does Keats draw attention to the form of the poem by its subtitle?

Close attention to the title takes us into answers to the riddles of the poem. Since there's no denotative significance in Keats's choice of language, it must be a sign of connection with "The Eve of St. Agnes," a sign that we're to link the two. The earlier poem gives us the figure of Porphyro who shows the amoral, cruel aspect of the faery, for he lies, bullies, voyeuristically spies, and rapes or at least seduces. This "fairy's child" does not, really, act to harm the knight. However, when we read backwards, we see that this ballad establishes without question that "The Eve of St. Agnes" is set within a faerie context. Keats was not writing metaphorically there about faeries, enchantments, and elfin-storms from faery land.

The lady without mercy... how this designation seems to recall all of the medieval cruel and capricious mistresses addressed by cast-off lovers.

Yet if one looks more closely at the meaning of "mercy," one sees that "the lady without mercy" is an accurate description of the faery's nature according to folk-tradition. "Mercy" means compassion shown to another being in one's power, who has no claim to any kindness and who should rightfully expect severity.[76] When the faery has the human in its power, the tradition held that the mortal could expect the worst: malicious tricks; food that seemed delicious but was made of disgusting substances; abduction with forcible retention; separation from loved ones as youth and time passed forever; at worst, the forfeiture to Hell. When we consider the behavior of this particular lady, we see that actually she is acting with "merci" as faeries sometimes choose to do. The title reminds us though of her original nature.

Keats's insistent reminder in the title that this is a *ballad* is really a reminder of its Celticism, for its title evokes Scott's revival of the old Gaelic ballads and "popular superstitions" in his own "Imitations of the ancient ballad" that were so well known from *Minstrelsy*. More specifically, it alludes to one famous ballad there about the figure beloved in Scottish history, that of "Thomas the Rhymer." This source for Keats's poem has been recognized by the folklorist Tristram P. Coffin, as part of his more general comparison of folk and literary ballads. He doesn't analyze either Scott's ballad or Keats's poem very closely, except to note that both employ the old story of the Faery Queen luring away the mortal man.[77] But Thomas the Rhymer's story is unique. The "queen of fair Elfland" takes "True Thomas" away, but releases him in the seventh year fearing that he will be chosen as the tithe; and he finally chooses to return after sojourning back in the human world. It was unusual for a faery queen to be kind in this way to her captive, and also for the captive to return to the faerie world willingly.

From the very first stanza of Keats's ballad there are parallels to Thomas the Rhymer, both the legendary person and the protagonist of Scott's ballad. His faery encounter was traditionally supposed to have taken place by the Eildon Tree located in a glen of the Eildon Hills, near the Bogle Burn (Brook). So in Part I of Scott's ballad, Thomas's adventure begins as he lies on "Huntlie bank" and sees "the Queen of fair Elfland . . . come riding / Down by the Eildon Tree" (I–IV). She asks him to "kiss [her] lips" so that "sure of your bodie I will be" (V); and when he does, they both "mount her milk-white steed" (VIII). As they ride, she speaks to him of the road to "fair Elfland" which "winds about the ferny brae [hillside]" (XIII).[78] When they reach "Elflyn land" she feeds him from a "garden green" (XVII), which gives him the gift of prophecy for which he was to become so renowned in Scottish legend. This is the last we see of him "till seven years were gane and past" (XX).[79]

The knight at arms questioned by Keats's interlocutor is similar in rank to Thomas since knights were highborn; and he is lingering by the sedge of the lake on the "cold hill's side," much as Thomas lay on Huntlie bank at the beginning of his adventure. This is where the knight had earlier met a lady in the "meads [meadows]" who took him to faeryland, as Thomas is taken by his Queen through the "ferny brae." Both encounters are initially sexual, for the knight's lady "did love, / And made sweet moan" (19–20), and then the two set off on the faery's steed while she sings or speaks to him. The "fairy's child" feeds the knight "roots of relish sweet" and "manna dew," as the Queen gives Thomas "an apple frae the tree" (XVII). Like the "elfin grot" of the knight's lady, Eildon Hills conceals the Queen's "Elflyn land."

Thus far, Keats's ballad follows Scott's ballad fairly faithfully. Where it diverges, of course, is in its conclusion. Scott divided his version of the old ballad into three parts, with the second "altered from ancient prophecies" and the third his own "modern" composition.[80] At the end of Part First, Thomas is in Elfland. He has left it in Part Second, which begins seven years later as "the sun blinked fair on pool and stream" while he "lay on Huntlie bank, / Like one awaken'd from a dream" (I); and for the rest of Part Second he busily makes his prophecies for his countrymen's benefit. Seven years later, in Part Third, Thomas is at a banquet still holding forth to his "armed lords" when the Queen's summoning comes, he leaps on his steed, and returns to Elfland. Keats takes these opening four lines of Part Second as the narrator's frame for his own ballad, with the knight's flashback modeled after Thomas's experience in Part First. "La Belle Dame" thus only follows the actual ancient ballad, which is provided in its original language by Scott in his Appendix to Part First, and is not concerned with Scott's own later "Imitations."

In "La Belle Dame sans Merci," Keats dwells on the interlude back on earth before Thomas is able to return to Elfland. Here, the narrator meets the knight at arms "loitering" near a lake, pale and ill with "fever dew" and fever's hectic "rose" in his cheeks. If he's deathly ill, then the "manna" and "honey dew" that he was given as food in faeryland was insubstantial as faery food usually is.[81] He's been taken out of the cycles of time too.[82] We find out from his story that he first left this world when the "meads" were full and he was able to make flower garlands and bracelets, and now he lingers here at the onset of winter when the grass is withered and the harvest has been gathered. This likely is an allusion to Hallowe'en. Traditionally, this is the only time that humans are able to leave the faerie world with the faeries on their Rade,[83] and this knight seems to have been such a captive. At the ballad's end, in lines echoing details of lines 1–4 of Scott's Part Second, the knight tells us that he has just awakened from "the latest dream I ever dream'd / On the cold hill's side" (35–6) near the lake. The kings, princes, and warriors in his dream who warn him of "La belle dame sans merci" must be other such captives since he dreams about them while in the "elfin grot."

This ballad may seem like the familiar folktale of the wayfarer who's captured into faeryland, and then ejected when the person shows the wrong attitude toward the faeries met there, such as curiosity, greed, or lack of trust.[84] But it's not. We simply don't know why he's been unwillingly left on the cold wintry hillside of his familiar human world. He hears the warnings of the other captives and sees them "in the gloam," the twilight atmosphere that supposedly is the perpetual light of the faerie world. But all his actions toward his "fairy's child" have been loving ones, as have hers to him. Nor do we know his reaction to those other captives' warnings. He hears the warnings and then he awakes.

Keats's ballad allows us to understand why Thomas the Rhymer was so unlike most of the other captives of the faeries in finally choosing the faery over the human world when he had known both. Here, the captive kings' and princes' "starv'd lips... gaped wide" suggesting that they too have been eating insubstantial faerie food, and they warn him that she has him "in thrall" (40) like a common serf.[85] But that's not how she has treated him. Nor has he acted as one in "thrall," or servitude. As Karen Swann has pointed out, "his first impulse is to control, to bind her" with his flowery crown, bracelets, and waist-shackle.[86] He is the one who sets her on his horse, and in her "grot" he is the one who kisses her asleep. For her part, her only actions are to "love" him, sing to him, feed him sweet food, and say "in language strange [which he evidently understands]... I love thee true" (27–8). And when his adventure is over, he is not disillusioned like those other captives. He waits to return to her, and so he "sojourn[s]... alone and palely loitering" (45–6).

The complete legend of Thomas the Rhymer haunts this poem that contains so many allusions to it, and we see why this knight is, as Keats states twice, "at arms." The first time that Thomas visited Elfland, he was given the gift of prophecy upon which later Scots relied. He finally was able to rejoin his "queen of fair Elfland," although he would leave again in the far future when the Scottish people most needed him. The tone of longing for the faery and her "elfin grot" in the knight's story is urgent. He *must* get back to her timeless place to be preserved for his future people.

Thus far, Keats's portrayal of the faerie may seem inconsistent, with some faeries malicious and even demonic, such as (probably) those that Calidore meets, Porphyro, Angela, and those in the dream related to Reynolds; and others kindly (though sometimes unintentionally injurious to the humans in their range), such as Cynthia, Old Meg the gipsey, and La Belle Dame. However, this shows that Keats knew the range of faery natures according to folk-tradition. Faeries generally were divided into those of the Seelie and the Unseelie Courts (or hosts), to use the British terms. They were indifferent to each other, if not actively hostile.[87] The Seelie faeries were primarily beneficial to mankind. The Unseelie were the feared malevolent spirits, solitary beings that emerged at nightfall, stealing humans, or working evil on them whenever possible. They were connected with the realm of the dead, and sometimes considered as the unsanctified dead themselves.[88]

This familiarity with the two faery Courts can be clearly seen in Keats's epistolary poem, "Song of Four Fairies: Fire, Air, Earth, and Water," that he wrote about the time that he wrote the two major faerie poems just discussed. These four faeries are the spirits of the natural elements, two with the characteristics of the Seelie and two the Unseelie, all of them playing and melding with an easy eroticism. The "Song" is a counterpoint of the four faery voices, with the male of each pair wooing the female. Each courtship is characteristic of their Seelie or Unseelie nature.

"Salamander" is the name for the first spirit and was the traditional name for fire faeries, probably because of the mythical fire-dwelling qualities of that beast.[89] This reptile also is phallic in appearance, and here are phallic overtones in his words to "Dusketha" whom he seeks in her "glooms" (3). Her name suggests the nighttime dear to the Unseelie faeries, as well as the earth's underworld.[90] Salamander too is a spirit associated with night (he compares his faery's wing to "a bat's" [8]); and, in fairly transparent sexual overtones, he urges Dusketha to let him "nimbly fan your fiery spaces / ... Open eyes that never daze: / Let me see the myriad shapes / ... Portray'd in many a fiery den / ... Let me breathe upon their skies ..." (9–19). He terms her "adder-eyed Dusketha," and "enchantingly / Freckle-wing'd and lizard-sided" (68, 73–4).[91] From our perspective as a human listener to this "song," this may not seem alluring ... but of course these creatures are all lovely to fellow reptiles and night-dwellers. Dusketha for her part vows that "at thy supreme desire" she will "touch the very pulse of fire / With my bare unlidded eyes" (84–6), which manages to sound at once suggestive and unpleasant.

The other two faeries, "Zephyr" and "Breama," are milder spirits associated with daytime; and they lack the intensity of the demonic or even the longing that one expects from wooing lovers. The derivation of the name of the spirit of air is obvious enough, for zephyr means a light west wind. "Breama" may be intended to refer to the bream, a silvery fish native to Europe that lurks at the bottom of ponds and lakes. She calls Zephyr to look at her apparent dwelling place, a "sedge-buried urn" resting in the water among mints and watercresses and flowers. This is as suggestively yonic in its own pleasant way as Dusketha's "fiery dens." Breama sounds like an undine in her "green-weed rivers bright" (4), and later Zephyr refers to her "watry hair" in "ringlets" (56–7). Her "Queen" evidently is the Shakespearean Titania since Oberon is said to "tease" her (37–8).

Zephyr calls her to follow him to his "home far, far in the west," the direction associated with the Otherworld,[92] to his "fragrant pallaces" (45–9) that sound like the faerie realms of *Endymion.* Nighttime for him is the "gently drowsed" time when "the fays...sleep" (54–5). This horrifies Salamander, who has other ideas for nighttime when "we / Bedded in tongued flames will be" (92–3). Breama for her part seeks a mildly sensuous, drifting union with Zephyr that will lead to clouds of rain and mist, and also to "blooms" and "flowers" (95–6). Keats gives us the permanently dual sides of the faerie here, the demonic and enchanting, and the playful and kind. The Seelie and the Unseelie faeries are repelled by each other. Each has its own realm that seems alien somehow to our experience of love. Humans don't belong in either one.

Nor do humans belong in the faerie realm of the woods in "Ode to a Nightingale" either, as the last stanza of that ode makes clear. Most critics have seen how strongly this ode is influenced by *A Midsummer Night's Dream,* whose woodland faerie realm also proves unsettling and even unfriendly to the humans who wander into it. This was the Shakespearean play perhaps most beloved by Keats, and also one of the established literary classics most popularly associated with the faerie during the nineteenth century. Shakespeare's portrayal of faeries in that play shaped our idea of the faerie from the Renaissance onward. It was not the faerie of folk-tradition although some traditional elements were present.[93] The faeries in *A Midsummer Night's Dream* are benevolent, harmless, small nature-spirits, although Titania must be a shape-shifter since she sleeps in flowers but also loves the human, Bottom.[94] This became the long-lived popular idea of faeries. It certainly was the one held during the nineteenth century.[95] Productions of the play usually emphasized the faeries and their world above all other elements of the work.[96] It was considered to be mainly an extravagant affair of music and faery dance, ending with a general display of happiness.[97]

We know, from his many allusions to it in letters and also from his markings in his own copy of Shakespeare, that *A Midsummer Night's Dream* was one of Keats's favorite plays by Shakespeare.[98] Keats's annotations and underscorings in his Shakespeare clearly show which plays were read and reread, and which passages most drew his attention. The two plays that dealt most prominently with faeries, *The Tempest* and *A Midsummer Night's Dream*, were the most worn and most marked.[99] In the second play, the passages he marked or underlined were the faery songs and speeches, especially in Act II.[100]

All of this needs to be remembered while considering Keats's version of it in "Ode to a Nightingale." Certain allusions to *A Midsummer Night's Dream* in this ode have usually been acknowledged, though generally critics have followed the direction of R.S. White who concludes that the influence of Shakespeare's play here is primarily seen in the similarity of language.[101] Others consider the similarities as atmospheric, particularly in stanzas four and five.[102] There are the obvious references to Shakespeare's faeries from the beginning to the end of the ode: the "light-winged Dryad of the trees" in stanza one; "the Queen-Moon" with her attending "starry fays" in stanza four (which shows that Keats was well aware that Titania's name derived from Ovid's designation for Diana); the named flowers of the "eglantine," "violets," and "musk-rose" in stanza five that Oberon said were part of Titania's bower;[103] and the nightingale now termed an "elf" in the concluding stanza eight. There are also the other references to faeries, such as the "magic casements" and the "faery lands forlorn" in stanza seven.

But the parallels go far deeper than this. Shakespeare's play takes place during Midsummer Eve, a time like Hallowe'en when the veil between the human and the faerie worlds is very thin.[104] Keats's ode also was written around this time, in May 1819, and makes it clear that this is the time "of summer" (10). The general situations of the ode and the play are similar, for one is a dream-poem as the other is a dream-play and both are dreamt in the woods. All of the play's characters enter the woods where the faeries dwell to experience the midsummer night's dream that is the play.[105] Similarly, the ode opens at twilight with the poet listening to the nightingale, which flies into the woods with the poet following; and that is the setting for the rest of the ode. Nighttime is a particularly potent time for magic.[106] In the final lines, Keats asks whether his experience has been "a vision, or a waking dream?" This is the dazed question posed too by most of the play's human characters at the end.

The nightingale itself has its origins in Shakespeare's play, where it sets in motion the subplot of Titania and Bottom, with its laughable human lout who unintentionally becomes involved with the world of the faerie. At the beginning of the second scene of Act II, Titania enters with her faery train and commands them to sing her asleep in her bower, which Oberon at the end of the previous scene has told us is a bank of "the nodding violet" that's "over-canopied with…sweet musk-roses and with eglantine" (II.i.250–2). They summon "Philomel, with melody / Sing in our sweet lullaby" (II.ii.13–14), an address they sing twice for emphasis. A direct result of this "lullaby" is that it enables Oberon to drug the sleeping Titania by "squeezing" the flower love-in-idleness on her eyelids.

Keats's ode opens with the poet listening to the nightingale, with the song drugging him as though he had drunk "hemlock" or some "dull opiate" (1–3). And he longs for the juice of the squeezed grape, "a draught of vintage… / Tasting of Flora," so that he too might go with the nightingale "into the forest dim" (11–20).[107] He does so "on the viewless wings of Poesy," which seems like another allusion to *A Midsummer Night's Dream*; and he remarks that for the nightingale, "tender is the night" and "the Queen-Moon is on her throne / Clustered around by all her starry Fays" (35–7). This setting duplicates the scene in the play in which "Philomel" is singing to Titania surrounded by her faery attendants. There, we know that the night is "tender," or young, because in the previous scene, one of Titania's fairies has been hanging "dewdrops" on the flowers (II.ii.8–15). As "Philomel" sings Titania to sleep, her faeries encircle her also singing.

There are these direct echoes of Titania in her bower. But the ode also registers the negative aspects of the faerie present in Shakespeare's play that were not emphasized in stage-productions or by critics until the twentieth century. Keats does not do this in a literal way but rather alludes to the unpleasant realities within the play that the faeries and the play's dream-like quality somehow elide, somewhat in the manner of Keats's own "Eve of St. Agnes."

When Titania's faeries sing her to sleep, they first evoke sinister creatures in order to forbid them entrance to her bower. One might say that of these the "snake with double tongue" in fact is not warned off since one of her faeries, who is supposed to stand sentinel, exits with the rest and thus Oberon is able to enter without any alarm sounded. Of course the very use of the name of "Philomel" rather than "nightingale," a word that would scan the same as the name, itself calls up the experiences of betrayal, rape, and death that the myth of Philomel contains. These experiences appear in the play, although without any lasting ill effect for the faeries involved. Oberon betrays Titania by drugging her, and one could say without too much exaggeration that her ensuing union with Bottom is against her conscious will and thus a form of rape. The changeling so glibly claimed by Titania and Oberon originally became Titania's servant because his mother died in childbirth, and Titania stole him from his human father with a faery substitute left behind ("A lovely boy, stolen from an Indian king; / She never had so sweet a changeling" [*MND*. II.i.22–3]).

Keats's ode also evokes betrayal and death, at least, as well as human sadness at our transience, experiences that "thou among the leaves [the nightingale] hast never known" (22). It's everything that midsummer dreams leave out, a world where the young die, Beauty fades and so does "new Love," and "where but to think is to be full of sorrow" (27). In stanzas three and four, the poet longs to join the nightingale in its realm, which stanza four directly connects with the sleeping Titania and her world of the faerie. Stanza five continues this link but with an unmistakable shift, for the faerie becomes as alien for the poet as Titania's world was for Bottom. There is no midsummer moon at all here for the poet, for he cannot see the flowers around him "in embalmed darkness" (43). Does that rather queasy adjective relate to the nature of the darkness or to himself? The flowers specified here are those of Titania's bower and all have intense fragrances like those of embalming spices. But Keats adds to them the "white hawthorn," a faery tree that is usually hostile to humans caught near it, and the "flies [of] summer eves" (50), an insect long associated with death and also evil spirits.[108]

Faerie music was thought to enchant the one who hears it, even to lure the human listener off to faeryland.[109] According to folk-tradition, some old melodies still sung, such as the "Londonderry Air," have derived from faery music that was remembered after the listener safely returned to the human world.[110] The pull of the faerie realm conjured by the faery music of the nightingale is rendered perfectly in stanza six of Keats's ode. It's a "midnight" world that, like life in faeryland, is "rich," "easeful," and painless, with a sinister drawing power ("now more than ever seems it rich to die," 55).[111] It's also timeless, as we can see in stanza seven.[112] The passing cycles of human life listen to the nightingale's alluring music that's the same for all the "hungry generations," the "emperor and clown" from "ancient days" (an allusion to Shakespeare's Theseus and Bottom?), the homesick Biblical Ruth, and the present poet. It's the same music heard in faeryland that charms "magic casements" opening on "perilous seas, in faery lands forlorn" (69–70),[113] a warning reminder that those in the "lands" can't leave.

"Forlorn" in its fullest sense is a word used of a place as well as a person that's abandoned, deserted, or left alone.[114] Here Keats adds, "Forlorn! the very word is like a bell/ To toll me back from thee to my sole self!" (71–2).[115] And with this bell sounding in the last stanza of the poem, Keats closely follows the resolution of *A Midsummer Night's Dream* that begins in Act IV. In the play, the characters in the woods begin to wake after Oberon releases Titania from her spell and she commands music to be played. Their responses are similar to Keats's here in the final lines of the Ode, from Bottom who declares on waking, "I have had a most rare vision. I have had a dream, past the wit of man to say what dream it was" (IV.i.201–2), to Lysander who says to Theseus, "Half sleep, half waking: but as yet, I swear, / I cannot truly say how I came here" (IV.i.146–7). Robin Goodfellow ends the entire play by inviting the audience to think "that you have but slumber'd here / While these visions did appear. / And this weak and idle theme, / No more yielding but a dream" (V.i.I.416–19).

Keats in his turn also questions if he has had "a vision, or a waking dream" (79). Awakened, he declares that "fancy" cannot really "cheat" him, and terms the nightingale "deceiving elf" as it flies off and away from him. These last lines describing the nightingale as it leaves "past the near meadows, over the still stream, / Up the hill-side . . . / In the next valley-glades" (76–8) are very close to the play's lines that originally introduced us to the world of the faeries in the woods, as one of Titania's faeries says to Robin that it wanders "over hill, over dale, / Thorough bush, thorough brier, / Over park, over pale" (II.i.2–4). We are full circle in Keats's ode, for it begins with the "Dryad" and ends with the "elf" that both wander everywhere. But Keats cannot be glamoured away this time as he was in the beginning lines. The world of the faerie alienates and isolates all it touches ("Forlorn!"), despite its strong allure of timelessness. The ode shows us human experience from the faery's chill, indifferent perspective, as does *A Midsummer Night's Dream*.

The folklore motifs that dominate these 1819 poems are mostly, though not completely, those that dwell on the sinister aspect of the faerie. Zephyr and Breama of "Song of Four Fairies" are Seelie faeries; and the "fairy's child" of "La Belle Dame" also may be one, although we can't be sure. But Salamander and Dusketha are fairly clearly identified with the Unseelie Host. The faeries in "The Faery's court" don't seem likely to welcome the intrusion on their privacy when they return from their Rade, to judge from the faery-struck companions of the Princess. Porphyro is a demon-lover or at the very least a faery intent on luring Madeline away to faeryland; and Angela is a witch. The song of the "elf" that is the nightingale entices the Ode's speaker away to a realm where he's "half in love with easeful Death." And the realm of faerie is dangerous too, with the predominant motifs of these poems those that relate to the sorrowful captivity of mortals in faeryland, the supernatural lapse of time in faeryland, and its similarity to the land of the dead.

These 1819 faerie poems show much that is attractive about the world of faerie, particularly its trickster aspect. Keats seems to love this trickster side more than anything else about the faerie. Here, the highborn are the faeries' particular targets: the "fretful Princess" with her faery-struck princes and kings who's about to be struck herself, one is sure; Madeline with the family scutcheons of queens and kings portrayed on her bedroom window; the knight at arms, and other kings and princes, who are "in thrall" to La Belle Dame; the "emperor" who listened "in ancient days" to the nightingale that is the "deceiving elf." But still, the faerie world seems inimical to the human one.

6
Privileging the Celtic

The context of Keats's final great faerie works, *Lamia* and *The Fall of Hyperion: A Dream*, was the mounting pressure of practical exigency on all sides. The continuing problem of securing remittances from Abbey, the guardian of the Keats estate, grew worse as it became clear to Abbey that when Keats decided to forego the profession of apothecary for that of poet, he was not assuring himself of a steady or even intermittent income. At various times, Abbey counseled him to be a hat-maker, bookseller, and tea-broker.[1] The possibility of any marriage to Fanny Brawne depended upon his ability to support her. And then, of course, there were the constant reminders of his worsening health, although the definitive hemorrhage of arterial blood that he termed "my death-warrant" did not occur until 3 February 1820.[2]

As a result of these pressures, Keats resolved to seek for commercial success through his writing as the only avenue left to him. In late September, 1819, he resolutely wrote to Charles Brown: "I have never yet exerted myself.... In no period of my life have I acted with any self will, but in throwing up the apothecary-profession. That I do not repent of.... My occupation is entirely literary; I will do so too. I will write, on the liberal side of the question, for whoever will pay me.... When I can afford to compose deliberate poems I will." He had decided to be a hack journalist, and added, "I shall not suffer my pride to hinder me. The whisper may go round; I shall not hear it. If I can get an article in the 'Edinburg[h]', I will. One must not be delicate."[3] On the same day he wrote to Charles Dilke about "a resolution I have taken to endeavor to acqu[i]re something by temporary writing in periodical works.... I would willingly have recourse to other means. I cannot; I am fit for nothing but literature."[4]

That last sentence, however, shows his inner sense of his real measure, for "literature" is not the same as "temporary writing." He had just finished the play *Otho the Great: A Tragedy in Five Acts* in collaboration with Charles Brown, solely as a vehicle for the famous Shakespearean actor Edmund Kean who they hoped would guarantee the play's long-running success. This collaboration itself was a sign of his determination to make some money. Yet as he confessed about the same time to George and Georgiana Keats who were far away in America and thus the perfect confidants: "Were [*Otho*] to succeed even there it would lift me out of the mire. I mean the mire of a bad reputation which is continually rising against me. My name with the literary fashionables is vulgar — I am a weaver boy to them — a Tragedy would lift me out of this mess."[5]

Most of what writing time he had left was spent in working on projects that he hoped would be commercially successful. The only exception was *The Fall of Hyperion*, abandoned for good after two months. All were tragedies of various sorts, except the very last poem that he left unfinished because he was too ill even to dictate it further to Brown. Two months before he wrote about his new resolution to Brown and Dilke, he began to compose *Lamia*. He wrote it "with great hopes of success," and added, "but in Case of failure with the world, I shall find my content."[6] As he wrote more expansively to George and Georgiana Keats: "I am certain there is that sort of fire in [*Lamia*] which must take hold of people in some way — give them either pleasant or unpleasant sensation. What they want is a sensation of some sort."[7] Spice it up! And the work does have a curious edge of perversity about it, with Lamia portrayed as the technical virgin who is erotically proficient.

Otho being the more pressing project, Keats completed it first and then *Lamia* soon after. He gave up trying to finish *Fall of Hyperion* a few weeks later. The last few months of 1819 were spent readying *Otho* to be sent to Drury Lane for consideration, reading Holinshed's *Chronicles* in preparation for an historical play, and writing a few scenes of another historical play suggested to him by Brown. *Otho* was indeed accepted by Drury Lane for the next season; however (presumably needing a more immediate commercial success), they withdrew it and sent it to Covent Garden. It was speedily rejected, and, worse luck, Kean departed for an American tour. Again at the suggestion of Brown, Keats began *The Cap and Bells; Or, the Jealousies. A Faery Tale, by Lucy Vaughan Lloyd of China Walk, Lambeth*, a long rambling poem probably modeled after the first Canto of Byron's *Don Juan* that had just been published and was selling well. *The Cap and Bells* attempted, not with an equal success, the same witty jibes and veiled allusions to the Regency.

Even so, he managed to create "deliberate poems" in *Lamia* and *The Fall of Hyperion*. These last two of his great faerie poems work primarily with the folklore motifs so familiar by now: the faery that glamours the man away to faeryland, the taboos enforcing faery privacy, the faerie realm with its captives and its links to the dead. In both poems, the narrative action is made possible by the faerie. Lamia is a member of the "faery brood" mentioned in the first line of her poem, and it's her faery powers of casting illusory spells that enlists Hermes' aid. Mythological lamias had no such abilities. The narrator of *The Fall* must pass through the bordering faerie realm in the flowering woods with its feast and enchanting potion before he joins Moneta in her timeless Otherworld that has so many associations with death.

Keats returned again in both faerie poems to the priority of the native Celtic experience, for both are set during the time of the Celtic revolts in the British Isles during the Roman conquest. This is clear from internal details within each. The dwindled present-day time of the narrator is the frame of *The Fall of Hyperion* as it was not in *Hyperion*. But we can deduce the general time of the saga told by Moneta. Here Keats returns to the story of the Titans that he began in *Hyperion*, and again associates the Titans with the Celts. Moneta, who has somehow survived from that time, begins to tell their history to the narrator, and at that point Keats breaks off the poem as he did before. Many commentators assume that "Moneta" is a slip of the pen for the character "Mnemosyne" in Book III of Hyperion. But this confusion of names must be deliberate. She's named Moneta throughout the narrator's encounter with her in the sanctuary, then Mnemosyne in I.331, Moneta a few lines later in I.337, and again Mnemosyne near the end in II.50. Moneta is the Roman name for Mnemosyne. As an original Titaness, she also retains her associations with the Celts that the Greek Titans had.

She may be the "sole priestess of [Saturn's] desolation" left, as she states in I.226–7. But she won't be telling the narrator of Saturn's initial fall, the first defeat in "the thunder of a war / Foughten long since" (I.222–3). The title of this revisited epic tells us that the fall will be Hyperion's, at the end of the long decline of the Titans/Celts. Additionally, we know from her name that Keats intended her recollection to date from the later period when the Romans had renamed her. We've advanced to the time when they battled the British Celts; and these revolts took place during the first century AD. Mnemosyne's Roman name emphasizes that she exists in the time of imperial Rome, but Keats's double slip suggests that she still keeps her original identity as resister to it. As Keats had written just before he began *Hyperion*, "There is a pleasure on the heath where Druids old have been, / Where mantles grey have rustled by and swept the nettles green" ("There is a joy in footing slow," 3–4).

Lamia dates from that century as well, and Keats provides insistent reminders to emphasize that. As its first lines tell us, the action takes place when "the faery broods" co-existed with nymphs, satyrs, and Hermes, during the time "*before* King Oberon's bright diadem, / . . . frighted away the Dryads and the Fauns / From rushes green, and brakes, and cowslip'd lawns" [italics mine] (I.1–6). The classical apparatus of nymphs and gods disappeared everywhere when the Roman Empire fell. They departed from the British Isles when the Romans left and the Christian missionaries arrived soon after. Oberon as the king of the faeries dates at least from that period or more probably later, since he was most commonly associated with Shakespeare's faeries. The mention of "cowslip'd lawns" underscores this, as an allusion to the busy faery "hang[ing] a pearl in every cowslip's ear" in Act II of *A Midsummer Night's Dream*. In fact, although Keats may not have known this, King Oberon was an invention from Renaissance romance.[8] So we know that Lamia's story is set sometime before AD 409 when the Romans left the Isles.

We learn this even more conclusively from the note that Keats added at the conclusion. Ostensibly, this note provides the source for his story of the encounter between Lamia and Apollonius — namely, Burton's *Anatomy of Melancholy* which relates the episode as taken from Philostratus's *de Vita Apollonii*. But something else is accomplished besides establishing the literary precedents for Lamia's story, for this note also provides the general date of the encounter. Apollonius was a fairly common ancient name, but the only one who was the subject of a biography by the well-known Philostratus was Apollonius of Tyana, who lived in the second half of the first century AD. Keats would have found this information in his well-worn Lemprière, where it is noted that Philostratus was a famous Sophist who wrote a biography of Apollonius of Tyana. And under the entry for "Apollonius of Tyana," Lemprière states that he lived during the time of the emperor Domitian, who died in AD 96.

Lamia's story is told from her perspective, and we sympathize with her throughout the poem. This is something of a surprise. Keats is not ambiguous about her nature, for her name is "Lamia" and when we meet her she looks like one with her serpent's body and woman's face (although she lacks the traditional row of multiple breasts).[9] Lamias are unquestionably malevolent faeries in all traditions. They're witches that steal and devour children; demons who lure and then devour their lovers; vampire goddesses; and hideous flying snake-monsters with scales, multiple breasts, and a woman's face.[10] But from the beginning of Keats's poem, this lamia seems vaguely British or at least Celtic, for she belongs to that "faery brood." Again and again Keats uses the word "fairy" to describe her, and motifs relating to the faerie run through her story. "King Oberon" who later disposed of the classical nymphs and fauns must be her king too. She has the magical powers that faeries have, and she certainly acts in the mercurial way that we expect of faeries.[11]

The only faery power she seems to lack is shape-shifting, for as a lamia she is bound to her "serpent prison-house" (I.203). However, her "spirit" can range far and wide like the faery's, and so she spied Lycius of Corinth and decided she loved him.[12] But her other faery powers are evidently prior or at least superior to that of the classical god Hermes, for he has to seek her assistance in finding the elusive nymph who's so weary of all the eager satyrs. Hermes has odd parallels to Lamia, like a weaker version of her. He carries the caduceus with its entwined snakes; and in his role as messenger between heaven and earth he flies about as Lamia's spirit did when she first saw Lycius. His situation is an echo of hers, for he too is "bent warm on amorous theft" of one who's indifferent to him. There's something faintly humorous about this Hermes, although he's one of the Olympians.

Generally considered a trickster and known as god of the thieves, as Keats's favored source Tooke notes,[13] this messenger of the gods is also a truant. He's trying to avoid errands from Jove by stealing off behind Jove's legendary thunderclouds to look for a nymph he knows only by reputation (I.7–11). As he flits along looking for her, he's not a very confident Olympian. He thinks of all his rivals and "a celestial heat" burns upward "to either ear," which, as Stillinger points out, is an inherently funny idea. (Ears, as he notes, are simply unpoetic by nature.)[14] Hermes jealously considers his possible rivals to be "the Wood-Gods and even the very trees" (I.34). He's in this state when he hears Lamia. He most likely mistakes her for the nymph he seeks, for he listens to her "like a stoop'd falcon ere he takes his prey" (I.67).

And rather than the usual demon or witch or vampire, this lamia is enchantingly beautiful to see and to hear. Keats never even alludes to her most fearsome aspect in the tradition, her penchant for stealing and eating children.[15] When we see her she is a glowing vision found by Hermes that is "palpitating" and "cirque-couchant" or lying coiled in circles, a yonic sight. Her appearance is at once a sign that she is a faery and not a faery's transformed victim, for her skin is mixed with opposites of stripes and freckles, and iridescent with gem-like colors and "silver moons."[16] Her mouth and eyes are those of a woman; and her voice is vaguely human as it warbles "as through bubbling honey." Lest we mistake her nature, Keats tells us that she seemed "some penanced lady elf" or "demon's mistress, or the demon's self" (I.45–65).

His character Lamia is usually considered by critics to be manipulative and treacherous, like a traditional lamia. However, if we look closely at her interactions with others, we can see that she does not deceive so much as knowingly personify others' mistaken perceptions of her. She deceives those who deserve to be deceived. Hermes intends to betray the solitary nymph once he finds her, and he himself is fooled by Lamia's initial cry that she's been forced out of her usual "sweet body" and longs to return to it. She suggests that she has been faery-struck into the form of a snake, transformed into "this wreathed tomb" and longing to resume her actual human form (I.38–41). But if she is a lamia, this is her natural form.

She shows her faery nature at once, for she's able to tell Hermes why he's there in Crete and, more, how her "power" (I.100) has made invisible the very nymph he wants. This particular spell of invisibility is itself a widespread faery spell.[17] Here, she performed it by "steep[ing] / Her hair in weïrd syrops" (I.106–7), and the word "weird" suggests enchantment or, in archaic Scottish usage (Scott, for example, revives the old word in his ballads), the fates or the uncanny. The effect on Hermes is that he is "charmed" (I.112), and Keats means that word precisely. It may seem that the nymph is here betrayed by Lamia, but in fact the nymph is invisibly watching the entire scene "near-smiling on the green" (I.125).

Hermes casually changes Lamia's form (he "turn'd / To the swoon'd serpent, and with languid arm, / Delicate, put to proof the lythe Caducean charm," I.131–3), and then rushes off to his nymph. Lamia's transformation into the human is remarkable, although the motif of the faery that becomes mortal is fairly familiar.[18] Here, it involves a physical pain close to death that's alien to the faery nature and presages Lycius's own death in the last few lines. "Her elfin blood" changes; her "melancholy eyes" (as the charmed Hermes had termed them) become fixed "with lid-lashes all sear," like Apollonius's eyes later described by Lycius as "demon eyes" with "lashless eyelids" (II.288–9). The faery gold turns to its reality, the transformed withered leaf or even dung in the folktales.[19] So the beauty of her form leaves, and she's only a snake-woman again: "in moments few, she was undrest / Of all her sapphires, greens, and amethyst, / And rubious-argent: of all these bereft, / Nothing but pain and ugliness were left" (I.161–4).

Then Lamia assumes the form of the virginal yet knowing young woman. Here again, in this new form she deceives by embodying others' mistaken perceptions, or perhaps one should say perverse perceptions. Like some masochistic Justine out of the Marquis de Sade, this young virgin with her hair in braids is "purest lipp'd" and the sort to listen to minstrel ballads in her "green kirtle" while sitting "on spring-flowered lea,"[20] while having a "sciental brain / To unperplex bliss from its neighbor pain" (I.186–92). This last characteristic proves a curious echo of Apollonius, with his "cold philosophy" that analyzes the rainbow (II.230–1).

And off she flies to Corinth in human form, the real reason why she had asked Hermes to transform her. For when she had the form of a snake, "how, ever, where she will'd, her spirit went" (I.205), and one place she visited was Corinth. Why did she choose Corinth? Probably because Corinth was renowned for holding the Isthmian Games, and it's well known that faeries love games.[21] Corinth was also famous through the ancient world for its luxury, even decadence, and its Temple of Aphrodite ("Venus' temple," I.317) with temple prostitutes. There she saw Lycius "charioting foremost in the envious race, / Like a young Jove with calm uneager face, / And fell into a swooning love of him" (I.217–19). What seems to provoke her insistent interest, with such unfortunate consequences for him, is his self-sufficient indifference even though he's first in a highly competitive chariot race. This desire to pre-empt the attention and capture the will of the proud human also is characteristic of faeries.[22]

This Corinthian charioting race is another indication of *Lamia*'s time-period. Lycius must be participating in the panhellenic Isthmian Games, which included charioting races and normally took place in Spring. These Games had taken place in Corinth for centuries until Rome took them over in the second century BC. A century later Corinth resumed the hosting. By the first century AD, Corinth was part of the Roman Empire.[23] We know from the note at the end that the poem's Apollonius is Apollonius of Tyana; so Keats is making it doubly clear that *Lamia* must be set around the first century AD when Corinth was part of the Roman Empire, as was most of Britain. The powers of this Celtic faery prove to be prior and superior to the classical figures surrounding her, as are those of the Roman Moneta who is really Mnemosyne.

A subtle irony ripples through Keats' entire account of Lycius's sojourn with Lamia, a savoring of the pretensions of the learned who are sure their intellect is adequate to all challenges. We might recall here the famous case of the Reverend Robert Kirk of seventeenth-century Scotland, the noted scholar who wrote extensively about the faerie in *The Secret Commonwealth of Elves and Fairies* and soon after mysteriously died near a faery mound. Supposedly he had so annoyed the faeries that they carried him off to faeryland where he still remains, with stones left behind in his coffin.[24] Lycius is the sort of protégé of a famous person who doesn't doubt his own mental powers precisely because he is that person's protégé. As the transformed Lamia hovers nearby while Lycius walks past this second time, still with an "indifference drear" (I.238), Keats reminds us of her real nature as he tells that "this fair creature chose so *fairily*" [italics mine] (I.200) to linger along the roadside in Corinth. She's waiting for him "on the moth-time of that evening dim" (I.220), an efficient reminder of her real nature since twilight is the faeries' favored time when they emerge as do the moths that lore connected with disguised faeries.[25]

For all his proud superiority, he succumbs to her blandishments at once when she speaks to him, appropriately enough since he is a follower of the rhetorician Apollonius. At first he sees her nature clearly enough to be something other than human, but he quickly loses that initial clarity as she glamours him away. He takes her for a naiad or a Pleiade that will soon fade and leave for her own ethereal realm; and Lamia agrees that she needs a "taste of purer air . . . to soothe [her] essence" (I.282–3). Even in this seemingly inconsequential detail, she deceives by personifying the mistaken perception. We know from the opening lines of Part I that she's not one of these classical nature-spirits, but one of the faeries who will drive them off. She goes on to flatter him, again with a certain irony: "Thou art a scholar, Lycius, and must know / That finer spirits cannot breathe below / In human climes, and live" (I.279–81). His scholarship is wide-ranging enough to include faeries and goddesses? In fact, if he were versed in the subject, he would know that her statement was false.

She sings her faery music of enchantment ("too sweet for earthly lyres," I.299)[26] and then sensibly sees that she is frightening him with her non-human powers, another wry touch. Her story that she had long seen him in Corinth, and fell in love when she saw him leaning against "Venus' temple porch" on "the night before / The Adonian feast"

(I.316–20) is certainly designed to allay any such fears. This Feast of Adonis that was celebrated throughout the Roman Empire took place the night before the spring equinox, and on that night Corinthian women took strangers for lovers. As Lycius and Lamia return to Corinth, this "scholar" never notices that "by a spell" the nine-mile distance ("the triple league") becomes a few steps and that no one notices them enter the city because they are "noiseless."[27] Along the way to her destination, they pass his mentor Apollonius looking very like the stereotype of the classical philosopher, with his "philosophic gown," sharp gaze, dignified mien, and — why this undignified detail? — bald head.

When Lamia and Lycius arrive at her palace, it's clearly been produced by magic;[28] and Keats again creates for us the experience of the human in faeryland. This evocation of the scene in which the human enters the faery realm, conjured up so often in *Endymion*, is again seen in *Lamia*. It's a place where laws of cause and effect are suspended, and so are those of time and space. No one can say where this palace exists.[29] Only two "Persian mutes" who venture into the markets know, probably human servants in faeryland whose secrecy has been horribly enforced,[30] as well as the "flitter-winged verse" relating this story to those who would really rather not know the "woe [that] afterwards befell" poor Lycius (I.390–5). "Flitter-winged" is an odd adjective. It makes the poem itself seem a faery that glamours us away from remembering the other side of faerie with its traditional connection with the world of the dead, though the last few lines of the poem remind us.

Part II opens with a chilling reminder of this connection that Lycius will learn by the end. Human love ("love in a hut, with water and a crust") versus faery love ("love in a palace") — that's the choice for us, though few understand this "doubtful tale from faery land" (II.1–5). Most of the "non-elect" who've never sojourned in this other realm would choose it over the human one although Lycius might have corrected them "had [he] liv'd to hand his story down" (II.7).[31] And then we zero in upon these two lovers in faery land at the point when Lycius fails to observe the faery taboos, as most humans inevitably do.

It's during summer at the faery time of twilight ("in the even tide") as the two lie pretending sleep so as to spy on the other, an unsettling detail in itself. Lycius hears the sound of distant trumpets, and thinks for the first time of that outside world — the human who doubts, however briefly, the seeming faerie reality around him.[32] Lamia reacts at once by teasingly threatening to leave. He in turn violates the taboo that enjoins faery privacy and punishes those who tell others of the ways of the faeries, such as the Reverend Robert Kirk: he seeks to display her like a trophy in her "bridal car."[33] Like other faeries in the folktales whose human lovers wish to wed them, Lamia weeps and tries to avoid this.[34] Lycius, provoked by her weeping, turns on his Justine ("he took delight/Luxurious in her sorrows") and insists on enforcing his will. This is not wise with faeries. Lamia "burn[s], she lov[es] the tyranny," and she agrees (II.72–81). Again, she deceives those who deserve to be deceived.

From this point on, the unmistakable signs of the faerie become increasingly ominous. He asks her name so he may invite her friends, and she sidesteps by answering that she has no friends or kin in Corinth — the faery always resists being named since naming gives control.[35] While Lycius goes off in "pompousness" to invite all to view his triumph, Lamia prepares her palace.[36] Keats's description of it stresses that ambiguous quality of the faerie that he has grown so proficient at suggesting. The music is "haunting," a word which takes on an eerier meaning when the music becomes the "lone supportress of the faery-roof" and a "moan" as if "fearful the whole charm might fade" (II.122–4).[37] One thinks of the role of music in spells, the witches calling up storms by whistling like the wind, the banshees wailing for imminent deaths, the mermaids singing their songs to lure sailors onto the rocks.[38] North Temperate cedar, "mimicking" tropical palms and plantains, forms a processional aisle for the bride. The feast is "teeming" with odors, an unpleasant word; and Lamia wanders through calling for more dramatic effects from her "viewless servants." Not only are there "mutes" who cannot reveal the directions to the palace but the blinded who cannot bear witness to what's done within it, all of them familiar faery-captive types in folktales.[39]

This faery wedding-feast must take place near or during Midsummer Eve, the same time as the weddings of *Midsummer Night's Dream* and the traditional time when the faeries come out. The two lovers met on the night before the spring equinox. We don't know exactly how long they were sequestered away after that, but Lycius became restive sometime near the time of summer (II.21). Indeed, *Lamia* echoes *A Midsummer Night's Dream* in many ways. *Lamia* also includes the opening references to King Oberon and "the faery broods," the love of the faery for the obtuse human, the wedding arranged by faeries at the conclusion, and the general mixing of the faery and the human realms. However, Lamia is no Titania, drugged, tricked, and compliant to her King's will. She chooses her human lover. She's rather like King Oberon himself, with the same qualities of dominance and trickery. This Midsummer Eve looses the same confusion of dream and reality, the same confounding of the human by the faerie, as did the one of Shakespeare's play; but no Robin Goodfellow appears at this poem's conclusion to wipe over the darker faerie truths revealed, and "sweep the dust behind the door" (*MND*, V.i.381).

For the "herd" comes to this wedding-feast, gaping (unlike Lycius) at this palace that seems built where none existed before, the old story of faeryland concealed in the familiar. Lycius's mentor Apollonius has come uninvited like the disbelieving intruder who's also a common feature in folktales, and only he understands what he sees. This shouldn't be surprising, because he himself is not so different from Lamia. The historical Apollonius of Tyana was well known as a miracle-worker. Lemprière noted that Apollonius was said to be "well skilled in the secret arts of magic" and was termed a "magician."[40] Keats refers to him as a Sophist several times (II.172, 285, 291), a detail not given by Lemprière. This also implies his connection with Lamia. Sophism as a branch of rhetoric dealt with surfaces and the verbal magic of making things appear to be what they are not. Sophists did the same with rhetoric and argument that Lamia did with charms and spells when she created her illusory palace.

Keats returns to his familiar pleasure of imagining the human suddenly plunged into the faery realm, as the wedding guests begin their faery feast.[41] It's reminiscent of the one that Porphryo spread before the sleeping Madeline in "The Eve of St. Agnes." The banquet room is filled with incense from the censers everywhere. As the guests eat and drink the faery food, with the faery music that comes from mysteriously hidden "powerful instruments," the spell intensifies to draw in the human guests as they drink their wine.[42] Baskets of woven gold with flowers and wreathes of branches from all climes appear.[43] The wreaths for Lamia, Lycius, and Apollonius are appropriate for the natures of each.

Lamia's is made from the willow, one of the trees frequented by faeries, and adder's tongue, a plant which not only refers to her lamia-nature but is a type of fern, that faery plant whose seed is believed to make one invisible.[44] Lycius's wreath is uncomplicatedly from the thyrsus, the staff carried by Dionysus, for he is downing the wine. The "sage," a designation for Apollonius evidently intended ironically given lines 229–38, wears "spear-grass and the spiteful thistle" which sounds most uncomfortable for him.[45] Both are weeds, and another common name for spear-grass was witch-grass. These sharp-edged plants may seem appropriate for this "sharp eyed" philosopher who presumes to "clip an Angel's wings," "unweave the rainbow," rid the air of spirits and the earth of gnomes, and, ultimately, turn Lamia into a "shade" (II.234–8). But Apollonius is a Sophist, the follower of what is generally considered a specious philosophy. The angels, spirits, gnomes, and Lamia only seem to disappear through the inadequate tricks of language.

The unmasking of Lamia by Apollonius is the expected climax of this scene with the faery, the human, and the disbeliever all sitting at the same wedding table. Robert Burton approvingly notes in his concluding quotation that Apollonius finds this "phantasm" and all her furnishings to be "no substance but mere illusions." She disappears, and Burton does not consider the results upon the young Menippus Lycius. Keats gives us something quite different. We see the scene from a perspective sympathetic to Lamia. Her opponent Apollonius staring at her is "wrinkled," "the bald-head philosopher" — again, that unseemly detail of baldness. Lamia is termed "poor Lamia," transfixed as she gradually metamorphosizes to the creature between the human and the faery that we saw back in I.146–64.[46]

Lycius cries, "Begone, foul dream!" and it seems at first that he's addressing Lamia, for we expect his accusatory language to be addressed to her. But then he goes on, and we realize that his sudden recognition of the reality is directed at Apollonius. He curses Apollonius with blindness for "all thine impious proud-heart sophistries" and charges him with "unlawful magic and enticing lies," terming him at last a "demon" (II.285–9).[47] Throughout these final lines, Apollonius is described in words recalling a snake. He "fix'd his eye, without a twinkle or stir" II.244–5) upon Lamia, with his "lashless eyelids" (II.288) hypnotizing his prey.[48] Still looking at her with his Evil Eye (the espied faery was believed to escape once one blinked one's eyes)[49] he violates the naming taboo by telling Lycius that he has been "a serpent's prey." Lycius also breaks the taboo by repeating, "A Serpent!" and Lamia vanishes.[50]

But Burton's ending is not Keats's ending, for Lycius seems to die although it's not clear how. Keats notes that his "limbs...were empty... of life," and that when his friends return that night (presumably after fleeing the feast in horror), they find that his "heavy body" is without any pulse or breath and wrapped around by his marriage robe (II.308–11). This could mean that the dead Lycius himself looks like a snake, and the protégé now resembles the faery who bewitched him...or his mentor. There is another possible understanding of these last lines. Lycius wed Lamia before Apollonius fatally named her. Perhaps Lycius isn't dead. Perhaps the faeries have exchanged another form for him such as a block of wood and left it wound in his robe while he is a captive in the faery world forever, as happened to the Reverend Kirk.[51] It's left ambiguous. But it's an inevitable ending, for the faerie world has long had associations with the realm of death.[52]

This folklore motif, increasingly familiar in Keats's works, dominates his last great poem. *The Fall of Hyperion: A Dream* is another attempt to write the story of *Hyperion*, abandoned after about two months. The imminence of Keats's death truly seems to haunt this epic fragment, beginning with the reminder in the opening lines of the first Canto that the true worth of this "dream" will not be known until "this warm scribe my hand is in the grave" (I.16–18). As the narrator relates this "dream," he begins moving back in time till he's in faeryland once again.

First he finds himself in a bordering realm where all about him are "trees of every clime," with both tropical and hardwood impossibly growing in one place at one time, some with fruit ("plantane") and some with flowers ("spice blossoms").[53] There's the sound of fountains everywhere, that feature of the otherworld familiar from Endymion's quest through faeryland.[54] There's the "arbour with a drooping roof" and the unidentifiable fragrance of the blooms hanging from that arbor ("scent, not far from roses").[55] It's summertime produced by magic, for there's a tempting "feast of summer fruits" which has been laid out for an oddly departed multitude; and the narrator cannot resist tasting it.[56] This unearthly food ("whose pure kinds I could not know") is like the "banqueting / For Proserpine return'd to her own fields" (I.36–7), Proserpine the Queen of the Dead come back from Hades.[57] There's the potion, not really the "poison" of the "jealous caliphat" since it leaves the "wander'd bee" unaffected, that the narrator drinks while "pledging all the mortals of the world / And all the dead whose names are in our lips" (I.44–5). (This is curious: why aren't the dead names *on* his lips?)

This drink "rapt unwilling life away" (I.51) and he swoons backwards to the otherworld that is the setting for the rest of the poem.[58] For most of *The Fall* the narrator is thus a captive in faeryland, where he will encounter Moneta and learn with fascination the history of her people. So the Celtic faeries have made it possible for him to reach this figure who proves to be a Druidess. The many folk-beliefs linking the faeries and the Druids should be recalled, particularly those holding that Druids controlled faeries or, alternately, that the Druids *were* faeries.[59]

Reading this poem, the reader gets the sense that the human conventions of time don't exist as we hurtle back before history, and neither do those of space. We're transported into faeryland along with the narrator. Our scope of perspective keeps widening up and out in a dizzying way, as we seem to look out in space toward the stars. First there's the enclosing forest, and within that the roofed arbor with its tempting feast that drugs the narrator asleep; and then when he awakens the arbor has expanded into a realm that's timeless and incorruptible. It possibly includes death for the narrator as he discovers after meeting Moneta, or at the least a permanent captivity in that strange land.[60] He's in "an old sanctuary" with "carved sides" and a "roof august," an "eternal domed monument"; and indeed, "so old the place was, I remembered none / The like upon the earth" (I.61–71). In fact, it is very like a tumulus, one of the prehistoric burial mounds found all across the British Isles and widely believed to be the places where faeries lived.[61]

This "old sanctuary" predates any he's ever seen in "grey cathedrals, buttress'd walls, rent towers," which seems to be a reference to the Gothic churches of medieval and Renaissance Europe. Above his head the roof extends far into space, and the "massy range of columns" is arranged to the north and south with "eastward" gates "shut against the sunrise evermore" (I.67–86). In this sanctuary is the marble-stepped altar that he'll come to know well, with a "sacrificial fire" (I.102) burning at a shrine on the altar and heaps of "spice-wood" and "faggots of cinnamon" on the floor nearby (I.235–6). At his feet is a jumble of unfamiliar ritual objects too: "strange vessels," robes, linens that have remained white and unravaged by insects, censers, chafing dishes, chains, and "holy jewelries."

All of this corresponds fairly closely to contemporary accounts of Druid temples and rituals. As most authors since classical days had noted, the Druids held their rites deep in remote forest recesses. The seventeenth-century antiquarian John Aubrey first associated the megalithic ruins at Stonehenge with the Druids; and as the craze for Druidism spread during the eighteenth century, such ruins were believed to be former Druid temples.[62] The details of Keats's "old sanctuary" with its "carved sides" and high roof sound very much like those of such a Druid temple back in the ancient days when it was in use. The "massy columns" like menhirs, the "domed monument" that was circular, the orientation of the columns to north and south and the gates to solar directions, all are reminiscent of this. He notes that "eastward... black gates were shut against the sunrise evermore." Antiquarians had long seen that the center stone posts at Stonehenge seemed to mark sunrise and sunset positions, with the stone arches framing midwinter sunsets and midsummer sunrises.

Those religious objects lying at his feet all had their place in Druid rituals, and so did the altar and fire. Pliny had first reported the Druids' annual rite of harvesting the sacred mistletoe with a golden sickle, catching it in white linen. Long known too were the gold neck torques that the priests and priestesses wore, and the cauldron (or the "chafing dish") used with burning spice-wood twigs and perfumes to perform magic. "Golden tongs" presumably were needed for that chafing dish. Most of the classical authors who described the Druids noted their ritual human sacrifices, although quite often that historical aspect was downplayed by the eighteenth- and nineteenth-century English enthusiasts. However, Keats makes it a central feature of *The Fall.*

That's the sudden horror for the narrator who is pulled into the scene that he's been viewing with the objectivity of a Romantic antiquarian. He approaches the altar and smells the incense from the "sacrificial fire" (I.102) that is so enchanting that "even the dying man forgets his shroud." Then he hears Moneta's chilling voice from the shrine command him to climb the altar steps or "die on that marble where thou art" (I.108). His bones and flesh will vanish there so that "not the quickest eye could find a grain / Of what thou now art," and he'll be out of time too since "no hand in the universe can turn / Thy hour glass" if he can't mount the first step (I.110–16). There follows the remarkable and prolonged anticipation by Keats of the death-experience, as the narrator tries and nearly fails to touch the first step. As he steps onto the pavement by the altar he suddenly feels the "palsied chill," the cold that literally seems to chill his blood ("those streams that pulse beside the throat"), the "stifling, suffocating" cold at the heart (I.122–30). It's the cold of the otherworld again that permeated "The Eve of St. Agnes."[63] He's in danger of becoming a captive in faeryland forever, without any chance of rescue because no one will even know he's there.[64]

So Moneta is introduced to us. As with *Lamia, The Fall of Hyperion* attempts to convince us of the precedence and superior power of the Celtic to the classical. Its central character Moneta may bear the Roman name for the Greek Titaness Mnemosyne, but her identity is Celtic rather than Greek although she includes the characteristics of that Titaness as part of her nature. This was true too for Keats's Mnemosyne in Book III of *Hyperion.* Both Mnemosyne of *Hyperion* and Moneta of *The Fall* are like the Greek Mnemosyne who was goddess of memory, vividly recollecting the past that still exists like pictures in the mind, blotting out the present. And like the Mnemosyne who was mother of the Greek Muses, both have a good knowledge of the nature of poetic identity. But there are significant differences between the classical Titaness, and Keats's Mnemosyne and Moneta.

When Mnemosyne first meets the untransformed Apollo in *Hyperion,* she tells him that she has had "prophecies of thee" (*Hyp.* III.78); and when he does undergo his painful deification she "upheld / Her arms as one who prophesied" (*Hyp.* III.133–4). Again in *The Fall*, Keats terms Moneta a "High Prophetess" (I.145). The Titaness Mnemosyne, as the goddess of memory, could well recall the history of her own race of beings, but she could not foretell its future. Further, Moneta calls herself a "priestess" (I.227), which the Titaness Mnemosyne never was. That Mnemosyne was a sister of the Titan Saturn, not his priestess. Mnemosyne of *Hyperion* must be a Druidess who possesses divinatory powers, and Moneta of *The Fall* must also be such an ancient Celtic priestess.[65] A Druidess would be well acquainted with bards since they were Druidical disciples in her society.

Moneta is the last of the Druids or as the narrator calls her, "the pale Omega of a wither'd race" (I.288). This figure of the last of a race or people has a compelling fascination of its own, as Stafford has shown so well.[66] This was a large part of the interest that the Celtic Britons commanded in eighteenth- and early nineteenth-century Britain, since "the genius of the Celts could only be reached imaginatively and there was no real hope of recovering their secrets."[67] The situation of such a survivor assures that their hard-won experience will also remain secret since they have no listeners. As Stafford also notes, the stories of these figures were very often created as "fantasies to repair ... self-esteem after a damaging experience of loss."[68] There's a kind of sympathetic identification with this survivor. Simply as a psychological expression of the stubborn need for preservation of the Self, the Celticists' association of the vanquished Celts with the huge and famed Titans was inevitable. And of course, Keats's own situation in late 1819 demanded that he try to cope with the imminent loss he faced in every area of his life.

Moneta assumes the central place in *The Fall*, although her counterpart does not in *Hyperion*; and her story, which is the narrative of *Hyperion*, is the core of *The Fall of Hyperion*. But Keats approaches this narrative through frame after doubting frame. In the opening 18 lines of *The Fall*, we start in the contemporary present with the dying poet transcribing the lines of what he self-effacingly terms in the subtitle *A Dream*. These 18 lines are a fine argument for the necessity of preserving history and lore through "Poesy" and "words," and not only through the oral transmission of adepts. We might say that the entire process of *The Fall* is the creation of such an adept in the narrator, who by the end of the truncated Canto II shares the vision of what Moneta sees unscrolling in her "globed brain" (I.245).

She acts as a Druidess throughout this scene of confrontal with the narrator, with the same magisterial authority and special powers that the Druid held in the Celtic society. Because of their divinatory abilities Druids were adjudicators who determined the sacrificial victims; and as such they excommunicated from the Celtic society where necessary, sometimes by means of curses and invective. Here, she's judging whether the narrator is to be sacrificed at the altar by deciding whether or not he belongs to the poet's "tribe," as revealed by his ability to climb the altar steps. Their ensuing dialogue raises the same questions about the nature of the poet in contemporary times as the opening frame of the poem. Like the Druid who had the role of educating the young, she teaches the narrator how to identify the true poet. The Greek Mnemosyne as mother of the Muses would have had a general understanding of those poets whom her daughters were likely to inspire. But Keats's Moneta seems to have an intimate and intuitive knowledge of the nature of the true poet that goes beyond that of the mother.

She speaks to the narrator in I.147–76 with the imperiousness of one who has known those who were bards; and in her accusations Keats expresses his own self-doubts that he voiced in the opening 18 lines of this Canto. Her denunciations of the dreamers who "thoughtless sleep away their days" effectively excludes them from the poet's "tribe," and also echo Keats's worst fears about himself ("a pet-lamb in a sentimental farce!" as he wrote in "Ode on Indolence" about six months earlier). Her admonition that poets are "those to whom the miseries of the world / Are misery, and will not let them rest" (II.148–9) may be more than a reference to the sad history of the Celts that she's about to relate. It could also allude more immediately to those who blandly ignore the "miseries" of the present colonized Celts.

Moneta may seem to address the narrator slightingly, even contemptuously, in I.162–76 for being "a dreaming thing" who's in her secluded sanctuary rather than out in the world, but she needs him there to listen to her story. As was widely known, Druidical lore was orally transmitted, committed to memory and never to paper.[69] The bards' primary role was the preservation of this history and wisdom through their poetry. As the "sole priestess of [Saturn's] desolation" (I.227), Moneta is the last of her people. Their history can only be preserved through the words of the bard, and it's urgent for her to find such a contemporary bard . . . if indeed any exist. The dominant question of *The Fall* is whether the narrator is such a poet. Does he have the power to tell their story when he returns to earth from faeryland?[70]

She goads him by taunting, "Art thou not of the dreamer tribe?," and then posing the apparent contradiction that the poet and the dreamer must be "antipodes" since "the one pours out a balm upon the world, / The other vexes it" (I.200–2). Keats's referents here have certainly proved vexing for critics trying to sort out which is which, for if the true poet feels the "miseries" of others in lines 148–9 then any "balm" would seem to be a palliative. However, the parallelism of the referents lets us know that the "dreamer" is the one vexing the world... or at least vexing those in the world who suffer the miseries ignored by the dreamers. And we can't mistake the conviction in the narrator's reply that the so-called poets of his time are self-absorbed "dreamers." There's a topical bitterness in his allusion to the contemporary "mock lyrists, large self worshipers, / And careless hectorers in proud bad verse," the false poets whom he wishes to be poisoned by the fumes from Apollo's shrine since they haven't been inspired like his oracle "Pythia" (I.204–8). The narrator may be no better than those he is cursing ("though I breathe death with them") but it doesn't matter any more, for he simply wants to know the story of Moneta and her people.

This in itself is the attitude of the Celtic bard, the receptive vessel for the Muse's tragic history of dead heroes and a vanquished people. The change in the stern Druidess is immediate, for her voice becomes "so much more earnest" and she weeps as she succinctly relates the outlines of her race's ancient war with its ruler still mourned by her. She and the narrator now share the same perspective. There's no more consideration of the abstract question of whether the narrator is a dreamer or a poet, nor concern about the diminished nature of contemporary poets either. There is "silence" while the fire at the altar burns low, and then "sad Moneta crie[s], / 'The sacrifice is done' " (I.240–1). What is this "sacrifice"? That of the "giant hierarchy" long ago? The narrator's artistic ego preoccupied with his own poetic identity? Something has made him worthy to hear her story and see her memories unfold through her "hollow brain" with his own "dull mortal eyes" — namely, his "good will" (I.242–7) toward her ancient cause.

To hear and see this, he must face her unveiled; and when she draws aside her cowl (itself part of the usual image of the Druid) he sees that she's blind. The blindness is to be expected, as prophets often were portrayed with their lack of physical vision compensated by their second sight.[71] Macpherson's Ossian was blind. But her face is "deathwards progressing / To no death" (I.260–1). Her face looks like that of a consumptive, as the tubercular were then called, a prophecy of what Keats most feared. It's "wan," "bright blanched / By an immortal sickness," "it had passed the lily and the snow" (I.256–62). She's the intimate fear he knows; and that constant awareness of death is part of

Celtic history, the "wither'd race." It's also part of the faery-faith, which associated faeries with the souls of the dead and faeryland with the world of the dead.[72]

Moneta has memories of the "high tragedy" of her "fallen house" to unfold before him; and that word "house" could allude to the Gaelic clans as well as the royal families of classical Greece. Then the poem shifts further back in time, and we begin the opening lines of *Hyperion* again (II.294ff.). Keats adds about 50 lines and revises some others, but the additions primarily are interjected reminders that this is a story related to the narrator of the far past rather than a straightforward narrative of present events. Descriptions of Saturn (I.438–54) still echo Ossian's *Fragments of Ancient Poetry*, most notably Fragment VIII. He no longer has "Druid locks," but during his laments Keats refers to their "dolorous accent from a tragic harp" (I.444).

There are some added lines near the end of Canto II that further emphasize the connection between this faerie realm and the land of the dead. As the narrator looks at the opening tableau from *Hyperion* of the immobilized Saturn and the sorrowing Thea (here, Moneta), he himself begins to become like the spirits he watches: "gaunt and ghostly," while he prays "that death would take me from the vale" (I.396–7). And near the end of the few lines that Keats composed for Canto II, Moneta is called "Mnemosyne" again, thus regressing backward in time; and the narrator sees her "sitting on a square edg'd polished stone" that "reflected pure / Her priestess-garments" (II.51–3). This seems to be one of the burial slabs from ancient times, for headstones came with Christianity. Keats would have seen these slabs on his walking tour when he and Brown stopped at Iona, and saw those of the kings of the Scots and the Picts, and the Highland chieftains.[73] Those stone slabs of such great age were seamed and worn, but of course back when they were new they would have been like polished mirrors, as this one is for Mnemosyne. But otherwise, the changes to the narrative of *Hyperion* are negligible.

However, this time there isn't any question about whether we are to sympathize with the Titans or with the Olympians. All of the elaborate frames of *The Fall* assure that the primary focus here remains on the Titans who are conflated with the Celts, and not the classical Olympians. Keats's contemporizing of *Hyperion* — the opening mention of "this warm scribe my hand" soon to be "in the grave," the continued dialogue about whether or not the true poet is alert to "the miseries of the world," the allusions to present-day poets — thrusts the entire project into the immediate historical context of England's present Celtic colonies. The narrator of *The Fall* who's caught in faeryland and learning Moneta's history is not so different from Thomas the Rhymer, also lingering under the Eildon Hills learning his lore from the faeries until the Celts needed him.

Keats abandoned this revision of *Hyperion* after only a few months. He had spent much of his most mature energies on this attempted epic, first in 1818 when he was fresh from his walking tour through Scotland and now near the end of 1819 and what was left of his health. His account to John Reynolds of why he had "given up Hyperion" is usually taken to mean that he intended finally to cast off any Miltonic influence, for he declared that "there were too many Miltonic inversions in it — Miltonic verse cannot be written but in an artful or rather artist's humour... Every now & then there is a Miltonic intonation."[74] But this is almost surely a deliberately off-handed way of hiding the real reasons. Or perhaps it's the literal truth: the completed *Fall of Hyperion* would have inverted all that Milton attempted in *Paradise Lost*, in a most dangerous way.

For *Paradise Lost* proceeded inevitably, and comfortably for the nineteenth-century reader, to "assert Eternal Providence, / And justify the ways of God to men" (*PL*. I.25–6). But if *The Fall of Hyperion* had incorporated the rest of *Hyperion* and continued on the course which Keats apparently set for it, we'd have a magnificent epic about the rebellion of the ancient Celtic peoples against the imperial forces of the classical world and then Christian Britain, enduring through the centuries to the present. It would be difficult for Keats to argue that "Eternal Providence" had decreed the present state of the Celtic people, after creating a lasting sympathy for them in *The Fall of Hyperion*. *Paradise Lost* could not well be written by a Celticist.

Keats wrote another, very late work based on faery motifs, although it's not really one of his faerie poems: *The Cap and Bells; Or, the Jealousies: A Faery Tale, by Lucy Vaughan Lloyd of China Walk, Lambeth*. This long, jumbled, unfinished poem is rarely considered by critics, but its setting is ostensibly faeryland and all but one of its characters are faeries. He began it in late February, 1820, after he had the severe hemorrhage that he called his "death warrant." He had offered to break off his engagement to Fanny Brawne, and was more or less confined to his sitting room for several weeks by his doctor. He wrote about the same time to Fanny Brawne: "I am reccommended [*sic*] not even to read poetry much less write it."[75] Charles Brown encouraged him to compose *Cap and Bells* as a cheering diversion and Keats dictated the stanzas to him, sometimes twelve in a single morning.[76] There was the hope even here that it might make them some money, for it's a transparent satire on the current scandals of the Prince Regent as well as the contemporary literary scene.

Briefly, in it the King of Faeries Elfinan (the Prince Regent) longs for a human woman Bertha Pearl (the Catholic commoner Maria Fitzherbert whom the Prince secretly and illegally married) although it's against faery law, while he also seeks to marry the faery Princess Bellanaine (Princess Caroline of Brunswick). The Chancellor Crafticanto is sent to bring Bellanaine to Panthea (London) for their wedding while one of Elfinan's slaves leaves with Elfinan to seduce away Bertha from Canterbury by magic. After a long journey (Princess Caroline slowly traveling from Germany to England for her wedding with the Regent), the Chancellor and Bellanaine reach Panthea with tumultuous crowds greeting them only to find that Elfinan's gone...and the whole meringue collapses suddenly as *Cap and Bells* ends after almost 800 lines.[77]

To an extent, *Cap and Bells* is a parody of Keats's own past faerie poems where the faery seeks the human with inevitably unfortunate results, such as "The Eve of St. Agnes," "La Belle Dame sans Merci," and *Lamia*. Like many of his faerie poems, it has echoes of *A Midsummer Night's Dream*.[78] But still it's a curious work, this sharp political satire laid in faeryland. It implies that the Regency court is as illusory as a faery court, with its royal extravagances like faery gold that turns to dead leaves and its amoral, capricious Faery King that all obey because of his faery powers. The moral stature of the court and its Regent is as diminutive as the physical stature of these faeries; and they have as little concern for their subjects as the faeries have for humans, too. The faerie materials lie at hand for Keats here, so familiar and well-worn from his earlier poems. But he doesn't use the esoteric motifs and allusions, only those well known to the most general reader: the love of faeries for humans even when beautiful faeries are available, the taboo against marriage between faeries and humans, and the faery abilities to change shape and to travel through the air. These are the tiny Shakespearean faeries that haven't appeared in Keats's poems since "Had I a man's fair form" of 1815.

The title, *Cap and Bells*, is especially appropriate because here Keats is the traditional jester in the royal court who alone speaks the unpleasant truth to his ruler that the surrounding couriers are afraid to speak, the truth disguised as jest.[79] In this last poem, Keats again alludes to the faerie and the Celtic in order to ridicule the upper class and nobility.[80] One remembers what Keats wrote to his brother a little earlier, "My name with the literary fashionables is vulgar — I am a weaver boy to them." Indeed, in *Cap and Bells* he's really playing the role of the faery that's punishing the presumptuous human as he writes what he thinks about the Regent's fussy, libidinous, tyrannical ways. There are many motifs about faery revenge that are relevant here, all called forth when the one of the "Little People" is disparaged or ignored by the human. Keats would have been well aware that faeries usually act this way when the human dishonors them, teases them, slights them, or treats other mortals badly; and that faeries are capable of making trouble for these humans in many inventive ways.[81] The faerie tradition, here as elsewhere in so much of his poetry, is used to mock human assumptions about world rank and status, much as the Celticist did the presumptions of superiority held by the English ruling class.

We should consider here the persona who supposedly tells the entire "faery tale," Lucy Vaughan Lloyd of China Walk, Lambeth. Some see her presence as Keats's joke on contemporary "women poetasters," or even as a satiric comment on "peasant poetesses" with her name an allusion to Wordsworth's Lucy figure.[82] There's another possibility. Wordsworth's Lucy is a simple country figure, but one with an intrinsic worth. "Vaughan" and "Lloyd" are Welsh names.[83] China Walk, Lambeth, was the site of the first English commercial pottery factory. Keats's "Lucy Vaughan Lloyd" probably came from rural Wales to become one of the hardworking, badly paid pottery workers of China Walk. Such a figure would be likely to have the faery-faith that runs through the poem, as well as its sharp-edged view of royalty.

Lucy Vaughan Lloyd is one more element in the satire — a native Celtic element, again. It was exactly such Londoners who greeted with swooning excitement the procession of Princess Caroline to St. James Palace for her wedding, so like the crowds following the Princess Bellanaine to her wedding. The well-recognized folly of the Prince Regent, and the popularly received entrance of Princess Caroline into London for their wedding, is served up to us by the working-class Welsh migrant to Cockney London. Keats may seem to be irreverently playing with his knowledge of the faeries in *Cap and Bells*, but at this point he's almost part of their realm that's so associated with the timeless, with death really. Again and again in his poetry he returned to variants on the particular folklore motif that associated the world of faerie with the land of the dead, Motif F160.0.2. He must have taken a double-edged pleasure in writing this satire, for it was certainly unlikely that he would be prosecuted for royal libel under the "Gagging Acts." What could the authorities do to him that was worse than his actual circumstances?

The faerie presence continued for Keats until the end. About a month after he began *Cap and Bells*, he wrote to Fanny Brawne of his wasting health with the old metaphor from sympathetic magic: "I have no need of an enchanted wax figure to duplicate me for I am melting in my proper person before the fire."[84] In Rome, Severn linked together candles so that as one burned down another was lit, to prevent Keats from waking in the darkness that he feared; and once Keats cried: "Severn! Severn! there's a little faery lamp-lighter actually has lit up another candle."[85] Near the end, Severn reported that once at four-thirty in the morning Keats suddenly roused up and said: "I think a malignant being must have power over us — over whom the Almighty has little or no influence."[86]

One of Keats's final wishes during the terrible process of his dying was that his grave be covered with daisies.[87] The doctor who had attended him remembered this and asked the Italian gravediggers to put turfs of daisies over it, so that the flowers bloomed as soon as the burial was complete.[88] It should be noted that the daisy has long been considered a potent sun-symbol, and an ancient protection against the faeries.[89]

Notes

All quotations from Keats's poetry are taken from the edition by Jack Stillinger, *John Keats: Complete Poems*, Cambridge, MA and London, England: Belknap Press of Harvard University Press, 1982. All quotations from Keats's letters are taken from *The Letters of John Keats*, ed. Hyder E. Rollins, 2 vols, Cambridge, MA: Harvard University Press, 1972. All references to folklore motifs are taken from Stith Thompson's major reference source, *Motif-Index of Folk-Literature: A Classification of Narrative Elements in Folktales, Ballads, Myths, Fables, Medieval Romances, Exempla, Fabliaux, Jest-Books, and Local Legends*, rev. edn, 6 vols, Bloomington, Indiana, and London: Indiana University Press, 1975.

1 The Evidence for Celticism in Keats

1. Motif C432, Tabu: uttering name of supernatural creature.
2. Motif F160.0.2, Fairy otherworld confused with land of the dead.
3. For a key example of a critic "demonstrating" Keats's supposed class anxiety in this regard, see Marjorie Levinson, *Keats's Life of Allegory: The Origins of a Style*, Oxford: Basil Blackwell, 1988.
4. J.A. Simpson and E.S.C. Weiner, *Oxford English Dictionary*, 5, Oxford: Clarendon Press and New York: Oxford University, 1989, p. 662.
5. Motif F172, No time, no birth, no death in otherworld.
6. Motif F377, Supernatural lapse of time in fairyland.
7. Katharine Briggs, *An Encyclopedia of Fairies: Hobgoblins, Brownies, Bogies, and Other Supernatural Creatures*, New York: Pantheon Books, 1976, p. 167. And see her study of the beginnings of the literary-faery tradition in *The Anatomy of Puck: An Examination of Fairy Beliefs among Shakespeare's Contemporaries and Successors*, London: Routledge & Paul, 1959.
8. Maureen Duffy, *The Erotic World of Faery*, London: Hodder & Stoughton, 1972, p. 244.
9. J. Burke Severs, "Keats's Fairy Sonnet," *Keats-Shelley Journal* VI (1957), p. 111.
10. There are few bibliographies or encyclopedias about the general subject of folklore and literature. *Encyclopedia of Folklore and Literature*, eds Mary Ellen Brown and Bruce A. Rosenberg, Santa Barbara, CA: ABC-CLIO, 1998, contains no references to Keats. Its entries are general and short, and its treatment of the subjects is fairly cursory. Its audience seems to be college undergraduates, not scholars in the field. This is not the case for *Folklore and Literature of the British Isles: An Annotated Bibliography*, edited by Florence E. Baer, New York and London: Garland, 1986, which is solid and detailed. It lists several article entries for Keats.

    As early as 1917, the intriguing suggestion is made by Sidney Colvin that a possible source for the "magic casements... in faery lands forlorn" in "Ode to a Nightingale" is a legend that Keats might have heard in crossing Kerrara to the Isle of Mull, connected with the Gylen Castle whose faery-mistress supposedly threw herself from a window into the sea when her nature was discovered (*John Keats: His Life and Poetry, His Friends, Critics and After-Fame*, London: Macmillan Press, 1917, p. 291). Forty-five years later a further connection between Keats and the world of the faerie is made by the prominent folklorist Tristram P. Coffin, who argues that the legend of Thomas the Rhymer (Child #37) is the source for "La Belle Dame" ("The Folk Ballad and the Literary Ballad: An Essay in Classification," in *Folklore in Action: Essays for Discussion in Honor of MacEdward Leach*, ed. Horace P. Beck, Philadelphia: American Folklore Society, 1962). See also Paul Edward's discussion of Thomas the Rhymer in relation to "La Belle Dame" ("Ambiguous Seductions: 'La Belle Dame,' 'The Faerie Queene,' and 'Thomas the Rhymer.'" *Durham University Journal*, Vol. 51, No. 2 [1990 July], pp. 199–203). Stuart P. Sperry comments on Keats's use of "Celtic lore" in "La Belle Dame," but restricts his use of the lore to this poem (*Keats the Poet*, Princeton: Princeton University Press, 1973, pp. 233–40). Coleman O. Parsons gives a thorough study of the secrecy taboo, familiar in folklore, as it operates in *Lamia* ("Primitive Sense in 'Lamia.'" *Folklore* 88 [1977], pp. 203–10). "The Eve of St. Agnes" is studied at length by Karen J. Harvey for its treatment of the faerie world ("The Trouble about Merlin: The Theme of Enchantment in 'The Eve of St. Agnes.'" *Keats-Shelley Journal* 34 [1985], pp. 83–94). David B. Pirie notes the many folk-legends surrounding "The Eve of St. Mark" and "The Eve of St. Agnes" ("Old Saints and Young Lovers: Keats's 'Eve of St. Mark' and Popular Culture," in *Keats: Bicentenary Readings*, ed. Michael O'Neill, Edinburgh: Edinburgh Press for the University of Durham, 1997).

11. The term "Celtic fringe" is used to designate Wales, Scotland, and Ireland, and sometimes Cornwall and the Isle of Man. It has the rather pejorative implication that England is the center of, and the other regions are only peripheral to, the British Isles.
12. Motif F381.6, Fairy leaves after Druid spell; Motif F389.5, Fairy defeated by druid's magic; Motif F394.1.1, Druid directs fairies; Motif F251.12, Fairies are druids.
13. Jeffrey C. Robinson, *Reception and Poetics in Keats: 'My Ended Poet,'* London: Macmillan Press, and New York: St. Martin's Press, 1998.
14. Ibid., p. 7.
15. There are several excellent summaries of the recent developments in Keats criticism that began with Jerome McGann's opening salvo in 1979. See Donald C. Goellnicht, "The Politics of Reading and Writing: Political Reviews of Keats's *Poems* (1817)," in *New Romanticisms: Theory and Critical Practice*, eds David L. Clark and Donald C. Goellnicht, Toronto: University of Toronto Press, 1994, pp. 101–5; and Nicholas Roe, "Introduction," in *Keats and History*, ed. Nicholas Roe, Cambridge: Cambridge University Press, 1995, pp. 1–8.
16. Robinson, p. 3.
17. *The Keats Circle: Letters and Papers and More Letters and Poems of the Keats Circle*, ed. Hyder Edward Rollins, 2nd edn, Vol. I, Cambridge, MA: Harvard University Press, 1965, pp. 253–60.
18. Fortunately for contemporary scholars, all of the books cited by Clarke from the Enfield School library and many from Keats's own library were of general enough interest during the eighteenth and nineteenth centuries to be published now as period reprints so we may read them for ourselves. Of the

books to be discussed, those by Tooke, Spence, and Davies have been published as part of Garland Publishing Company's ongoing series of period reprints; Burnet, by Georg Olms Publishers; and Lemprière, Robertson, Beveridge, and Hunt's *Juvenilia* by the Readex Microprint Series. Lemprière has also been published in a new revised edition as *Classical Dictionary of Proper Names Mentioned in Ancient Authors, with a Chronological Table*, 1788; edited by F.A. Wright, New York: Dutton, 1949.

19. Andrew Motion, *Keats*, New York: Farrar, Straus, and Giroux, 1997, p. 37.
20. Charles Cowden and Mary Clarke, *Recollections of Writers* (ptd. 1878), Sussex: Centaur Press, 1969, p. 147.
21. Lemprière, p. 103.
22. Andrew Tooke, *The Pantheon, Representing the Fabulous Histories of the Heathen Gods and Most Illustrious Heroes*, London: C. Harper, 1713; rpt. New York and London: Garland, 1976, p. 254.
23. Joseph Spence, *Polymetis: Or, An Enquiry Concerning the Agreement between the Works of the Roman Poets, and the Remains of the Antient Artists*, London: R. Dodsley, 1747; rpt. New York: Garland, 1976.
24. Clarke, p. 124.
25. Spence, p. 288, no. 4.
26. Ibid., p. 289.
27. This legend is similar to that surrounding Thomas of Ercildoune (Thomas the Rhymer). Both are a nexus of folk-literature motifs: Motif F323, Fairy women take body of dead hero to fairyland; Motif F399.1, Fairies bear dead warrior to fairyland; Motif A581.1, Culture hero returns and assists mortals; Motif F349.2, Fairy aids mortal in battle.
28. Edward Davies, *Celtic Researches, on the Origin, Traditions & Language of the Ancient Britons; with some Introductory Sketches on Primitive Society*, London: J. Booth, 1804; rpt., introduction by Burton Feldman, New York and London: Garland Publishing, 1979.
29. Ibid., p. 104.
30. Ibid., p. 148.
31. Ibid., p. 119.
32. Ibid., p. 140ff.
33. Bernard Blackstone, *The Consecrated Urn: An Interpretation of Keats in Terms of Growth and Form*, London: Longman's and Green, 1959, p. 387.
34. Ibid., p. 401.
35. Fiona Stafford, "*Fingal* and the Fallen Angels: Macpherson, Milton and Romantic Titanism," in *From Gaelic to Romantic: Ossianic Translations*, eds Fiona Stafford and Howard Gaskill, Amsterdam and Atlanta, GA: Rodolpi Press, 1998, pp. 176–8.
36. The first to do so was Edward Snyder, *The Celtic Revival in English Literature, 1760–1800*, Cambridge, MA: Harvard University Press, 1923.
37. Laura Doyle, "The Racial Sublime," in *Romanticism, Race, and Imperial Culture 1780–1834*, eds Alan Richardson and Sonia Hofkosh, Bloomington: Indiana University Press, 1996, pp. 22–5.
38. Michael Hechter advanced the argument that the Celtic fringe countries had a common experience in their relation to the English core that was colonial in nature. See Michael Hechter, *Internal Colonialism: The Celtic Fringe in British National Development*, Berkeley, CA: University of California Press, 1975.

39. Clarkes, p. 124.
40. Leigh Hunt, *The Autobiography of Leigh Hunt, with Reminiscences of Friends and Contemporaries*, 1850; rpt. New York: AMS Press, 1965, p. 278.
41. Pirie, p. 64.
42. Cox, p. 34.
43. Ibid., p. 85.
44. Nicholas Roe, "Leigh Hunt: Some Early Matters," in *Leigh Hunt: Life, Poetics, Politics*, ed. Nicholas Roe, London and New York: Routledge, 2003, p. 27.
45. Leigh Hunt, *Juvenilia, or A Collection of Poems Written Between the Ages of Twelve and Sixteen by J.H.L. Hunt*, Philadelphia: Printed and published for the author by H. Maxwell, 1804; rpt. microfiche (New Canaan, CT: Readex Microprint, 1987–1992). Ossian's influence may be seen in "Odes. To the Evening Star. From Ossian," and Gray's in "To Honor" and "Elegy. Written in Poets' Corner, Westminster Abbey."
46. Hunt, *Autobiography*, p. 124.
47. Ibid., pp. 128–36.
48. Leigh Hunt, *Lord Byron and Some of His Contemporaries*, London: Colburn, 1828; rpt. AMS Press, 1966, p. 247.
49. Rollins, I, p. 257.
50. "Calidore: A Fragment" is based on Book VI of Spenser's *The Faerie Queene*; and "Imitation of Spenser," "On Receiving a Curious Shell," and "Had I a man's fair form" were either sent to close friends along with letters or occasioned by exchanges with friends.
51. Cox, pp. 88, 110. By "pagan myth," Cox means classical myth; however, the Hunt circle would also have included the native non-Christian myths as pagan too.
52. "I feel it would be no bad thing to be the favorite of some Fairy, who would give one the power of seeing how our Friends got on, at a Distance," Keats wrote to Reynolds in 1817 (*Letters*, I, p. 132). About the same time he signed a letter to Hunt, "Your sincere friend John Keats alias Junkets," with the term explained by his friend Richard Milnes as "an appellation given him in play upon his name, and in allusion to his friends of Fairy-land." Hunt also referred to Keats upon occasion as "Junkets" (Ibid., p. 140). They all had in mind the widespread country habit of leaving out milk at night for the faeries. And when Keats wrote in 1819 to George and Georgiana Keats of their infant daughter, he described her as a faery: "O the little span long elf.... Let her only have delicate nails both on hands and feet, and teeth as small as a May-fly's. who will live you his life on a square inch of oak-leaf" (*Letters*, II, 189). He is alluding to the old rhyme: "Turn your clokes / For fairy folks / Live in old oakes." Turning one's clothes inside-out was thought a protection against faeries (Motif F385.1, Fairy spell averted by turning coat).
53. These include "Dear Reynolds, as last night I lay in bed" (1818); the poems from the 1818 walking tour, "Old Meg," "'To Ailsa Rock," "There is a joy in footing slow across a silent plain"; "'Tis the 'witching time of night'" (1818); "When they were come unto the Faery's court" (1819); and "Song of Four Fairies" (1819).
54. Nicholas Roe, *John Keats and the Culture of Dissent*, Oxford: Clarendon Press, 1997. The first two chapters are particularly valuable in establishing the extent to which Keats's republicanism was formed and nourished by Enfield School.

55. Clarke, p. 147.
56. Ibid., p. 124.
57. William Robertson, *The History of Scotland: During the Reigns of Queen Mary and King James VI, till His Ascension to the Crown of England*, 3rd edn, A. Millar, 1760, Vol. I, p. 3.
58. Ibid., p. 260.
59. Bishop Gilbert Burnet, *Bishop Burnet's History of His Own Time*, 2nd edn, 6 vols, London: Oxford University Press, 1833.
60. Ibid., I, p. 16.
61. Keats, *Letters*, I, p. 130. See also Robert Gittings, *John Keats*, Boston, MA: Little, Brown and Company, 1968, p. 127.
62. Napoleon carried the eight volumes of *The Poems of Ossian* (a translated French version of Macpherson's supposed translation from the Gaelic) with him on several military campaigns; and Thomas Jefferson termed Ossian "the greatest poet that has ever existed" (Paul M. Allen and Joan deRis Allen, *Fingal's Cave, the Poems of Ossian, and Celtic Christianity*, New York: Continuum, 1999, pp. 152–3).
63. Fiona J. Stafford, *The Sublime Savage: A Study of James Macpherson and the Poems of Ossian*, Edinburgh: Edinburgh University Press, 1988, p. 164.
64. Fiona Stafford, "*Fingal* and the Fallen Angels," p. 176.
65. Jerome McGann, *The Poetics of Sensibility: A Revolution in Literary Style*, Oxford: Clarendon Press, 1996, p. 33.
66. *The Complete Works of William Hazlitt*, Centenary Edition, ed. P.P. Howe, 1930; rpt. New York: AMS Press, 1967, Vol. V, p. 15.
67. Ibid., p. 18.
68. Keats, *Letters*, II, p. 16.
69. The first edition of *Minstrelsy* was sold out in six months; and *Last Minstrel* was an immediate phenomenon, with six editions within three years.
70. Sir Walter Scott, *Minstrelsy of the Scottish Border*, 1902; ed. T.F. Henderson, Detroit: Singing Tree Press, 1968, Vol. I, p. 18.
71. Ibid., IV, pp. 79–137.
72. See the brief allusion to parallels between Thomas and Endymion in Nancy Moore Goslee, *Scott the Rhymer*, Lexington, KY: University of Kentucky, 1988, p. 207; and in her essay, "The Envisioning of Women: From *Endymion* to the Later Romances," in *Approaches to Teaching Keats's Poetry*, eds Walter H. Evert and Jack W. Rhodes, New York: Modern Language Association, 1991, pp. 112–15. See also the equally brief comparison of "Thomas the Rhymer" and "La Belle Dame sans Merci" by Tristram Coffin, p. 67.
73. Charles G. Zug, III, "The Ballad Editor as Antiquary: Scott and the *Minstrelsy*," *Journal of the Folklore Institute*, Vol. 13, No. 1 (1976), p. 70.
74. W.H. Nicolaisen, "Scott and the Folk Tradition," in *Sir Walter Scott: The Long-Forgotten Melody*, ed. Alan Bold, Totowa, NJ: Barnes and Noble, 1983, p. 131.
75. Scott, II, pp. 300–87.
76. Keats, *Letters*, I, p. 323.
77. Mary Ellen Brown, *Burns and Tradition*, Urbana and Chicago: University of Illinois Press, 1984, p. 23.
78. Ibid., p. 45.
79. Rollins, I, pp. 253–4. The edition of *Celtic Researches* in Keats's library, listed by Brown, is marked "m" for "mine."

80. *Letters of Keats*, I, p. 347.
81. Ibid., p. 268.
82. Ibid., II, pp. 167–8.
83. Ibid., I, p. 264.
84. Ibid., I, p. 58; II, p. 288.
85. Murray G.H. Pittock, *Celtic Identity and the British Image*, Manchester: Manchester University Press and New York: St. Martin's Press, 1999, p. 39.
86. Robert Gittings, *John Keats*, Boston: Little, Brown and Company, 1968, pp. 230–1.
87. Keats, *Letters*, I, p. 306.
88. Ibid., I, p. 307.
89. Ibid., I, p. 309; Brown's comment is found in n1.
90. Ibid., I, p. 321.
91. Declan Kiberd, cited in Fiona Stafford, *Starting Lines in Scottish, Irish, and English Poetry: From Burns to Heaney*, Oxford: Oxford University Press, 2000, p. 252. Stafford agrees with Kiberd, commenting that "Keats [was] representative of the problematic attitudes encountered by the Irish over so many years" (252).
92. Declan Kiberd, "The Fall of the Stage Irishman," in *The Genres of the Irish Literary Revival*, ed. Ronald Schleifer, Norman, Oklahoma: Pilgrim Books, and Dublin, Ireland: Wolfhound Press, 1980, p. 43.
93. Keats, *Letters*, I, pp. 330–1.
94. Ibid., pp. 346–7.
95. Motif F211.0.1, Prehistoric burial mounds as dwellings of fairies.
96. Jennifer Westwood, *Albion: A Guide to Legendary Britain*, Salem, NH: Salem House, 1985, p. 399. Motifs F420.1.1, Water-spirit as man; Motif F420.1.6.1, Water-spirits are dressed like people of surroundings; Motif F420.4.7, Seeing and observing of water-spirits has fatal consequences; and Motif F422, Marsh-spirit.
97. Diane Purkiss, *At the Bottom of the Garden: A History of Fairies, Hobgoblins and Other Troublesome Things*, New York: New York University Press, 2001. Scott had noted this earlier "... the character of the Scottish Fairy is more harsh and terrific than that which is ascribed to the elves of our sister kingdom [England]" (*Minstrelsy*, II, p. 351).
98. Motif F369.7, Fairies lead travelers astray; Motif F402.1.1, Spirit leads person astray; Motif F234.0.2, Fairy as shape-shifter; Motif D1812.5.1.13, Fairy music as an evil omen; Motif F262.1, Fairies sing; Motif F362, Fairies cause disease.
99. Keats, *Letters*, I, p. 392.
100. Andrew Motion states decisively: "It was on Mull that [Keats's] short life started to end, and his slow death began" (p. 290).
101. John Gregorson Campbell, *Superstitions of the Highlands and Islands of Scotland: Collected Entirely from Oral Sources*, Glasgow: James MacLehose and Sons, 1900; rpt. Detroit: Singing Tree Press, 1970, p. 23.
102. Ibid., pp. 42, 89, 97, 103, 105, 145, 179–80, 208.
103. Motif F211, Fairyland under hollow knoll.
104. Campbell, p. 75.
105. Ibid., pp. 179–80.

2 Romantic Celticism in Context

1. W.Y. Evans-Wentz, *The Fairy-Faith in Celtic Countries*, London: Oxford University Press, 1911.
2. As Keats wrote to Benjamin Bailey: "You know my ideas about Religion — I do not think myself more in the right than other people and that nothing in this world is proveable. . . . We take but three steps from feathers to iron" (*Letters*, I, pp. 242–3). This is quite congenial with the amorphous, amoral qualities of faeries.
3. See Edward Snyder, *The Celtic Revival in English Literature, 1760–1800*, Cambridge, MA: Harvard University Press, 1923. This is "still the authority in the field" as of the mid-1990s, according to Sam Smiles, *The Image of Antiquity: Ancient Britain and the Romantic Imagination*, New Haven and London: Yale University Press, 1994, p. 48. Snyder confines himself to a strictly literary discussion of the influence of Thomas Gray and James Macpherson upon later eighteenth-century writers who wrote in the Ossianic vein.
4. Smiles, p. 48.
5. See Stephen Pattison's excellent, thorough, and engagingly written analysis of this emotion that has too often been conflated with guilt in *Shame: Theory, Therapy, Theology*, Cambridge: Cambridge University Press, 2000.
6. Ibid., pp. 162–3.
7. "Cockney: strictly (according to Minsheu), 'one born within the sound of Bow Bells' " (*Oxford English Dictionary*, 3, p. 419). The "sound of Bow Bells" meant "within a quarter mile of St. Mary-le-Bow in Cheapside, not far from London Bridge, Billingsgate fish-market, and the Mansion House" (Peter Wright, *Cockney Dialect and Slang*, London: B.T. Batsford Ltd, 1981, p. 11). One can see that Keats's birthplace did indeed fit this restricted definition if one checks the map of Keats's London that is conveniently provided on the inside covers of *The Letters of John Keats*.
8. The "cockney" dialect became a farcical, satirical, or otherwise "humorous" indicator of lower-class characters in plays and novels by the mid-eighteenth century. See William Matthews, *Cockney Past and Present: A Short History of the Dialect of London*, London: Routledge & Sons, 1938, pp. 31ff.
9. Rollins, I, *The Keats Circle*, p. 93.
10. Ibid., pp. 223–6.
11. Gerry Kearns, "Biology, Class and the Urban Penalty," in *Urbanising Britain: Essays on Class and Community in the Nineteenth Century*, eds Gerry Kearns and Charles W.J. Withers, Cambridge: Cambridge University Press, 1991, pp. 15–16.
12. Keats, *Letters*, I, p. 291.
13. Ibid., II, p. 61.
14. Ibid., p. 275.
15. John Rule, *The Laboring Classes in Early Industrial England 1750–1850*, London and New York: Longman, 1986, p. 379.
16. John Gibson Lockhart's review of *Poems* and *Endymion* (*Blackwood's Edinburgh Magazine*, III, July 1818), in *The Romantics Reviewed: Contemporary Reviews of British Romantic Writers*, ed. Donald H. Reiman, Part C. Vol. I, New York and London: Garland, 1972, pp. 86–93.

17. Ibid., p. 90.
18. Rollins, ed., *The Keats Circle*, I, p. 43.
19. Nicholas Roe, *John Keats and the Culture of Dissent*, Oxford: Clarendon Press, 1997; and Jeffrey N. Cox, *Poetry and Politics in the Cockney School: Keats, Shelley, Hunt and Their Circle*, Cambridge: Cambridge University Press, 1998. Cox's first chapter (pp. 16–37) admirably gives the literary and political implications of the term "Cockney School."
20. Emily Lorraine de Montluzin, "Killing the Cockneys: Blackwood's Weapons of Choice against Hunt, Hazlitt, and Keats," *Keats-Shelley Journal*, XLVII (1998), pp. 87–107.
21. Edward John Trelawny, *Records of Shelley, Byron, and the Author*, Vol. I, 1878; rpt. New York: Benjamin Blom, 1968, p. 39.
22. *Byron's Letters and Journals*, 7, ed. Leslie A. Marchand, Cambridge, MA: Harvard University Press, 1977, p. 200.
23. Ibid., p. 216.
24. Ibid., p. 225.
25. *The Confessions of Lord Byron, A Collection of His Private Opinions of Men and of Matters*, ed. W.A. Lewis Bettany, 1905; rpt. New York: Haskell House, 1973, pp. 200–2.
26. *Oxford English Dictionary*, 2, p. 247.
27. *Byron's Letters and Journals*, 8, p. 102.
28. Keats, *Letters*, II, p. 162.
29. Ibid., p. 174.
30. Kelvin Everest, "Isabella in the Market-Place: Keats and Feminism," in *Keats and History*, ed. Nicholas Roe, Cambridge: Cambridge University Press, 1995.
31. James Chandler, *England in 1819: The Politics of Literary Culture and the Case of Romantic Historicism*, Chicago: University of Chicago, 1998, p. 402. Chapter 7 is excellent on the general subject of Keats's fear of writing "smokeable" poetry.
32. Lockhart, p. 93.
33. Murray G.H. Pittock, *Celtic Identity and the British Image*, Manchester: Manchester University Press and New York: St. Martin's Press, 1999, p. 25.
34. Pittock, pp. 25–9.
35. Linda Colley, *Britons: Forging the Nation 1707–1837*, New Haven and London: Yale University Press, 1992, p. 13.
36. Colin Kidd, *British Identities before Nationalism: Ethnicity and Nationhood in the Atlantic World, 1600–1800*, Cambridge: Cambridge University Press, 1999, p. 69.
37. For a good discussion of the class implications of Romantic classicism, see the chapter "Classicism as Cultural Luxury," in Ayumi Mizukoshi's study of the Cockney poets "in the light of a rising bourgeois consumer culture" (7): *Keats, Hunt, and the Aesthetics of Pleasure*. New York: Palgrave, 2001.
38. Colley, p. 168.
39. For an excellent discussion of this Romantic shift of emphasis away from classical Greece to the native culture of the ancient Britons, see Laura Doyle, "The Racial Sublime," in *Romanticism, Race, and Imperial Culture, 1780–1834*, eds Alan Richardson and Sonia Hofkosh, Bloomington: Indiana University Press, 1996, especially pp. 19–26.
40. The terms "Celtic" and "Gallic" generally were used interchangeably until the eighteenth century. Stuart Piggott, *Celts, Saxons, and the Early Antiquaries*, O'Donnell Lecture, 1966: Edinburgh, 1967, p. 11, cited in Kidd, p. 189.

41. Kidd, p. 178.
42. Ibid., pp. 123–4.
43. Stuart Piggott, *Ancient Britons and the Antiquarian Imagination: Ideas from the Renaissance to the Regency*, New York: Thames and Hudson, 1989, p. 34.
44. Ibid., pp. 39–40.
45. Pittock, p. 61.
46. Kidd, p. 68.
47. Davies, pp. vi–vii.
48. Ibid., pp. 81–5.
49. Ibid., p. 130.
50. Ibid., p. 181.
51. Ibid., p. 147.
52. Rollins, *Keats Circle*, I, p. 253.
53. Motion notes that Brown met Keats walking on the Hampstead Road (p. 195). The composition dates of the books of *Endymion* are given in the chronology of Keats's life to be found in Keats, *Letters*, I (p. 35).
54. Davies, p. 119.
55. Ibid., p. 309.
56. Lemprière, p. 216.
57. Davies, p. 246.
58. "By the term, *Bards*, the *Welsh* do not understand merely *poets*; but persons regularly instructed in the institutes, and mysteries, of the original and primitive *Britons*" [italics his]. Davies, p. 270.
59. Ibid., pp. 182–3.
60. Excellent discussions of this cultural fervor that was not limited to antiquarians may be found in Piggott, *Ancient Britons*, and, especially, Smiles.
61. Miranda J. Green, *The World of the Druids*, London: Thames and Hudson, 1997, p. 43. Karen J. Harvey notes that the figure of Merlin prevailing in late eighteenth-century popular culture was that of the prophet or seer, which corresponded also to the figure then popularly held of the Druid (p. 88).
62. Lemprière, p. 216.
63. Motif M301.3, Druids as prophets; Motif D1711.4, Druid as magician.
64. Motif F251.12, Fairies are druids; Motif F394.1.1, Druids direct fairies; Motif F389.5, Fairy defeated by Druid magic.
65. Motif D2031.0.4, Druids cause illusions; Motif D2031.0.2, Fairies cause illusions; Motif D1981.3, Magic invisibility of Druids; Motif F235.1, Fairies invisible; Motif A974.1, Certain stones are druids transformed by the power of a saint. Westwood notes that several of the stone circles in the Isles are said to be petrified witches, such as Long Meg and her Daughters in Cumbria (pp. 310–11) and Mitchell's Fold in Shropshire (pp. 257–9), trows such as the Haltadans on the Shetlands (pp. 408–9), or giants such as the Callendish Standing Stones on the Western Isles (pp. 398–9).
66. Katie Trumpener, *Bardic Nationalism: The Romantic Novel and the British Empire*, Princeton, NJ: Princeton University Press, 1997, pp. 7–8.
67. Smiles, pp. 48–9.
68. One significant reason for this has been that there has not been a reliable modern edition of Macpherson's Ossianic works. This lack has been redressed with *The Poems of Ossian and Related Works*, ed. Howard Gaskill and Introduction by Fiona Stafford, Edinburgh: Edinburgh University Press, 1996.

69. There are several studies of Macpherson that reconsider his creation of Ossian from the viewpoint of the modern Scottish critic interested in eighteenth- and nineteenth-century Gaelic culture. See Fiona Stafford, *The Sublime Savage: A Study of James Macpherson and the Poems of Ossian*, Edinburgh: Edinburgh University Press, 1988; *Ossian Revisited*, ed. Howard Gaskill, Edinburgh: Edinburgh University Press, 1991; and the excellent overview in Fiona Stafford's Introduction to *The Poems of Ossian*, pp. v–xxi. See also *Journal of American Folklore*, Fall 2001, Vol. 114, No. 454, a special issue that is devoted to the contributions of Macpherson to the field of folklore.
70. The National Library of Scotland possesses sixteen of the manuscripts; the National Museum of Antiquities in Edinburgh, one; the Scottish Record Office, one; Trinity College in Dublin, one; and the Royal Irish Academy in Dublin, seven, in several folios (Stafford, *Sublime Savage*, p. 184).
71. Ibid., p. 171.

3 Keats as Bard

1. Evans-Wentz, p. 477, cited in Gregory Çastle, *Modernism and the Celtic Revival*, Cambridge: Cambridge University Press, 2001, p. 41.
2. Edward Hirsch, " 'Contention is Better than Loneliness': The Poet as Folklorist," in *The Genres of the Irish Literary Revival*, ed. Ronald Schleifer, Dublin: Wolfhound Press and Norman, OK: Pilgrim Books, 1980, p. 13.
3. Gregory Castle, *Modernism and the Celtic Revival*, Cambridge: Cambridge University Press, 2001, p. 58.
4. Hirsch, pp. 19–23.
5. The taboo on faery privacy was a widespread one, as Yeats should have recalled if he genuinely believed faeries existed (Motif F361.3, Fairies take revenge on person who spies on them). W.B. Yeats, ed., *Fairy and Folk Tales of Ireland*, intro. Yeats, 1888; rpt. Gerrards Cross: Colin Smythe Ltd, 1973. Thus he classifies faeries as either the "trooping" ones who go about together, or the solitary ones who tend to be malicious and evil. Yeats's taxonomy is continued by Katharine Briggs in her *Encyclopedia of Fairies*, although she does not attribute those terms to Yeats.
6. Yeats, *Fairy and Folk Tales of Ireland*, pp. 7–8.
7. Yeats, "The Message of the Folk-lorist" (1883), in *Uncollected Prose*, collected and ed. John P. Frayne, I, New York: Columbia University Press, 1970, pp. 284–8.
8. Purkiss, p. 297.
9. Frank Kinahan, *Yeats, Folklore, and Occultism: Contexts of the Early Works and Thought*, Boston: Unwin Hyman, 1988, p. 52.
10. Yeats, *Uncollected Prose*, "Irish Fairies, Ghosts, Witches, Etc." (1899), I, p. 133.
11. *Oxford English Dictionary*, 6, p. 53.
12. Purkiss, p. 297.
13. See Gregory Castle's excellent study of the influence of anthropology on the Irish Celtic Revival.
14. For two incisive demonstrations of just how much of a construct Yeats's peasant was, see Edward Hirsch, "The Imaginary Irish Peasant," PMLA 106, No. 5 (October 1991), pp. 1116–33; and Deborah Fleming, *"A man who does*

not exist": The Irish Peasant in the Work of W.B. Yeats and J.M. Synge, Ann Arbor, MI: University of Michigan Press, 1995.

15. Hirsch, "Contention is Better than Loneliness," p. 19.
16. For a thorough discussion of the inadequacy of Shakespeare as an accurate source for the folkloric traditions surrounding the faerie, see Briggs, *The Anatomy of Puck*.
17. As T.F. Henderson, editor of the 1902 edition of *Minstrelsy*, noted: "The most valuable and original portion of Scott's undertaking was the preservation and annotation of ballads specially connected with the Borders" (I, xiv).
18. Scott, *Minstrelsy*, II, p. 344.
19. Ibid., p. 351.
20. Motif V236.1, Fallen angels become fairies.
21. Motif F257, Tribute taken from fairies by fiend at stated periods.
22. Motif F321.1, Changeling.
23. Motif F211, Fairyland under hollow knoll; Motif F221.3, Fairies have a pretty room in hill.
24. Scott, *Minstrelsy*, II, p. 358. This has proved to be a common motif in folklore (Motif F211.0.1, Prehistoric burial mounds as dwellings of fairies) and connected to the widespread belief that the faerie world was close to the realm of the dead (Motif F160.0.2, Fairy otherworld confused with land of the dead).
25. Motif F165.6.1, Otherworld (fairyland) as place of sorrowful captivity.
26. Motif C211.1, Eating in fairyland; Motif C516, Tabu: lying under tree. Girl who does so carried off by fairies; Motif F218, Entrance to fairyland through fairy ring (for reference to this motif see Motif F261.1, Fairy rings on grass); Motif F262.9, Fairy music makes seven years seem like one day to mortal hearer.
27. Motif D2011, Years thought days. Years spent in the otherworld or asleep seem as days because of magic forgetfulness; Motif F377, Supernatural lapse of time in fairyland.
28. Motif D1293.2, Green as Magic Color; Motif F178.2, Green as otherworld color; Motif F212, Fairyland under water; Motif H1286.0.1, Quest to fairyland at bottom of lake.
29. See Scott's essays in *Minstrelsy*: "Introductory Remarks on Popular Poetry" (I, pp. 1–54); "Introduction to the Tale of Tamlane" (II, pp. 300–87); "Thomas the Rhymer" (IV, pp. 79–137); and "The Mermaid" (IV, pp. 277–83). Faeries were well known as "White Ladies" in many cultures (Motif F233.2, Silver-colored fairy; Motif F233.6, Fairies fair [fine, white]).
30. Katharine Briggs, *Anatomy of Puck*, pp. 45–6. See also Purkiss, who sarcastically comments that it was due to Shakespeare's influence that faeries have been seen as tiny and "freakish" (158), and merely "tiresome little wingy thingies" (8).
31. Jonathan Bate, *Shakespeare and Ovid*, Oxford: Oxford University Press, 1993, p. 136. Bates remarks that "Shakespeare was well versed in Ovid" (24), and "the fact of Shakespeare's imitation of Ovid is beyond dispute" (9).
32. Bate, p. 136. See Purkiss, pp. 176–80, for a good analysis of the implications of this Ovidian parentage.
33. Motif E545.8, Fairy converses with dead; Motif F160.0.2, Fairy otherworld confused with land of dead; Motif F251.2, Fairies as souls of departed.
34. Motif F302.3.1, Fairy entices man into fairyland.
35. Stillinger, ed., *John Keats: Complete Poems*, p. 417.

36. Motif F262.3.1, Fairy as harper.
37. Motif F262.3.4, Fairy music causes sleep.
38. Motif F225, Fairy lives in a shell.
39. J. Burke Severs, "Keats's Fairy Sonnet," *Keats-Shelley Journal*, VI (Winter, 1957), pp. 109–13. As Severs points out, although most readers of the poem have simplistically read it as a biographical lament for Keats's shortness of stature and lack of attractiveness to women, there is no mention in the poem of tallness or shortness but rather the plain statement that the speaker does not even have a man's form or, as Severs reads it, a human form.
40. Motif F241.1, Fairies' horses.
41. Severs, pp. 112–13.
42. Motif F221.3, Fairies have a pretty room in hill.
43. Motif H1286.0.1, Quest to fairyland at bottom of lake.
44. Motif D1293.1, Red as magic color; Motif D1293.2, Green as magic color; Motif F178.2, Green as otherworld color; Motif F233.1, Green fairy; Motif F236.1.1, Fairies in red clothes; Motif F236.3.2, Fairies with red caps.
45. Motif F160.0.2, Fairy otherworld confused with land of the dead; Motif F172, No time, no birth, no death in otherworld.
46. Motif F213, Fairyland on island; Motif F213.1, Magic boat to fairyland.
47. Motif D2146.2, Night controlled by magic; Motif F235.2.1, Fairies visible only at night.
48. Motif D950.12, Magic birch tree; Motif F261.3.2, Fairies dance on foxgloves.
49. Motif F234.1, Fairy in form of animal; Motif G211.1.7, Witch in form of cat.
50. Motif F241.1.1.1, Fairies ride white horses.
51. Motif F222.1, Fairies' underground palace.
52. Briggs, *Encyclopedia of Fairies*, pp. 313–14. The oak was also a tree long associated with the Druids and their magic. Motif D950.2, Magic oak tree.
53. Motif F241.1.0.1, Fairy cavalcade.
54. Motif F211.1.1, Door to fairyland opens once a year.
55. Motif F165.6.1, Otherworld (fairyland) as place of sorrowful captivity; Motif F375, Mortals as captives in fairyland.
56. Motif E587.6, Ghosts walk at full moon; Motif F262.8, Fairy horns heard by mortal.
57. Robert F.Gleckner, "Keats's 'How Many Bards' and Poetic Tradition", *Keats-Shelley Journal*, Vol. XXVII (1978), p. 16.
58. Motif F262.3.4, Fairy music causes sleep.
59. Motif F233.2, Silver-colored fairy.
60. Motif C122, Tabu: kissing fairies. This puts one in their power; Motif F302.3.2, Fairy offers gifts to man to be her paramour; Motif F305, Offspring of fairy and mortal.
61. In this poem, Keats "produce[d] a distinctly original, shrewd, almost alchemical blending of Spenser and Milton into characteristic Keats" (Gleckner, p. 22).
62. Gleckner, p. 16. He also cites Harold Bloom and W.J. Bate in support of this reading of a poem that few have remarked.
63. Ibid.
64. See the introductory chapter, "Harps Hung Upon the Willow," of Trumpener's *Bardic Nationalism* for a good analysis of what "the bardic institution" (3) meant for the Celtic nationalist movements of the late eighteenth and early nineteenth centuries.

65. *Oxford English Dictionary*, 6, p. 508.
66. Ibid., 8, p. 652.
67. Ibid., 13, p. 342.
68. Davies, p. 150.
69. For an incisive analysis of the class-implications of Keats's passage boldly locating himself thus, see Elizabeth Jones, "Keats in the Suburbs", *Keats-Shelley Journal*, XLV (1996), pp. 23–43.
70. Davies, pp. 196–7 and p. 1 of his eccentric "Index."
71. Motif F379.1, Return from fairyland.
72. Scott, *Minstrelsy*, II, p. 325.
73. Ibid., IV, p. 79.
74. Motif R112.3, Rescue of prisoners from fairy stronghold.
75. Motif F329.1, Fairies carry off youth; he has gift of prophecy when he returns to earth (Thomas the Rhymer) [parenthesis by Thompson].
76. Motif A571.1, Culture hero still alive inside hollow hill; Motif F211, Fairyland under a hollow knoll; Motif A581.1, Culture hero returns and assists mortals.
77. Tourists to Ercildoune today may visit the "Rhymer's castle," now a picturesque ruin, and the "Eildon Tree Stone" that commemorates the Eildon Tree beneath which Thomas delivered his prophecies. The Eildon Hills are nearby, outside town.
78. Scott, *Minstrelsy*, IV, pp. 79–127.
79. Goslee, "The Envisioning of Women," p. 112.
80. Goslee, *Scott the Rhymer*, p. 159. This book looks at the enchantress figure in Scott's poetry from a feminist point of view, finding "a particularly important subject matter in the stereotypes or archetypes of romance" (p. 3).
81. Scott, *Minstrelsy*, II, pp. 336–78.
82. Ibid., p. 325.
83. All quotes from "Thomas the Rhymer" and "Tamlane" are from the versions by Scott in *Minstrelsy* in IV and II, respectively.
84. Motif C122, Tabu: kissing fairies. This puts one in their power.
85. Motif D683.7, Transformation by fairy; Motif F302.3.3.1, Fairy avenges herself on inconstant lover; Motif Q247, Punishment for desertion of fairy mistress.
86. Briggs, *An Encyclopedia of Fairies*, p. 233. Motif F361.3, Fairies take revenge on person spying on them; Motif C311.1.2, Tabu: looking at fairies; Motif F348.5, Mortal not to recognize fairy who gives him gift; Motif F348.5.1, Mortal not to reveal secret of fairies' gift; Motif F348.5.2, Mortal not to thank fairy for gifts. And see Coleman O. Parsons for an overview of the secrecy tabu in folklore.
87. Motif F379.1, Return from fairyland.
88. Dittany was a plant of Crete that was famous from ancient times for its medicinal qualities and ability to staunch blood, and as such was used as a metaphor from the seventeenth through the early nineteenth centuries (*Oxford English Dictionary*, 4, p. 880). Keats would have been likely to know this from his medicinal background.
89. Motif F302.3.0.1, Fairy visits mortal and becomes his mistress.
90. Motif D1293.3, White as magic color; Motif F233.6, Fairies fair (fine, white); Motif F236.1.3, Fairies in white clothes.
91. Motif F131, Otherworld in hollow mountain; Motif F211, Fairyland under hollow knoll; F211.3, Fairies live under earth.

92. Motif D1364.3, Flowers cause magical sleep; Motif F302.3.4.4, Fairy takes lover back to fairyland in magic sleep.
93. *Oxford English Dictionary*, 5, p. 400.
94. Ibid., 4, p. 893.
95. Ibid., 1, p. 300.
96. Motif H1381.3.8, Quest for queen of fairies.
97. We know that Keats was familiar with this falsely beckoning shape taken by fairies that was so common to folktales, because of later lines from Book II referring to it: "A mad-pursuing of the fog-born elf, / Whose flitting lantern, through rude nettle-briar, Cheats us into a swamp, into a fire, / Into the bosom of a hated thing" (II.277–80). Motif F369.7, Fairies lead travelers astray; Motif F491.1, Will-o'-the-Wisp leads people astray.
98. Motif F262.3.4, Fairy music causes sleep; Motif F302.3.4.4, Fairy takes lover back to fairyland in magic sleep.
99. Scott, IV, p. 94. Motif F302.3.4.4, Fairy takes lover back to fairyland in magic sleep; Motif F219.2, Garden in fairyland.
100. Motif F361.17.3, Fairies pinch as revenge.
101. Motif F222.1, Fairies' underground palace.
102. Motif F162.8, Magic fountain in otherworld.
103. Motif D2031.0.2, Fairies cause illusions.
104. Motif F219.2, Garden in fairyland.
105. Motif F305, Offspring of fairy and mortal; Motif F305.2, Offspring of fairy and mortal extraordinarily beautiful.
106. Motif F348.7, Tabu: telling of fairy gifts; the gifts cease.
107. Scott, *Minstrelsy*, II, pp. 317, 352–3.
108. Motif H1286.0.1, Quest to fairyland under lake.
109. Scott, *Minstrelsy*, IV, p. 83.
110. Motif F420.3.3, Water-spirits have kingdom under water.
111. Motif E587.6, Ghosts walk at full moon.
112. Motif F302.3.3.1, Fairy avenges herself on an inconstant lover.
113. Motif F165.6.1, Fairyland as place of sorrowful captivity.
114. Motif F236.1.2, Fairies in blue clothes; Motif F251.12, Fairies are Druids; Motif F394.1.1, Druid directs fairies.
115. Motif C311.1.2, Tabu: looking at fairies.
116. Motif C943, Loss of sight for breaking tabu; Motif D772, Disenchantment by naming; Motif D2062.2, Blinding by magic; Motif F362.1, Fairies cause blindness.
117. Motif D1855.1, Witch delays person's death; Motif F377, Supernatural lapse of time in fairyland.
118. Motif G269.8, Witch causes shipwreck.
119. Motif G283, Witches have control over weather; Motif G283.3, Witch produces rain or snow.
120. Motif D1711.4, Druid as magician; Motif D1810.0.8, Magic knowledge of druid.
121. Motif R112.3, Rescue of prisoners from fairy stronghold.
122. Motif F162.2.2, Rivers of wine in otherworld; Motif F162.5.1, Well of wine in otherworld.
123. Motif F420.3.3, Water-spirits have kingdom under water; Motif F420.3.5, Water-spirits visited by mortal.

124. Motif F212, Fairyland under water.
125. Motif F420.4.8, Water-spirits have treasures under water.
126. Motif F173.3, Perpetual feasts in otherworld.
127. Motif F373, Mortal abandons world to live in fairyland.
128. Keats probably got this detail of Bacchus riding through India "with Asian elephants" (IV.246) from Tooke, p. 75.
129. Motif A171.1, God rides through air on wind-swift horse; Motif B542.2, Escape on flying horse.
130. Motif T111.2.2, Marriage of mortal and moon.
131. Motif F282, Fairies travel through air.
132. Motif F411.0.1, Spirit travels with extraordinary speed.
133. Motif F130.1, Land of India as otherworld ["Irish myth," notes Thompson].
134. Motif F302.3.3.1, Fairy avenges herself on inconstant lover (husband); Motif Q247, Punishment for deserting fairy mistress.
135. There are examples of stylistic awkwardness throughout. Among Pan's subjects in Book I is "the *squatted* hare" (I.265). Endymion measures the denseness of the forest outside Latona's temple to Peona by stating that with "spreaded tail, a *vulture* could not glide/Past" (I.867–8). Endymion's state of mind is dominated by "the *pest* of love" (II.365). Glaucis states that during his stay with Circe, he sought for her "to slake / My greedy thirst with nectarous *camel-draughts*" (III.479). When all the lovers finally are awakened undersea by Endymion, they follow Scylla like "swans upon a gentle *waterfall*" (III.817) which presumably sail over the edge of the fall to a watery confusion. King Oceanus is serenaded with "the Eolian *twang* of Love's own bow" (III.973). Cynthia expresses her lasting love for Endymion by predicting that she'll "kissing *snatch* / Thee into endless heaven" (III.1026–7). And when Endymion first sees the Indian maid she's lying on "new-made *hay*" (IV.102).
136. Susan J. Wolfson, ed., *The Cambridge Companion to Keats*, Cambridge: Cambridge University Press, 2001, p. xxiv.
137. *Letters*, I, p. 170.
138. Ibid., p. 146.
139. Ibid., p. 166.
140. Ibid., p. 168.
141. Ibid., p. 175.
142. Ibid., p. 170.

4 The Native Muse

1. In the accompanying letter, Keats writes: "You know, I am sure, Claude's Enchanted Castle and I wish you may be pleased with my remembrance of it" (*Letters*, I, p. 263).
2. Motif A671.0.1, Hell located to the North; Motif G633, North as abode of evil spirits.
3. Motif F213, Fairyland on island; Motif F213.1, Magic boat to fairyland; Motif F222, Fairy castle.
4. Motif F160.0.2, Fairy otherworld confused with land of the dead; Motif F211.0.1, Prehistoric burial mounds as dwellings of fairies.

5. Motif F222.2, Fairy stronghold.
6. Motif D1645.3, Magic castle shines from afar; Motif F771.4.7, Castle inhabited by enchanted princess.
7. Motif D1123, Magic ship; Motif D1523.2, Self-propelling ship.
8. Motif E535.3, Ghost ship.
9. Motif D1812.5.1.13, Fairy music as evil omen.
10. Keats, *Letters*, I, p. 193.
11. Motif F222.1, Fairies' underground palace.
12. Joan Coldwell, " 'Meg Merrilies': Scott's Gipsey Tamed," *Keats-Shelley Memorial Bulletin*, XXXII (1981), p. 33.
13. Keats, *Letters*, I, p. 317.
14. During the time when Keats attended Guy's Hospital medical students were usually trained in botany also, particularly in the medicinal use of poisonous plants. Keats drew on this medical knowledge in the references to poisonous plants in his "Ode to a Nightingale" and "Ode to Melancholy." See Gareth Evans for a detailed discussion of Keats's probable knowledge of medical botany ("John Keats and the Botanic Pharmacy," *Keats-Shelley Review* 16 [2002], pp. 31–55).
15. Motif E545.8, Fairy converses with dead.
16. Motif D950.14, Magic yew tree.
17. Motif F236.1.1, Fairies in red clothes.
18. Motif F271.4.2, Fairies skillful as weavers; Motif F343.5, Fairies give beautiful clothes.
19. Keats, *Letters*, I, p. 264.
20. Ibid., p. 348.
21. Fiona Stafford, "*Fingal* and the Fallen Angels," p. 178.
22. Davies, p. 146.
23. Motif A974.1, Certain stones are druids transformed by power of saint.
24. Homer Sykes, *Celtic Britain*, London: Weidenfeld & Nicolson, 1997, pp. 10, 47.
25. Motif F375, Mortals as captives in fairyland.
26. Motif C712.1, Tabu: staying too long in fairyland; Motif F165.6.1, Otherworld (fairyland) as place of sorrowful captivity.
27. Keats, *Letters*, II, p. 174.
28. Lockhart, *The Romantics Reviewed*, Part C, Vol. I, p. 93.
29. By now, *Paradise Lost* is a generally assumed model for *Hyperion*. Beth Lau demonstrates its general importance as a source for Keats of parallels, allusions, and images with her analysis of the marginalia in Keats's copy of *Paradise Lost* (*Keats's 'Paradise Lost,'* Gainesville, FL: University Press of Florida, 1998).
30. Ibid., p. 3.
31. Ibid., p. 35.
32. Scott, *Minstrelsy*, II, p. 328.
33. Ibid., p. 62.
34. Daniel Watkins, *Keats's Poetry and the Politics of the Imagination*, Cranbury, NJ: Fairleigh Dickinson University Press, 1989, p. 100.
35. Others have developed this interpretation with more detailed historical readings. Michael O'Neill suggests that Saturn may be viewed as a Napoleonic figure and the context of the nearly completed Olympian revolution that of post-Waterloo Britain (" 'When this warm scribe my hand': writing and history in *Hyperion* and *Fall of Hyperion*," in *Keats and History*, ed. Roe, p. 158);

and Nicola Trott compares the Titans to the *ancien regime* ("Keats and the prison house of memory," in *Keats and History*, p. 268). Vincent Newey also holds that Keats in this work followed "a Republican, anti-Monarchal view," and notes that Keats abandoned the "*Hyperion* project" just after the Peterloo crisis in 1819 ("*Hyperion, The Fall of Hyperion* and Keats's Epic Ambitions," in *The Cambridge Companion to Keats*, ed. Wolfson, p. 73).

36. Stafford, "*Fingal* and the Fallen Angels," p. 176.
37. Ibid., p. 177.
38. Watkins, p. 90.
39. Stafford, "*Fingal* and the Fallen Angels," p. 179.
40. See Macpherson, *The Poems of Ossian*, ed. Gaskill.
41. Tooke, p. 300.
42. Hesiod, *Theogony; Works and Days; Shield*, trans. Apostolos N. Athanassakis, Baltimore: Johns Hopkins Press, 1983.
43. Ibid., p. 51.
44. Stafford, "*Fingal* and the Fallen Angels," p. 179.
45. Davies, p. 141.
46. Ibid., pp. 120, 149, 150, 197, and *passim*.
47. Donald C. Goellnicht, *The Poet-Physician: Keats and Medical Science*, Pittsburgh: University of Pittsburgh Press, 1984, p. 216.
48. Davies, p. 142.
49. Ibid., p. 185.
50. The editor of the Hampstead Edition of Keats notes: "The unfinished line and sentence is filled up in pencil in the Woodhouse transcript, wherein we read: 'At length / Apollo shriek'd — and lo from all his limbs / Celestial Glory dawn'd: he was a god!' " (*The Poetical Works and Other Writings of John Keats*, ed. H. Buxton Forman, III, New York: Phaeton Press, 1970, p. 252.) However, it seems as likely to be an addition by Woodhouse as by Keats.
51. This reading is tactfully suggested in the Hampstead Edition of Keats when the editor comments: "I confess that I should be disposed to rank all these symptoms of convulsion and hysteria in the same category as the fainting of lovers" (p. 253).
52. Goellnicht, *The Poet-Physician*, p. 221.

5 Faery Lands Forlorn

1. C.G. Jung, "On the Psychology of the Trickster-Figure," in *Archetypes and the Collective Unconscious*, Princeton, NJ: Princeton University Press, 1959; 2nd edn, 1977, p. 256.
2. Keats, *Letters*, II, p. 80.
3. Stillinger, ed., *John Keats: Complete Poems*, p. 417.
4. Motif F268, Burial among otherworld folk.
5. Motif F233.2, Silver-colored fairy.
6. Lemprière, p. 673.
7. Motif A692.1, Otherworld in west; Motif E481.6.2, Land of dead in west.
8. Motif E545.8, Fairy converses with dead; Motif F160.0.2, Fairy otherworld confused with land of the dead.
9. Keats, *Letters*, II, p. 85.

10. There are so many editions available of this poem then so popular that it may be arbitrary to choose one. However, the one cited here appears in Volume XLVIII of *The Works of Sir Walter Scott,* Boston and New York: Houghton Mifflin Company, 1913. The "Fairy Ballad" occurs in Canto Four, stanza xv, pp. 124–5.
11. Thompson devotes the entire section of D0-D699 to motifs of transformation, noting that "no real difference seems to exist between transformation and enchantment" (II, p. 8).
12. Motif F241.1.0.1, Fairy cavalcade.
13. Motif F165.2, Otherworld dwellings open only at certain times; Motif 211.1.1, Door to fairyland opens once a year.
14. Motif A2221.2.2, Blood from cross on robin red breast; Motif A2353.2, Why robin has red breast.
15. Motif F383.2, Fairy unable to cross running stream; Motif G303.16.19.13, Devil cannot cross running water.
16. Motif F361.2, Fairy takes revenge for theft.
17. Motif F218, Entrance to fairyland through fairy ring (see Motif F261.1, Fairy rings on grass); Motif F361.4, Fairies take revenge on trespassers on ground they claim as theirs.
18. Motif F361.3, Fairies take revenge on person who spies on them.
19. With this old-fashioned toy, a small whip was used to make the top keep on spinning.
20. Motif D950.1, Magic hazel tree.
21. Motif F211.1, Entrance to fairyland through door in knoll.
22. Motif F216, Fairies live in forest. Consider also the old couplet: "Fairy folks / Are in old oaks." See Briggs, *Encyclopedia of Fairies*, pp. 159–61.
23. Motif F262.1, Fairies sing.
24. Scott noted, "The Daemon-Lover was taken down from recitation by Mr. William Laidlaw, a tenant at Traquaire-Knowe" (*Minstrelsy*, III, p. 246), and that "The Eve of St. John" "was first printed in Mr. Lewis's *Tales of Wonder*" (*Minstrelsy*, IV, p. 159).
25. Francis Jeffrey, "Review of Keats's *Lamia, Isabella, The Eve of St. Agnes, and Other Poems*" (*Edinburgh Review*, XXXIV, August 1820), in *The Romantics Reviewed*, ed. Reiman, Part C, Vol. I, p. 390.
26. Scott, *Minstrelsy*, I, p. 173.
27. Ibid., I, pp. 172–3.
28. Ibid., I, p. 175.
29. Motif F211.1.1.2, Fairies emerge on St. John's night [Midsummer Eve].
30. The relevant lines from Scott's "The Eve of St. John" are:

> And I heard her name the midnight hour,
> And name this holy eve;
> And say, "Come this night to thy lady's bower;
> Ask no bold Baron's leave." . . .
>
> "I cannot come; I must not come;
> I dare not come to thee;
> On the eve of St. John I must wander alone:
> In thy bower I may not be." . . .

"Though the bloodhound be mute, and the rush beneath my foot,
And the warder his bugle should not blow,
Yet sleepeth a priest in the chamber to the east,
And my footstep he would know."

"O fear not the priest, who sleepeth to the east!
For to Dryburgh the way he has ta'en" . . .
"At the lone midnight hour, when bad spirits have power,
In thy chamber will I be." (XVI–XXIV)

31. The relevant lines from Scott's ballad "The Daemon-Lover" are:

The clouds grew dark, and the wind grew loud,
And the levin [lightning] fill'd her ee;
And waesome wail'd the snaw-white sprites
Upon the gurlie [stormy] sea. (XVIII)

32. Marcia Gilbreath, "The Etymology of Porphryro's Name in Keats's 'Eve of St. Agnes,' " *Keats-Shelley Journal*, Vol. 37 (1988), pp. 20–5.
33. Motif V236.1, Fallen angels become faeries.
34. Scott, *Minstrelsy*, II, pp. 328, 336, 368.
35. Stafford, "*Fingal* and the Fallen Angels", p. 171.
36. Motif F251.11, Fairies not good enough for heaven but not bad enough for hell.
37. *Oxford English Dictionary*, 5, p. 662.
38. Herbert G. Wright, "Has Keats's 'Eve of St. Agnes' A Tragic Ending?", *Modern Language Review*, Vol. 40, No. 2, 1945, pp. 90–4.
39. This is, for example, the strategy of Scott's three-part version of "Thomas the Rhymer." Part First begins with the encounter between "True Thomas" on his hillside and the highly ornamented "Queen of fair Elfland," and after a detailed voyage to Elfland and much dialogue it ends with a similarly distancing stanza and the last lines: "And, till seven years were gane and past, / True Thomas on earth was never seen" (XX).
40. Jack Stillinger, *Reading The Eve of St. Agnes: The Multiples of Complex Literary Transaction*, New York: Oxford University Press, 1999, pp. 133, 144.
41. See Stillinger's witty account of his rereading which changed the direction of Keats studies completely in 1971 (pp. 38–9). This was a valuable service to perform, given the ethereal and solely aesthetic portrayal of Keats which had taken hold for so long.
42. Motif F322.4, Abducted bride hidden in fairyland.
43. Motif F362.1, Fairies cause blindness; Motif F363.3, Sight of fairies fatal; Motif F372.1, Fairies take human midwife to attend fairy woman.
44. Motif F321.1, Changeling, fairy steals child from cradle and leaves fairy substitute.
45. Motif A671.3.1, Coldness in hell; Motif F169.7, Coldness of otherworld.
46. Westwood, p. 30. Motif G211.2.7, Witch in form of hare; Motif G211.4.4, Witch in form of owl. This was true for faeries as well (Motif F234.1, Fairy in form of animal).
47. Motif G263.6, Witchcraft causes maiden to hate lover.

48. *Oxford English Dictionary*, 7, p. 363. Motif D2031.0.2, Fairies cause illusions.
49. Motif E587.6, Ghosts walk at full moon; Motif F451.6.3.5, Dwarfs play in the moonlight; Motif F482.5.2, Brownies sew by moonlight.
50. Motif B521.3.1, Dogs warn against witch; Motif F381.9, Fairies will not approach when dogs are present; Motif F405.5.1, Dogs protect house from spirits.
51. Motif F271.4.3, Fairies spin. See also Briggs, *Encyclopedia of Fairies*, pp. 137–8. Associated with fairy cobwebs was the old folk-superstition that binding a wound with cobwebs would heal it.
52. Motif E587.6, Ghosts walk at full moon.
53. Briggs, *Encyclopedia of Fairies*, p. 25.
54. Ibid., p. 339.
55. Motif G303.4.8.8, Devil laughs when men weep.
56. Westwood, pp. 257–8. She only cites this tale as being from the one locale of Shropshire, but it was widespread throughout the Isles.
57. Motif G243.2, Parody of church ceremony at witch's Sabbath.
58. Motif F470.2, Night spirits dance.
59. Typical is the popular *Longman Anthology of British Literature: The Romantics and Their Contemporaries*, eds Susan J. Wolfson and Peter Manning, New York: Addison-Wesley Educational Publishers, 1999, p. 763.
60. *English Romantic Writers*, ed. David Perkins, New York: Harcourt Brace, 1967, 2nd edn, 1995, p. 1243.
61. Motif F282, Fairies travel through air.
62. Motif F95.4, Knots in grass mark path to underworld.
63. Motif F234.1.16.2, Fairy in form of moth.
64. Scott, *Minstrelsy*, III, p. 246.
65. Motif T521.1, Conception from moonlight. Madeline is still asleep under the "faded moon" when Porphyro joins her.
66. Motif F243, Fairies' food.
67. Motif C211.1, Tabu: eating in fairyland.
68. Motif F348.4, Gifts of gold and silver not to be accepted from fairies.
69. Motif F166.11, Abundant food in otherworld.
70. Motif D1469.15, Magic ship furnishes treasure.
71. Motif F262.3.4, Fairy music causes sleep.
72. Motif G283.1, Witch raises winds; Motif G283.3, Witch produces rain or snow.
73. Motif D2088, Locks opened by magic; Motif G249.8, Witches open doors and windows.
74. Motif D192.0.1, Transformation: demon (in human form) to worm; Motif F234.1.7, Fairy in form of worm (snake, serpent).
75. One classified folk-motif, G264, is designated "La Belle Dame sans Merci," with the description, "witch entices men with offers of love and then deserts or destroys them." But it isn't at all clear in Keats's ballad that this "Belle Dame" either deserts or destroys the knight.
76. *Oxford English Dictionary*, 9, p. 626.
77. Coffin, pp. 67–8. Paul Edwards later notes that "one of Keats' generally acknowledged sources for 'La Belle Dame sans Merci' [is] the ballad of Thomas the Rhymer," but gives no further particulars about such previous acknowledgements or why this is so except for the fact that Thomas meets the Queen of Fairy (p. 202).

78. Motif F302.3.1, Fairy entices man into fairyland.
79. All quotations are from "Thomas the Rhymer," Part First, in Scott, *Minstrelsy*, IV, pp. 86–90.
80. Ibid., pp. 98, 125.
81. Motif F343.19, Fairies give mortals fairy bread.
82. Motif F377, Supernatural lapse of time in fairyland.
83. Motif F211.1.1.1, Fairies emerge on Hallowe'en; Motif F255.4, Fairy army can go among mortals only on Hallowe'en.
84. Motif F378.0.1, Mortal expelled from fairyland for breaking tabu.
85. Motif F302.3.4, Fairies entice men and then harm them.
86. Karen Swann, "Harassing the Muse," in *Romanticism and Feminism*, ed. Anne K. Mellor, Bloomington, Indiana: Indiana University Press, 1988, p. 88.
87. Motif F277.0.3, Good and bad fairies battle.
88. Motif F160.0.2, Fairy otherworld confused with land of the dead; Motif F251.2, Fairies as souls of departed.
89. Motif B768.2, Salamander subsists on fire.
90. Motif D2146.2, Night controlled by magic.
91. Motif A1903, God makes birds, devil reptiles.
92. Motif A692.1, Overseas otherworld in the west.
93. Such traditions may be seen in the boggart tricks of Robin Goodfellow, the helpful household spirits, the faeries' shape-shifting powers and ability to raise storms, and the faery changeling. See the folklorist Katharine Briggs for a thorough discussion of this topic in *The Anatomy of Puck*. More recently and more tartly, Diane Purkiss has written of Shakespeare's responsibility for the popular understanding of the faerie. See her chapter, "The Fairy Goes Literary: Puck and Others."
94. Purkiss comments that the "fairy whose characteristics are . . . tininess, endearing sweetness — and freakiness . . . is largely introduced to the world — fabricated — by one man: William Shakespeare" (p. 158).
95. This view that the primary, most interesting figures in the play were the faeries continued through the century, as may be seen in the many late Romantic and Victorian "fairy paintings" based on this play by Henry Fuseli, Sir Joseph Noel Patton, Richard Dadd, John Simmons, and John Anser Fitzgerald, to name only the most prominent. The usual scenes portrayed were Titania in her bower, Titania and Bottom, or the reconciled Titania and Oberon. For a fuller understanding of this nineteenth-century view of the faerie, see the beautifully produced *Victorian Fairy Painting*, ed. Jane Martineau, London: Royal Academy of Arts, in association with Merrell Holbertson Publishers, 1997. The accompanying essays by Stella Beddoe, Charlotte Gere, Jeremy Maas, and Pamela White Trimpe are fine studies of the faerie and its significance in Victorian writers.
96. Dorothy Kehler, "*A Midsummer Night's Dream*: A Bibliographic Survey of the Criticism," in *A Midsummer Night's Dream: Critical Essays*, ed. Dorothy Kehler, New York and London: Garland Publishing, 1999, p. 51.
97. James L. Calderwood, "A Midsummer Night's Dream," New York: Twayne Publishers, 1992, p. xxii.
98. Six volumes of the seven-volume 1808 reprint of the 1623 folio edition were found posthumously in Keats's library. He had taken the missing one with him when he left with Severn for Italy, and gave it to Severn at the end in

Italy. On Severn's death it was sold, and the entire set eventually joined the library holdings of Princeton University. For a complete account of this, see Caroline F.E. Spurgeon, *Keats's Shakespeare: A Descriptive Study Based on New Material*, London: Oxford University Press, 1929.

99. Ibid., p. 5.
100. Ibid., p. 19.
101. R.S. White, *Keats as a Reader of Shakespeare*, Norman, Oklahoma and London: University of Oklahoma Press, 1987, p. 108.
102. Christopher Ricks comments about these stanzas, "the darkness of the night; the sweet that is not sickly, and the wild that is not dangerous: all these are transplanted from Shakespeare's garden to Keats's" (*Allusion to the Poets*, Oxford: Oxford University Press, 2002, p. 168).
103. Helen Vendler comments that these allusions "borrowed from Titania's bower in *A Midsummer Night's Dream*, described by Oberon (as this bower is described by Keats) from memory, not sight." Presumably she means that Keats errs by adding the "white hawthorn" (*The Odes of John Keats*, Cambridge, MA and London: Harvard University Press, 1983, p. 84). But why has he chosen to add this particular flower?
104. Motif F211.1.1.2, Fairies emerge on St. John's night [Midsummer Eve].
105. Motif F216, Fairies live in forest.
106. Motif D2146.2, Night controlled by magic; Motif F235.2.1, Fairies visible only at night.
107. This may have additional faerie overtones. Motif D555.2, Transformation [enchantment] by drinking wine; Motif F162.2.2, Rivers of wine in otherworld.
108. Motif F261.3.1.1, Fairies dance under hawthorne trees; Motif F234.1.16.1, Fairy in form of fly; Motif G303.3.3.4.4, Devil in form of fly.
109. Motif F262.5, Fairy music — person listening is without food or sleep for a year.
110. The Londonderry Air is perhaps better known in its adaptation as "Danny Boy." It seems to be an ancient Irish melody, taken down by a nineteenth-century collector of folk-songs from a blind itinerant musician who said it was an old melody he learned from a faery. The tune was used to accompany the lyrics to "Danny Boy" around the turn of the century. It is an interesting exercise to consider whether these familiar words, usually taken to be sung by a father to his son gone off to war, could instead be sung by a father to his son stolen by faeries to their timeless place.

    O Danny boy, the pipes, the pipes are calling
    From glen to glen and down the mountain side
    The summer's gone, and all the roses falling
    ''Tis you, 'tis you must go, and I must bide...

111. Motif F160.0.2, Fairy otherworld confused with land of dead.
112. Motif F377, Supernatural lapse of time in fairyland.
113. Motif F165.3.5, Windows in the otherworld.
114. *Oxford English Dictionary*, 6, p. 77.
115. Motif D789.10, Disenchantment by ringing bell.

6 Privileging the Celtic

1. Keats, *Letters*, II, pp. 77, 192, 230, 237. This last possibility was not as implausible as it sounds since Abbey himself was a wholesale tea dealer.
2. Ibid., p. 251, n3.
3. Ibid., pp. 176–7.
4. Ibid., pp. 178–9.
5. Ibid., p. 186.
6. Ibid., p. 128.
7. Ibid., p. 189.
8. Purkiss, p. 174.
9. Motif B29.1, Lamia. Face of woman, body of serpent. Briggs provides a woodcut of the lamia as it appeared in Topsell's *The History of Foure-Footed Beastes* (1607) that was a favorite of children as well as adults. Keats could have seen this, for it was a well-known illustration. Here the lamia also has scales, a row of multiple breasts, paws, hoofs and the sexual organs of both genders as it is hermaphroditic (*Encyclopedia of Fairies*, pp. 260–1). Purkiss also has a brief but valuable analysis of the lamia-figure as a female demon that went back before ancient Greece to Sumaria and Mesopotamia (pp. 31–5).
10. Motif G262.0.1, Lamia. Witch who eats children; Motif G262.0.1.1, Lamia devours her lover; Motif A139.4, Vampire goddess. Briggs here calls the lamia a faery (260).
11. Motif D1719.5, Magic power of fairy.
12. Motif F282, Fairies travel through air; Motif F302.3.1.4, Fairy abducts whomever she falls in love with.
13. Tooke, p. 62.
14. Jack Stillinger, "The 'Story' of Keats," in *The Cambridge Companion to Keats*, ed. Wolfson, p. 254.
15. Motif G262.0.1, Lamia. Witch who eats children.
16. Motif F233.7, Fairies are multicolored; Motif F236.1.7, Fairy wears multicolored dress.
17. Motif D1983.2, Invisibility conferred by fairy.
18. Motif F259.1.2, Fairy becomes mortal; Motif F234.0.1, Fairy transforms self.
19. Motif D475.1.3, Transformation: dead leaves to gold; Motif F342.1, Fairy gold.
20. Motif F262.10.2, Fairy music issues from fairy ring.
21. Motif F267, Fairies attend games.
22. Motif F302.3.3, Fairy avenges self on man who scorns her love; Motif F361.1, Fairy takes revenge for being slighted.
23. Elizabeth R. Gebhard, "The Isthmian Games and the Sanctuary of Poseidon in the Early Empire," originally published in *Journal of Roman Archaeology*, no. 8, 1993, and cited in http:/humanitiesuchicago.edu/orgs/isthmia/publications/is-roman/is-games.html.
24. Motif F322.1, Changeling bride; fairies steal bride and leave substitute; Motif F361.3, Fairies take revenge on person who spies on them.
25. Motif D2146.2, Night controlled by magic; Motif F235.2.1, Fairies only visible at night; Motif F234.1.16.2, Fairy in form of moth.
26. Motif F262.3.6, Fairy music causes joy.
27. Motif D2121.4, Magic journey by making distance vanish.
28. Motif D1132.1, Palace produced by magic.

29. Motif F221.1, Fairy house disappears at dawn; Motif F235.3, Fairies visible to one person alone.
30. Motif F362.4, Fairy causes mutilation (injury); Motif S160.3, Fairies mutilate mortals; Motif F376, Mortal as servant in fairyland.
31. Motif F160.0.2, Fairy otherworld confused with land of the dead; Motif F165.6.1, Otherworld (fairyland) as place of sorrowful captivity.
32. Motif D1812.5.1.13, Fairy music as evil omen.
33. Motif C311.1.2, Tabu: looking at fairies.
34. Motif C162.1.1, Tabu: fairy girl marrying mortal.
35. Motif F381.1, Fairy leaves when he is named.
36. Motif F303, Wedding of mortal and fairy.
37. Motif F271.2.0.1, Fairies build great structures in one night; Motif F346.2, Fairies build house for mortal.
38. Motif D1781, Magic results from singing; Motif D2142.1.6, Wind raised by whistling; Motif M301.6.1, Banshees as portents of misfortune; Motif B81.11, Mermaid's singing causes sleep.
39. Motif G263.0.1, Witch has persons she has enchanted as servants.
40. Lemprière, pp. 480, 63.
41. Motif C211.1, Tabu: eating in fairyland; Motif C242, Tabu: eating food of witch; Motif C243.1, Tabu: eating food of supernatural lover; Motif F243, Fairy food.
42. Motif F262.3.6, Fairy music causes joy.
43. Motif F271.3, Fairies skillful as smiths.
44. Motif D1361.5.1, Magic fern-seed renders invisible.
45. Motif G303.10.13, Thistles and nettles are the devil's vegetables.
46. Motif D513, Transformation by violation of looking tabu.
47. Motif F402.1.4, Demons assume human forms in order to deceive.
48. Motif D2072.1, Magic paralysis by Evil Eye.
49. Motif C311.1.2, Tabu: looking at fairies.
50. Motif D772, Disenchantment by naming; Motif F381.1, Fairy leaves when he is named.
51. Motif C644, Returning home after marrying fairy tabu; Motif F322.1, Changeling bride; fairies steal bride and leave a substitute.
52. Motif F160.0.2, Fairy otherworld confused with land of the dead.
53. Moltif F162.1.3, Trees bloom, others bear concurrently in otherworld garden.
54. Motif F162.8, Magic fountain in otherworld.
55. Motif F162.1.1, Everblooming garden in otherworld; Motif F219.2, Garden in fairyland.
56. Motif D2145.2, Summertime produced by magic; Motif F173.3, Perpetual feasts in otherworld.
57. Motif F160.0.2, Fairy otherworld confused with land of the dead.
58. Motif D1364.7, Drink causes magic sleep; Motif F302.3.4.4, Fairy takes lover back to fairyland in magic sleep; Motif F160.0.2, Fairy otherworld confused with land of the dead.
59. Motif F251.12, Fairies are Druids; Motif F394.1.1, Druid directs fairies.
60. Motif F222.1.1, Fairies' underground palace cannot be burned by fire nor destroyed by water; Motif F163.2, Church (chapel) in otherworld; Motif F377, Supernatural lapse of time in fairyland; Motif F160.0.2, Fairy otherworld confused with land of the dead.

61. Motif F211.0.1, Prehistoric burial mounds [tumuli] as dwellings of fairies; Motif F160.0.2, Fairy otherworld confused with land of the dead.
62. For an excellent summary of this Romantic preoccupation with the Druids and their supposed monuments left behind all over the Isles, see the chapter, "The Megalithic Landscape," in Smiles.
63. Motif F169.7, Coldness of the otherworld.
64. Motif F165.6.1, Otherworld (fairyland) as place of sorrowful captivity; Motif F379.1.1, No return from fairyland; Motif R112.3, Rescue of prisoners from fairy stronghold.
65. Motif P427.0.3, Women as Druids.
66. Fiona J. Stafford, *The Last of the Race: The Growth of a Myth from Milton to Darwin*, Oxford: Clarendon Press, 1994.
67. Ibid., p. 93.
68. Ibid., p. 7.
69. The Druids' aversion to preserving their secret lore in manuscript form was known since Roman days. Keats would have known it at least from Edward Davies, who notes that the Druids' "method of instruction was by *symbols* and by enigmas, or dark allegories, by ancient songs, and maxims orally delivered, and in private; but which they deemed it unlawful to reduce into writing, or communicate it out of their own pale" [italics his] (p. 150).
70. Motif F329.1, Fairies carry off youth; he has the gift of prophecy when he returns to earth.
71. See Katie Trumpener, pp. 96–100, for a good discussion of the late eighteenth-century linkage of blindness and second sight, particularly as it related to the supposed clairvoyance prevalent among the Scottish Highlanders.
72. Motif F160.0.2, Fairy otherworld confused with land of the dead; Motif F251.2, Fairies as souls of departed.
73. Keats, *Letters*, I, p. 348. See also the photographs of such burial slabs in Carol Kyros Walker's fine pictorial account of this walking tour in *Walking North with Keats*, New Haven and London: Yale, 1992, p. 120.
74. Keats, *Letters*, II, p. 167.
75. Ibid., p. 257.
76. Keats, *Letters*, I, pp. 56–7; and Motion, p. 482.
77. This view of the poem as a satire on the travails of the Prince Regent and Princess Caroline is the generally accepted reading by those few who have commented upon the poem. See Gittings, pp. 368–70; Stillinger, ed., *John Keats: Complete Poems*, pp. 482–4; and Motion, pp. 482–3. Stillinger notes that the journey of Bellanaine to Panthea parallels that of Princess Caroline from Brunswick to London for her wedding to the Prince Regent (p. 483).
78. White points out that the plots of Shakespeare's play and Keats's poem both employ the intermixing of faery and the human loves (pp. 102–3).
79. For a thorough discussion of these essential qualities of the court jester, both in Europe and in China, see Beatrice K. Otto, *Fools are Everywhere: The Court Jester Around the World*, Chicago and London: University of Chicago Press, 2001. There is also a fairly common motif in folk-literature that associates poets and fools (Motif P427.7.2.1.1, Poets and fools closely allied).
80. This is not so distant from the way in which the Druid used invective and satire against his ruler as a method of social control — here, Keats used the faerie materials he had at hand. Motif P427.4, Poet (Druid) as satirist.

81. Motif F361.1, Fairy takes revenge for being slighted; Motif F361.9, Fairies take revenge for being dishonored; Motif F361.10, Fairy takes revenge for being teased; Motif F361.16, Fairies punish person who needs punishment because of his treatment of other mortals; Motif F369.4, Fairy tricks mortal; Motif F399.4, Playful or troublesome fairies; Motif F399.4.1, Fairies sport with mortal.
82. Gittings thinks that this persona is a satire on Keats's contemporary "blue-stockings" (p. 372); as does Ralph Pite, "*The Cap and Bells; or, the Jealousies*: Satire, Irony and Parody", *Romanticism,* Vol. 2.1 (March 1996), p. 75; and Motion, p. 483.
83. "Vaughan" could well refer to the seventeenth-century Metaphysical poet William Vaughan. Coincidentally or not, he was a Welshman who was Celtic in his sympathies, affixing "the Silurist" to his name after the local Celtic tribe (the Silures).
84. Keats, *Letters*, II, p. 286.
85. Motion, p. 563.
86. Rollins, ed., *The Keats Circle,* I, p. 181.
87. Ibid., p. 224.
88. Gittings, p. 433.
89. Briggs, *Encyclopedia of Fairies,* pp. 335–6. Through sympathetic magic, the daisy with its strong solar resemblance probably was considered a protection against faeries because of the widespread belief that faeries disappear at dawn. (Motif C752.2.1, Tabu: supernatural creatures being abroad after sunrise; Motif F383.4, Fairies must leave at cockcrow; Motif F383.4.3, Sunlight fatal to fairies.)

Bibliography

Allen, Paul M. and Joan deRis Allen. *Fingal's Cave, the Poems of Ossian, and Celtic Christianity*. New York: Continuum, 1999.

Bate, Jonathan. *Shakespeare and Ovid*. Oxford: Oxford University Press, 1993.

Beck, Horace P., ed. *Folklore in Action: Essays for Discussion in Honor of MacEdward Leach*. Philadelphia: American Folklore Society, 1962.

Bettany, W.A. Lewis, ed. *The Confessions of Lord Byron: A Collection of his Private Opinions of Men and of Matters*, 1905; rpt. New York: Haskell House, 1973.

Blackstone, Bernard. *The Consecrated Urn: An Interpretation of Keats in Terms of Growth and Form*. London: Longman's and Green, 1959.

Bold, Alan, ed. *Sir Walter Scott: The Long-Forgotten Melody*. Totowa, NJ: Barnes and Noble, 1983.

Briggs, Katharine. *The Anatomy of Puck: An Examination of Fairy Beliefs Among Shakespeare's Contemporaries and Successors*. London: Routledge & Paul, 1959.

——. *An Encyclopedia of Fairies: Hobgoblins, Brownies, Bogies, and Other Supernatural Creatures*. New York: Pantheon Books, 1976.

Brown, Mary Ellen. *Burns and Tradition*. Urbana, Illinois: University of Illinois Press, 1984.

Burnet, Bishop Gilbert. *Bishop Burnet's History of His Own Time*. 2nd edn, 6 vols. London: Oxford University Press, 1833.

Calderwood, James L., ed. *A Midsummer Night's Dream*. New York: Twayne Publishers, 1992.

Campbell, John Gregorson. *Superstitions of the Highlands and Islands of Scotland: Collected Entirely from Oral Sources*, 1900; rpt. Detroit: Singing Tree Press, 1970.

Castle, Gregory. *Modernism and the Celtic Revival*. Cambridge: Cambridge University Press, 2001.

Chandler, James. *England in 1819: The Politics of Literary Culture and the Case of Romantic Historicism*. Chicago: University of Chicago, 1998.

Clark, David L. and Donald C. Goellnicht, eds. *New Romanticisms: Theory and Critical Practice*. Toronto: University of Toronto Press, 1994.

Clarke, Charles Cowden and Mary Cowden Clarke. *Recollections of Writers*, 1878; rpt. Sussex: Centaur Press, 1969.

Coffin, Tristram P. "The Folk Ballad and the Literary Ballad: An Essay in Classification." In *Folklore in Action*. Ed. Beck.

Coldwell, Joan. "'Meg Merrilies': Scott's Gipsey Tamed." *Keats-Shelley Memorial Bulletin* XXXII (1981): 30–7.

Colley, Linda. *Britons: Forging the Nation 1707–1837*. New Haven and London: Yale University Press, 1992.

Colvin, Sidney. *John Keats: His Life and Poetry, His Friends, Critics and After-Fame*. London: Macmillan Press, 1917.

Cox, Jeffrey N. *Poetry and Politics in the Cockney School: Keats, Shelley, Hunt, and Their Circle*. Cambridge: Cambridge University Press, 1998.

Davies, Edward. *Celtic Researches, on the Origin, Traditions & Language of the Ancient Britons; with some Introductory Sketches on Primitive Society*, 1804;

rpt. Introduction by Burton Feldman. New York and London: Garland Publishing, 1979.

de Montluzin, Emily Lorraine. "Killing the Cockneys: Blackwood's Weapons of Choice against Hunt, Hazlitt, and Keats." *Keats-Shelley Journal* XLVII (1998): 87–107.

Doyle, Laura. "The Racial Sublime." In *Romanticism, Race, and Imperial Culture.* Eds Richardson and Hofkosh.

Duffy, Maureen. *The Erotic World of Faery.* London: Hodder & Stoughton, 1972.

Edwards, Paul. "Ambiguous Seductions: 'La Belle Dame sans Merci,' 'The Faerie Queene' and 'Thomas the Rhymer.'" *The Durham University Journal,* Vol. 83, No. 2 (July 1990): 199–203.

Evans, Gareth. "John Keats and the Botanic Pharmacy." *Keats-Shelley Review* 16 (2002): 31–55.

Evans-Wentz, W.Y. *The Fairy-Faith in Celtic Countries.* London: Oxford University Press, 1911.

Everest, Kelvin. "Isabella in the Market-Place: Keats and Feminism." In *Keats and History.* Ed. Roe.

Evert, Walter H. and Jack W. Rhodes. *Approaches to Teaching Keats's Poetry.* New York: Modern Language Association, 1991.

Fleming, Deborah. *"A man who does not exist": The Irish Peasant in the Work of W.B. Yeats and J.M. Synge.* Ann Arbor, MI: University of Michigan Press, 1995.

Forman, H. Buxton, ed. *The Poetical Works and Other Writings of John Keats* (Hampstead Edition), 8 vols. New York: Scribner's, 1939.

Frayne, John P. *Uncollected Prose of W.B. Yeats,* 2 vols. New York: Columbia University Press, 1970.

Gaskill, Howard, ed. *Ossian Revisited.* Edinburgh: Edinburgh University Press, 1991.

——. *The Poems of Ossian and Related Works.* Edinburgh: Edinburgh University Press, 1996.

Gilbreath, Marcia. "The Etymology of Porphryro's Name in Keats's 'Eve of St. Agnes.'" *Keats-Shelley Journal* 37 (1988): 20–7.

Gittings, Robert. *John Keats.* Boston, MA: Little, Brown and Company, 1968.

Gleckner, Robert F. "Keats's 'How Many Bards' and Poetic Tradition." *Keats-Shelley Journal* XXVII (1978): 14–22.

Goellnicht, Donald C. *The Poet-Physician: Keats and Medical Science.* Pittsburgh: University of Pittsburgh Press, 1984.

——. "The Politics of Reading and Writing: Political Reviews of Keats's *Poems* (1817)." In *New Romanticisms.* Eds Clark and Goellnicht.

Goslee, Nancy Moore. *Scott the Rhymer.* Lexington, KY: University of Kentucky, 1988.

——. "The Envisioning of Women: From *Endymion* to the Later Romances." In *Approaches to Teaching Keats's Poetry.* Eds Evert and Rhodes.

Green, Miranda J. *The World of the Druids.* London: Thames and Hudson, 1997.

Harvey, Karen J. "The Trouble about Merlin: The Theme of Enchantment in 'The Eve of St. Agnes.'" *Keats-Shelley Journal* 34 (1985): 83–94.

Hazlitt, William. *The Complete Works.* Centenary Edition, ed. P.P. Howe, 1930, 21 vols. London: Taylor and Hessey, 1819; rpt. New York: AMS Press, 1967.

Hechter, Michael. *Internal Colonialism: The Celtic Fringe in British National Development.* Berkeley, CA: University of California Press, 1975.

Hesiod. *Theogony; Works and Days; Shield.* Trans. Apostolos N. Athanassakis. Baltimore: Johns Hopkins Press, 1983.

Hirsch, Edward. " 'Contention is Better than Loneliness': The Poet as Folklorist." In *The Genres of the Irish Literary Revival*. Ed. Schleifer.

——. "The Imaginary Irish Peasant." PMLA, Vol. 106, No. 5 (October 1991): 1116–33.

Hunt, Leigh. *The Autobiography of Leigh Hunt, with Reminiscences of Friends and Contemporaries*, 1850; rpt. 2 vols. New York: AMS Press, 1965.

——. *Lord Byron and Some of His Contemporaries*. London: Colburn, 1828; rpt. AMS Press, 1966.

——. *Juvenilia, or A Collection of Poems Written between the Ages of Twelve and Sixteen by J.H.L. Hunt*, 1804; rpt. (microfiche) New Canaan, CT: Readex Microprint, 1987–1992.

Jeffrey, Francis. "Review of Keats's *Lamia, Isabella, The Eve of St. Agnes, and Other Poems*" (*Edinburgh Review*, XXXIV, August 1820). In *The Romantics Reviewed*. Ed. Reiman.

Jones, Elizabeth. "Keats in the Suburbs." *Keats-Shelley Journal* XLV (1996): 23–43.

Jung, C.G. *Archetypes and the Collective Unconscious*. Princeton: Princeton University Press, 1959; 2nd edn, 1977.

Kearns, Gerry. "Biology, Class and the Urban Penalty." In *Urbanising Britain*. Eds Kearns and Withers.

Kearns, Gerry and W.J. Withers. *Urbanising Britain: Essays on Class and Community in the Nineteenth Century*. Cambridge: Cambridge University Press, 1991.

Kehler, Dorothy. "*A Midsummer Night's Dream*: A Bibliographic Survey of the Criticism." In *A Midsummer Night's Dream: Critical Essays*. Ed. Kehler.

——. ed. *A Midsummer Night's Dream: Critical Essays*. New York and London: Garland Publishing, 1999.

Kiberd, Declan. "The Fall of the Stage Irishman." In *The Genres of the Irish Literary Revival*. Ed. Schleifer.

Kidd, Colin. *British Identities before Nationalism: Ethnicity and Nationhood in the Atlantic World, 1600–1800*. Cambridge: Cambridge University Press, 1999.

Kinahan, Frank. *Yeats, Folklore, and Occultism: Contexts of the Early Works and Thought*. Boston: Unwin Hyman, 1988.

Lau, Beth. *Keats's 'Paradise Lost.'* Gainesville, FL: University Press of Florida, 1998.

Lemprière, John. *Classical Dictionary of Proper Names Mentioned in Ancient Authors, with a Chronological Table*, 1788; rpt. ed. F.A. Wright. New York: Dutton, 1949.

Levinson, Marjorie. *Keats's Life of Allegory: The Origins of A Style*. Oxford: Basil Blackwell, 1988.

Lockhart, John Gibson. "Review of *Poems* and *Endymion*" (*Blackwood's Edinburgh Magazine*, III, July 1818). In *The Romantics Reviewed*. Ed. Reiman.

Macpherson, James. *The Poems of Ossian and Related Works*. Ed. Howard Gaskill. Edinburgh: Edinburgh University Press, 1996.

Marchand, Leslie A., ed. *Byron's Letters and Journals*, 12 vols. Cambridge, MA: Harvard University Press, 1973–1982.

Martineau, Jane, ed. *Victorian Fairy Painting*. London: Royal Academy of Arts, in association with Merrell Holbertson Publishers, 1997.

Matthews, William. *Cockney Past and Present: A Short History of the Dialect of London*. London: Routledge & Sons, 1938.

McGann, Jerome. *The Poetics of Sensibility: A Revolution in Literary Style*. Oxford: Clarendon Press, 1996.

Mellor, Anne K., ed. *Romanticism and Feminism*. Bloomington, Indiana: Indiana University Press, 1988.

Mizukoshi, Ayumi. *Keats, Hunt, and the Aesthetics of Pleasure*. New York: Palgrave Macmillan, 2001.

Motion, Andrew. *Keats*. New York: Farrar, Straus, and Giroux, 1997.

Newey, Vincent. "*Hyperion, The Fall of Hyperion* and Keats's Epic Ambitions." In *The Cambridge Companion to Keats*. Ed. Wolfson.

Nicolaisen, W.H. "Scott and the Folk Tradition." In *Sir Walter Scott*. Ed. Bold.

O'Neill, Michael, ed. *Keats: Bicentenary Readings*. Edinburgh: Edinburgh Press for the University of Durham, 1997.

——. " 'When this warm scribe my hand': Writing and History in *Hyperion* and *Fall of Hyperion*." In *Keats and History*. Ed. Roe.

Otto, Beatrice K. *Fools are Everywhere: The Court Jester Around the World*. Chicago and London: University of Chicago Press, 2001.

Parsons, Coleman O. "Primitive Sense in 'Lamia.' " *Folklore* 88 [1977]: pp. 203–10.

Pattison, Stephen. *Shame: Theory, Therapy, Theology*. Cambridge: Cambridge University Press, 2000.

Perkins, David, ed. *English Romantic Writers*. New York: Harcourt Brace, 1967.

Piggott, Stuart. *Ancient Britons and the Antiquarian Imagination: Ideas from the Renaissance to the Regency*. [London] New York: Thames and Hudson, 1989.

Pirie, David B. "Old Saints and Young Lovers: Keats's 'Eve of St. Mark' and Popular Culture." In *Keats: Bicentenary Readings*. Ed. O'Neill.

Pite, Ralph. "*The Cap and Bells; or, the Jealousies*: Satire, Irony and Parody." *Romanticism*, Vol. 2, No.1 (March 1996): 68–80.

Pittock, Murray G.H. *Celtic Identity and the British Image*. Manchester: Manchester University Press, and New York: St. Martin's Press, 1999.

Purkiss, Diane. *At the Bottom of the Garden: A History of Fairies, Hobgoblins and Other Troublesome Things*. New York: New York University Press, 2001.

Reiman, Donald H., ed. *The Romantics Reviewed; Contemporary Reviews of British Romantic Writers*, 9 vols. New York and London: Garland, 1972.

Richardson, Alan and Sonia Hofkosh, eds. *Romanticism, Race, and Imperial Culture 1780–1834*. Bloomington, Indiana: Indiana University Press, 1996.

Ricks, Christopher. *Allusion to the Poets*. Oxford and New York: Oxford University Press, 2002.

Robertson, William. *The History of Scotland: During the Reigns of Queen Mary and King James VI, till his Ascension to the Crown of England*. 3rd edn, 2 vols. A. Millar, 1760.

Robinson, Jeffrey C. *Reception and Poetics in Keats: 'My Ended Poet.'* London: Macmillan Press, and New York: St. Martin's Press, 1998.

Roe, Nicholas. *John Keats and the Culture of Dissent*. Oxford: Clarendon Press, 1997.

——, ed. *Keats and History*. Cambridge: Cambridge University Press, 1995.

——, ed. *Leigh Hunt: Life, Poetics, Politics*. London and New York: Routledge, 2003.

——. "Leigh Hunt: Some Early Matters." In *Leigh Hunt: Life, Poetics, Politics*. Ed. Roe.

Rollins, Hyder E. *The Keats Circle: Letters and Papers and More Letters and Poems of the Keats Circle*. 2nd edn, 2 vols. Cambridge, MA: Harvard University Press, 1965.

Rollins, Hyder E., ed. *The Letters of John Keats*, 2 vols. Cambridge, MA: Harvard University Press, 1972.

Rule, John. *The Laboring Classes in Early Industrial England 1750–1850*. London and New York: Longman, 1986.

Schleifer, Ronald, ed. *The Genres of the Irish Literary Revival*. Norman, Oklahoma: Pilgrim Books, and Dublin, Ireland: Wolfhound Press, 1980.

Scott, Sir Walter. *The Works of Sir Walter Scott*, 50 vols. Boston and New York: Houghton Mifflin, 1913.

——. *Minstrelsy of the Scottish Border*, 4 vols 1902; rpt. ed. T.F. Henderson, Detroit: Singing Tree Press, 1968.

Severs, J. Burke. "Keats's Fairy Sonnet." *Keats-Shelley Journal* VI (1957): 109–13.

Simpson, J.A. and E.S.C. Weiner. *Oxford English Dictionary*. 2nd edn, 20 vols. Oxford: Clarendon Press; New York: Oxford University, 1989.

Smiles, Sam. *The Image of Antiquity: Ancient Britain and the Romantic Imagination*. New Haven and London: Yale University Press, 1994.

Snyder, Edward. *The Celtic Revival in English Literature, 1760–1800*. Cambridge, MA: Harvard University Press, 1923.

Spence, Joseph. *Polymetis: Or, An Enquiry Concerning the Agreement between the Works of the Roman Poets, and the Remains of the Antient Artists*, 1747; rpt. New York: Garland, 1976.

Spurgeon, Caroline F.E. *Keats's Shakespeare: A Descriptive Study Based on New Material*. London: Oxford University Press, 1929.

Stafford, Fiona. *The Sublime Savage: A Study of James Macpherson and the Poems of Ossian*. Edinburgh: Edinburgh University Press, 1988.

——. *The Last of the Race: The Growth of a Myth from Milton to Darwin*. Oxford: Clarendon Press, 1994.

——. "*Fingal* and the Fallen Angels: Macpherson, Milton and Romantic Titanism." In *From Gaelic to Romantic*. Eds Stafford and Gaskill.

——. *Starting Lines in Scottish, Irish, and English Poetry: From Burns to Heaney*. Oxford: Oxford University Press, 2000.

Stafford, Fiona and Howard Gaskill, eds. *From Gaelic to Romantic: Ossianic Translations*. Amsterdam and Atlanta, GA: Rodolpi Press, 1998.

Stillinger, Jack. *John Keats: Complete Poems*. Cambridge, MA and London, England: Belknap Press of Harvard University Press, 1982.

——. *Reading The Eve of St. Agnes: The Multiples of Complex Literary Transaction*. New York: Oxford University Press, 1999.

——. "The 'Story' of Keats." In *The Cambridge Companion to Keats*. Ed. Wolfson.

Swann, Karen. "Harassing the Muse." In *Romanticism and Feminism*. Ed. Mellor.

Sykes, Homer. *Celtic Britain*. London: Weidenfeld & Nicolson, 1997.

Thompson, Stith. *Motif-Index of Folk-Literature: A Classification of Narrative Elements in Folktales, Ballads, Myths, Fables, Medieval Romances, Exempla, Fabliaux, Jest-Books, and Local Legends*. rev. edn, 6 vols. Bloomington: Indiana, and London: Indiana University Press, 1975.

Tooke, Andrew. *The Pantheon, Representing the Fabulous Histories of the Heathen Gods and Most Illustrious Heroes*, 1713; rpt. New York and London: Garland, 1976.

Trelawny, Edward John. *Records of Shelley, Byron, and the Author*, 1878; rpt. New York: Benjamin Blom, 1968.

Trott, Nicola. "Keats and the Prison House of Memory." In *Keats and History*. Ed. Roe.

Trumpener, Katie. *Bardic Nationalism: The Romantic Novel and the British Empire*. Princeton: Princeton University Press, 1997.

Vendler, Helen. *The Odes of John Keats*. Cambridge, MA and London: Harvard University Press, 1983.

Walker, Carol Kyros. *Walking North with Keats*. New Haven and London: Yale, 1992.

Watkins, Daniel. *Keats's Poetry and the Politics of the Imagination*. Cranbury, NJ: Fairleigh Dickinson University Press, 1989.

Westwood, Jennifer. *Albion: A Guide to Legendary Britain*. Salem, NH: Salem House, 1985.

White, R.S. *Keats as a Reader of Shakespeare*. Norman, Oklahoma, and London: University of Oklahoma Press, 1987.

Wolfson, Susan J., ed. *The Cambridge Companion to Keats*. Cambridge: Cambridge University Press, 2001.

Wolfson, Susan J. and Peter Manning, eds. *Longman Anthology of British Literature: The Romantics and Their Contemporaries*. New York: Addison-Wesley, 1999.

Wright, Herbert G. "Has Keats's 'Eve of St. Agnes' a Tragic Ending?" *Modern Language Review*, Vol. 40, No. 2 (1945): 90–4.

Wright, Peter. *Cockney Dialect and Slang*. London: B.T. Batsford Ltd, 1981.

Yeats, W.B., ed. *Fairy and Folk Tales of Ireland*, 1888; rpt. Gerrards Cross: Colin Smythe Ltd, 1973.

——. "The Message of the Folk-lorist" (1883). In *Uncollected Prose of Yeats*. Ed. Frayne.

Zug, Charles G. "The Ballad Editor as Antiquary: Scott and the *Minstrelsy*." *Journal of the Folklore Institute*, Vol. 13, No. 1 (1976): 57–73.

Index

Since the folklore motif numbers are not given in this index, the subcategories for "faeries" and "faeryland" are based on those of Stith Thompson.

Printed in the United States
71086LV00003B/64-66

9 781403 948519